Shame

Series Editors: Alex Thomson, Benjamin Arditi, Andrew Schaap
International Advisory Editors: Michael Dillon, Michael J. Shapiro, Jeremy Valentine

Offering New Perspectives on Contemporary Political Theory, books in this series 'take on' the political in accordance with the ambivalent colloquial sense of the phrase – as both an acceptance and a challenge. They interrogate received accounts of the relationship between political thought and political practice, criticise and engage with the contemporary political imagination, and reflect on the ongoing transformations of politics. Concise and polemical, the texts are oriented toward critique, developments in Continental thought, and the crossing of disciplinary borders.

Titles in the *Taking on the Political* series include:
Polemicization: The Contingency of the Commonplace
Benjamin Arditi and Jeremy Valentine

Cinematic Political Thought
Michael Shapiro

Untimely Politics
Samuel A. Chambers

Speaking Against Number: Heidegger, Language and the Politics of Calculation
Stuart Elden

Post-Marxism versus Cultural Studies
Paul Bowman

Post-Foundational Political Thought: Political Difference in Nancy, Lefort, Badiou and Laclau
Oliver Marchart

Democratic Piety: Complexity, Conflict and Violence
Adrian Little

Gillian Rose: A Good Enough Justice
Kate Schick

Ethics and Politics after Poststructuralism: Levinas, Derrida and Nancy
Madeleine Fagan

Space, Politics and Aesthetics
Mustafa Dikeç

History and Event: From Marxism to Contemporary French Theory
Nathan Coombs

www.edinburghuniversitypress.com/series/totp

Shame

A Genealogy of Queer Practices in the Nineteenth Century

Bogdan Popa

Edinburgh University Press is one of the leading university presses in the UK. We publish academic books and journals in our selected subject areas across the humanities and social sciences, combining cutting-edge scholarship with high editorial and production values to produce academic works of lasting importance. For more information visit our website: edinburghuniversitypress.com

© Bogdan Popa, 2017

Edinburgh University Press Ltd
The Tun – Holyrood Road
12(2f) Jackson's Entry
Edinburgh EH8 8PJ

Typeset in 11/13 Sabon by
IDSUK (DataConnection) Ltd

A CIP record for this book is available from the British Library

ISBN 978 1 4744 1982 6 (hardback)
ISBN 978 1 4744 1983 3 (webready PDF)
ISBN 978 1 4744 1984 0 (epub)

The right of Bogdan Popa to be identified as the author of this work has been asserted in accordance with the Copyright, Designs and Patents Act 1988, and the Copyright and Related Rights Regulations 2003 (SI No. 2498).

Contents

Foreword	vii
Acknowledgements	xii
List of Illustrations	xiv

Part I: Shame and Queer Political Theory

1   Queer Practices, or How to Unmoor Feminism from
    Liberal Feminism   3
    The Argument   3
    What is Shame?   8
    What is Queer Genealogy?   10
    Queer Practices   14
    Political Theory and *The Police*   17
    Why Nineteenth-Century Feminists?   22
    The Structure of the Book   25

2   How to do Queer Genealogy with J. S. Mill   41
    How to "Part Company with the World"   44
    Mill in Drag, Shame and Silence   53
    "Barbarians" and "Lunatics": Harsh Language and
        Mill's Rhetoric   63
    Conclusion   70

Part II: Counter-Figures

3   Disturbing Silence: Mill and the Radicals at the
    Monthly Repository   81
    Unitarian Radicals and Performativity   84
    Beyond Liberal Shame   90
    Mill's Disturbing Silence and the *Fox Affair*   97
    Conclusion   106

4	Performative Slurs: Political Rhetoric in Feminist Activism	115
	The Contagious Diseases Acts and Josephine Butler's Rhetoric of Humiliation	119
	Mill's Testimony against the Contagious Diseases Acts and the Policing of Feminist Activism	132
	Conclusion	146
5	Shame as a Line of Escape: Victoria Woodhull, Dispossession, and Free Love	151
	Woodhull's Shaming and Sexual Transgressions	154
	Shame as Dispossession	162
	The Police and How to Close the Lines of Escape	172
	Conclusion	177

Part III: Queering Shame

6	Does Queer Political Theory Have a Future?	183

References and Further Reading	194
Index	205

Foreword: "But Officer . . ."

> The moment when "explanations are in order" may rightly give rise to the desire to withhold . . . long enough, at any rate, to draw attention to what is most compelling in the demand for them.
>
> (Miller 1988: vii)

Shame has flourished as an academic topic during the last decade. This development is not shocking, given the circumstances prevailing in the academic market. Because neoliberal academia functions in a way that requires productive scholars, shame appears to encapsulate, in a strange manner, "a feel for the time." While many scholars seem to have more freedom to choose unconventional topics—such as affects, for example—it is also clear that they are pressured to produce more and more work. The freedom to create seems to generate more discipline and feelings of inferiority. As most of us know, if you do not want to feel unworthy or deficient, you have to produce quality work, an effort that paradoxically produces more anxiety and a greater sense of failure. In the writing of this book, I share this anxiety with my colleagues, but the additional step I want to take is to interrogate the conditions of its production.

Like many others, I feel ashamed not only when I have to live with the demand to be productive, but also when I am in direct encounters with direct mechanisms of repression. When I am stopped by the police, I face the demand to show my papers. Without exception, I always feel that I am doing something bad, or that I am somewhere I should not be. In responding to this feeling, I do sometimes question either the demand to open the trunk of my car or to tautologically repeat that I am a citizen at that special moment when I have to cross the border. I know I want to resist the demand to show my papers. "But officer . . ." is my hesitant effort to articulate what may count as resistance. Because my papers, like yours, are never without a flaw, I want to postpone the moment of showing to the police that I qualify as a moral person. And then I say:

But officer . . .

However reticent, my undecided "but officer . . ." disturbs the order of the police. It introduces a break in a logic that has its anticipated flow and structure. My reluctance to follow what I need to do seeks to take away space and time from an order that functions on the basis of hierarchy. It produces, unintentionally, a moment of equality, and it does so by producing a stage of contestation. Like Jacques Rancière, I believe that *the police* do not exist primarily to interpellate protesters but to reduce the possibility of the protest. The moment when my "but officer" is shut down—policed—is the moment when it is asserted that our roles should return to their natural order. When I articulate my reservation, I know I am interrupting a space that functions with proper roles. But it takes the policing moment to make invisible that which is not supposed to be seen, such as a citizen who is always deficient in front of the police.

I want to start from "but officer"—this break in the ritual of presenting our papers to the police—to think about queer political theory. In this sense, the first goal of this book is to reflect on the political capacity of feeling bad, or postponing a demand to appear normal and in order. Most accounts of shame in political theory discuss shame as a disciplinary mechanism that is deployed to produce hierarchy and order. In contrast, here I want to *queer* shame, to take shame out of its current understanding and theorize its capacity to interrupt *the police*. What I want to show is that shame has the capacity to surprise us. When shame is dislodged from its demarcated boundaries it *becomes* politics and interrupts a given order that is perceived as natural. Rather than thinking about shame as enforcing conventional norms, I want to reimagine shame as suspending the liberal regime of business-as-usual. My intention is to show political theorists that they need to be more curious about shame's unexpected intensity and effects. This curiosity may lead to grasping shame in its disruptive capacity, and as such, to see its opposition to mechanisms of repression. That is why I sought to show that new forms of political action emerge from feeling that one is *bad*, when one does what one is not expected to do.

While feeling bad could interrupt politics-as-usual, it does not follow that it repairs what is defective about a hierarchical order. If I see shame as opening our curiosity to what is possible, shame also fails to redeem. Laurent Berlant (2011: 124) observes that liberal narratives, such as John Stuart Mill's *Autobiography*, which locate the cultivated mind as the locus of good politics, have in common with certain scholarship on affect, which sees bodies and sexualities as a ground for anti-capitalist politics, an investment in better, intimate, and reparative politics. This politics seeks to establish hope that, if one feels what one should, then a better politics will emerge. Although in this book I wanted to talk about queer practices as interrupting liberal politics, these interruptions do not necessarily generate stories of achievement and success. Sometimes these practices can lead to a hard life, an institutional backlash, or historical amnesia. Like Berlant, I wanted to think about how "but officer ..." disturbs an aesthetic order of what is perceived, but I also sought to show that what it inaugurates is often awkward and precarious.

A second goal of the book is to offer a historicized account of the life of shame by paying attention to our neoliberal present. Some of us accept that capitalism changes us and that, historically, we are experiencing ourselves in ways that are unique to this century, but we do not extend this insight to feelings. What if feelings, like commodities or political systems, change their texture and materiality according to time and geography? What if even the category of shame, which we seem to know and understand, is produced historically and has particular textures and shapes?

Contemporary ways of talking about shame have a given tone, feel, and materiality I think a lot of us take for granted. That is why this is a book about historical interventions and practices that aims to change the current academic perception about shame. In our neoliberal time, it s*eems* that to feel deficient is a mistake—we are living, after all, in a culture that asks one to be happy, vibrant, and productive. Also, the demand is to see oneself on the right, progressive side of history. There is an important value, however, in making mistakes, in practices that, as Joseph Litvak (in Sedgwick 2003: 147) put it, "take the terror out of error" and make "the making of mistakes sexy, creative, even cognitively powerful." Although a lot of energy is today located in the performance of authority and expertise, shame, I felt, has an untapped potential to disrupt the willingness to be smart, heroic, and valuable. What if mistakes, instead of consolidating the canonical investment in heroes, have the capacity to undo the force of our present investment in success?

I imagined this book as an argument aimed at an audience for political theory. I began to think about it as I felt frustrated and angry with the predominant narrative in political theory. During my training I perceived my field as excessively invested in producing a story about successes and various sorts of heroes, ranging from Antigone and Socrates to Martin Luther King Jr. In contrast, my question became how to think about intellectual figures that we might not look up to, or that we might not want to emulate. I wanted to write about figures that I feel shame about and imagine a new kind of theory—queer political theory. While certain thinkers are part of the standard syllabus in political theory, they seem to be already unfashionable. The Victorians, for example, were important for second-wave feminists, who made a selective use of their reputation as champions of women's legal and political recognition. Yet Victorians have a strange status because they represent in many respects a past that we have overcome, that is no longer present. The stereotype that we have about their sex lives is that it was a disaster. When I teach nineteenth-century thinkers in my courses, my students have a hard time connecting to these figures. *I* feel like I make a mistake in talking about them. Their racial politics are odious, for activists such as J. S. Mill and Josephine Butler were invested in the success of British imperialism. Their class politics are scarcely any better, since they stem from their position in strongly classist societies. Also, we know that the canon selected its major figures as part of a project of Anglo-American domination and exploitation, which threw many queers, poor people, people of color, non-Europeans, and non-gender-conforming people into the dustbin of history. Why not reverse the operation? Why not abolish not only the presence of these individuals but also the canon itself?

Here is where I go back to my feeling of not feeling proud of the so-called first-wave feminists. I believe that the space of ambivalence that is opened up by shame is strangely generative. Perhaps queer political theory can emerge from our ambivalence about key canonical figures. I write about thinkers such as Mill, who were revitalized for a colonialist and second-wave feminist project, with a sense of shame. My impulse to abolish the canon is countered by an allegiance to the life and practices of a different temporal and geographical humanity, which I still struggle to grasp. It seems too easy to write about people that I can unambiguously draw upon to gesture toward a better progressive politics. I wanted to sit with and ruminate about thinkers that seem part of a history and a "structure of feeling" that is already gone.

This is why I wanted to talk about a group of figures that are more or less associated with the past of our contemporary predicament. There is something queer about *them* making mistakes, doing things they were not expected to do. I wanted to think about these figures in the moment when they feel bad in their interaction with *the police*, or when they respond to the impossible demand to present their papers. As such, their distinct ways of saying "but officer" can open up a new stage of contestation, which, as I will show, has unanticipated effects. I want to locate the possibility of queer feminist politics in this space of anticipation and unpredictability. But to do so this book needs to function as an intervention in what counts as visible and sayable. While I discuss nineteenth-century queer life, I also ask political theorists to turn a critical eye toward calls to successfully resist professionalization in political science departments. While these attempts to formulate an alternative imagine political theorists either as brave "unabashed mongrels" (Kaufman-Osborn 2010: 666) or intellectuals who need to speak to the public and hit the streets (Brown 2010: 684), I want to start from moments of feeling bad and making mistakes. To nervously mumble "but officer . . ." may initiate a disagreement that neither has the map of "coupling with other academic breeds" (Kaufman-Osborn 2010: 668) nor follows the heroic and seductive trajectory of the engaged intellectual (Brown 2010: 680–3). My contention is that from situations where one does what one does not know, or feels that an action might be shameful and mistaken, unfamiliar political theory can emerge. This book utilizes queer genealogy to capture those moments of a future that has not already been imagined.

Like most academic books, this one will be also judged on whether it says something new. Now it is the reader who needs to be convinced that they see and hear what they have neither seen nor heard before.

Acknowledgments

This book started as a Ph.D. dissertation, and I was lucky enough to have the support of several institutions that made this work possible. I wrote a first draft of the manuscript during my time as a graduate student at Indiana University, Bloomington. Bill Scheuerman has been a wonderful mentor who offered his time, patience and knowledge to guide me in this adventure. Without him this project would have never been possible. Russell Hanson, Jean Robinson, Jon Simons, Aurelian Crăiuțu, Jeffrey Isaac, Purnima Bose, Majed Akhter, Alex Tipei, Maria Bucur, Brendon Westler, Ahmed Khanani, Alfio Saitta, Padraic Kenney, and Judith Failer provided critical advice and encouragement while I lived in Bloomington. I also benefited from talking to outstanding academics at the University of Michigan, Ann Arbor, and Oberlin College, Ohio. Many thanks to those who conversed with me: Lisa Disch, Elisabeth Wingrove, Mariah Zeisberg, Harry Hirsch, Rostom Mesli, Greggor Matson, Evangeline Heiliger, Patrick O'Connor, Tina Botts, Mathew Senior, Danielle Skeehan, Gabriel Cooper, Carol Lasser, and Ann Cooper Albright.

This project has gained tremendously from the brilliant insights that my colleagues in political theory have shared with me. I want to thank Joe Fischel, Mihaela Mihai, Sam Chambers, Nina Hagel, Manu Samnotra, Tiffany Willoughby-Herard, Tamara Cărăuș, Jill Locke, Camil Ungureanu, Inés Valdez, Christina Tarnopolsky, Drew Walker, Benjamin McKean, and Lorna Bracewell. Also, I cannot forget my professors in Bucharest who taught me how to think, so thank you Ovidiu Caraiani and Cornel Mihai-Ionescu. While political theorists keep me alert, my students at Oberlin College are pushing me in ways I have not imagined. I am grateful to Waylon Cunningham, Michael Drougas, Paris Gravely, Laura Feyer, and Dylan Good.

I could not have done this work without the help of my parents, family, and friends. I want to thank my mom and dad, Mimi and Vali Popa, for their relentless trust in my strange professional life. A special shout out to my friends for making my life better: Nancy Wolfe, Irene Iniesta Arandia, Nic Dobrei, Elena Popa, and Quetzil Castañeda. Dorin Liviu-Bâtfoi and his web project, *Cafe Gradiva*, offered me the space to sketch various drafts for my arguments. James Hansell has shown me the importance of thinking about psychoanalysis and emotions. My psychoanalyst, Jane Hassinger, has been a wonderful therapist and human being who showed me how to take risks and enjoy it.

List of Illustrations

Figure 2.1: "Miss Mill joins the ladies" (*Judy, or The London serio-comic journal*, November 25, 1868: 46–7)   57
Photo courtesy of Indiana University Libraries

Figure 2.2: Mill "in drag" (*Judy, or The London serio-comic journal*, July 24, 1867: 156)   59
Photo courtesy of Indiana University Libraries

Figure 5.1: The Woodhull sisters (*The Days' Doing*, February 26, 1870)   156
Photo courtesy of Indiana University Libraries

PART I
SHAME AND QUEER POLITICAL THEORY

Chapter 1
Queer Practices, or How to Unmoor Feminism from Liberal Feminism

This introductory chapter clarifies the goals and the method of the book. My first claim here is that a genealogical approach pushes political theory away from traditional liberal models about politics. In doing genealogy, I put Jacques Rancière's work in conversation with queer theory and challenge a liberal feminist conception of shame, which understands shame as being primarily negative and dangerous for politics. In turn, I conceptualize shame as a political act which interrupts a given hierarchy of power and social roles. As such, shame articulates a wrong, disrupts an uninterrogated allegiance to a hierarchical identity, and creates the scene of a disagreement. My second claim is that I shift a conventional perception about political agency by rethinking the origins of Anglo-American feminism. Rather than highlighting the nineteenth-century contributions to a liberal conception of agency, I illuminate three counter-figures, disturbing silences, performative slurs, and non-conventional relationships, that challenge a contemporary brand of activism. I categorize these figures as nineteenth century queer practices and explain why shame functions as a political interruption of the liberal order.

Politics happens on the terrain of the police. (Chambers 2013: 64)

The Argument

This is a work of political theory that aims to rethink the relationship between shame and politics.[1] I draw from Jacques Rancière's philosophy of politics, queer feminist theory, Michel Foucault's practices of freedom, as well as from the actions of nineteenth-century theorists such as John Stuart Mill, to imagine interventions that have the potential to open up situations that are currently considered blocked and unchangeable.[2] The goal of this book is to imagine a new kind of queer political theory and, in doing so, to change the conventional perspective on shame as a negative and bad emotion for political action.[3] Shame, I argue, has a disturbing capacity to introduce an order of equality as an antidote to *the police*. To modify a widespread perception about shame, I challenge various feminist and queer theories that police this affect, by which I mean that they contain and restrict shame's capacity for political action.

This book intervenes both in queer feminist scholarship and in the history of feminist activism and theory. First, I see my argument as interrupting a certain mode of theorizing in queer feminist scholarship. I seek to resignify the term shame and give it a new meaning. The thesis that I advance is that shame is what interrupts *the police*.[4] In a provocative mode of address, Rancière wanted us to rethink what we call politics by flipping the current use of the word. For him, politics becomes *the police*, which is "the set of procedures whereby the aggregation and consent of collectivities is achieved, the organization of powers, the distribution of places and roles, and the systems for legitimizing this distribution" (Rancière 1999: 28). Politics, on the other hand, is what interrupts *the police*. Like Rancière, my reconceptualization of shame as a political act seeks to disturb a contemporary view that offers an account of good and bad forms of shame. If my argument is convincing, it calls upon political theorists to change their current view on the political productivity of shame.[5] To make this thesis not an abstract call but a performative intervention, I show the limitations of theories that police shame.

Secondly, I provide a genealogy of shame that traces practices from nineteenth-century activism and offers the possibility of novel contemporary interventions.[6] At the heart of these political interventions are what I call *queer practices*, which are risky for the subject who undertakes them. These practices, which are performative and which unsettle the natural organization of places and roles, include disturbing silences, performative slurs, and unconventional relationships. This historical account stems from the assumption that shame is an assertion of a wrong, is localized at a visceral level, and creates a party and stage for a political conflict.[7] My book operates as an intervention both in contemporary political theory and in a field of historical research, which both limit the political possibilities of shame.

To begin my account of how shame opens up a new field of possibilities for politics, I look to Michel Foucault's concept of *practices of freedom*. Foucault's concept of practices of freedom has been central to queer feminists' efforts to rethink the relationship between feminism and agency.[8] A practice of freedom is "an exercise of the self on the self by which one attempts to develop and transform oneself, and to attain to a certain mode of being" (1994: 282).[9] These practices have a dimension of risk where they open a situation and "[make] possible effects which are, precisely, not known" (2010: 62).[10] Like practices of freedom, practices of speaking the truth, such as parrhesia, constitute an "irruptive event opening up an undefined or poorly defined risk for the subject who speaks" (2010: 63). This possibility, this field of danger, is an upshot of freedom. These practices have at their core the insight that in order to generate a new field of possibilities, one must risk oneself. Under specific conditions of domination, relations of power are fixed so that they are "perpetually asymmetrical" and do not allow for free exchanges (1994: 292). Yet it is possible for us to wield power over one another in an "open-ended strategic game where the situation may be reversed" (1994: 298).

But practices of freedom are not enough to offer an account about how to interrupt the order of *the police*. I draw on Rancière's thought and queer theory to illuminate shame's potential to produce equality and shift power dynamics. In a Rancièrian mode, I conceptualize shame a practice which asserts a wrong and interrupts the order of domination. In his critique of Foucault, Rancière argues that "politics" is the site where *the police* and egalitarian logic meet (1999: 32). Politics is an "initial twist" that institutes it as "the deployment of a wrong or of a fundamental dispute" (Rancière 1999: 13). Like "politics," shame is a "twist" that creates a disagreement and a political scene. While Rancière is helpful for capturing shame's relationship to equality, queer theory offers the tools to describe and challenge inequality as an affective condition. Domination can suppress possibilities for living a queer life, but it also enables possibilities for reversing its effects. In this regard, shame has a great force to provoke political activism, leading to strategies for resignifying political norms that exclude sex and gender marginals.

By bringing together Rancière's interest in techniques of disrupting inequality and a queer interest in the performativity of shame, I conceptualize shame as a political affect that interrupts *the police*. This rethinking of shame draws both on the need to capture equality as an exercise and on the need to identify affects in their productive force. Unlike many queer theorists, Rancière offers a deep understanding of historical practices where subjects create themselves by asserting their equal status. In contrast with Judith Butler's work, I find in Rancière a stronger description of subjects who act in ways they are not supposed to and disrupt the naturalized order of *the police*. His emphasis on the theatrical production of subjects and the anarchic functions of the language is key to theorizing shame as disruptive. Yet Rancière's work lacks a theoretical interest in the life and the performativity of shame.[11] Eve Sedgwick (2009: 60) highlighted shame's role in unsettling rigid identities and its unique performative capacity to be "contagious from one person to another." Queer theory illuminates the pull to feel and think about wrongs that oppressive structures perpetuate as well as urging us to change their force and meaning. In cross-pollinating the Rancièrian and queer apparatuses I theorize shame as both an affect that creates new political subjects and the assertion of a wrong that resignifies norms.[12]

Also, I interrogate the relationship between sexuality, shame, and politics to offer an account of shame as a troublemaker. This particular theoretical intersection asks us to reconsider not only what counts as pleasure but also what incites political action. In some accounts in queer theory, sexual shame leads to an oppositional stance against those who are invested in policing sexuality from its abjection and negativity. Butler articulated the connection between sexual shame and activism when she analyzed the production of queers through shaming (1993: 172).[13] Leo Bersani showed that shame is a key site that challenges a redemptive and pastoral understanding of sexuality (2009: 22).[14] The value of sex lies in its capacity to shatter the self—or to produce a radical humiliation of the self (2009: 24). Tim Dean (2009: 20) sought to locate the appeal of shame not only in the individual psyche but also in communities such as the barebackers. In his argument, barebackers have used unprotected anal sex as a basis for an identity category, and in doing so, "resignified" sexual shame by making the abject attractive. As such, barebackers take a strong critical position with regard to gay norms, and their stance is antihomonormative (Dean 2009: 9).[15] Queer political theory shows that sexual shame is disruptive to a given order that stigmatizes queers and rejects risky sex.

My first target in this book is the belief that shame is primarily bad and normatively suspect, a belief that is shared to varying degrees by theorists such as Martha Nussbaum, Christina Tarnopolsky, and Jill Locke. While Nussbaum emphasizes the negative and threatening consequences of "primitive shame," Tarnopolsky offers ideal types such as *respectful shame* to mitigate the danger in shame.[16] In a stronger vein, Jill Locke (2007: 148) argues that shame and shaming should not "occupy a central position in feminist-democratic politics" and explicitly opposes shaming in favor of feminist-democratic tactics. It is here that I intend to contribute to queer feminist scholarship. Most feminist theorists have showed little interest in, if not outward hostility toward, strategies that deploy silence, humiliating slurs, or nonconventional relationships in political activism.[17]

The book's second target is a perception of shame and its queerness that is removed from its historical production. In political theory, queer had a "queer" trajectory because it arrived rather late. Wendy Brown was doing queer theory in the mid 1990s by challenging identity politics, and more recently, Sam Chambers has been mobilizing queerness to introduce the work of Rancière to political theorists.[18] They show the limits of "politicized identities" (Brown 1995: 54–5) or theorize about "queer" as a political strategy (Chambers 2013: 157–69) in order to point to a transformative politics that does not want to merely assimilate the minorities into liberal democracies. Their hope is that "queer" (Chambers 2013: 168) or the refusal of "the closure of identity" (Brown 1995: 75) will transform politics in unpredictable and radical ways.[19] My work here is motivated by Brown's effort to revive anti-identity politics against an established view of feminism as inherently political. In contrast with a vision of feminism as already political, I show that feminist activism is political when it challenges the order of a given partition of powers, places, and roles. Also, I draw on and develop Chambers' insights in order to establish points of alliance between Rancière's work and queer theory. While both Brown and Chambers are inspired by a historicized understanding of sexual and political identities, they do not, however, systematically investigate the formation of the identities they criticize, nor do they show historically how "queering" identities leads to unconventional politics.[20] Chambers (2013: 58) insightfully notices that the disruptive other is both part of and outside of *the police* order, and that politics is always impure. Yet he does not demonstrate how the category of politics functions throughout its history. Politics needs a genealogy so that political theory can understand the production of politics at specific times and locations.

In this book I mobilize queer genealogy to interrupt a current understanding of shame that seeks to deny its political potential. This genealogy of queer practices seeks to historicize and localize politics as a category of disruption. Although shame is an emotion that is produced by contemporary political discourses, and insults are considered bad, and humiliation is outlawed, shame also has a genealogy and has had shifts in its meaning. A genealogical inquiry would explore practices that could potentially change the widespread perception of shame and its political articulation, so that shame would not have to be defined only by accepted categories. As part of this inquiry, I seek to dislodge the view that illicit relationships, silence, and slurs should be seen as normatively bad. I follow Valerie Traub's injunction to practice a queer historicism dedicated "to showing how *categories . . . came to be*" (2016: 81).[21] As such, my queer historicist approach seeks to explain the force of a category such as shame and illuminate its contingent and historical nature.

What is Shame?

By *shame*, I mean two things. At a theoretical level, I deploy the term shame to talk about a *political affect* that disturbs an organization of politics that is articulated in various theories of shame. In its performative intention, my theoretical take on shame seeks to speak primarily to queer and feminist theorists because these thinkers take the political potential of affects seriously. I conceptualize shame as both the feeling that generates and produces the possibility of novel political actions and a component of their material formation. In the relationship between shame and politics, I see shame not primarily as a subject of politics, but only emerging by way of, through, and *after* politics.[22] Shame always occurs in history and is a political event. In this specific use of the term, shame is a key element in what I analyze as queer practices.

But this theoretical understanding of shame is directly related to a complex organization of psychological reactions such as silence, disgust, humiliation, contempt, and fear.[23] In a *psychological* sense, shame is a result of a relation between an individual and an actual person or an imagined other. Shame is an emotion that is relationally defined by various actors within a particular context.[24] One can be shamed by an individual and feel shame as a reaction to this specific person; one can feel shame when one's bodily or verbal act does not correspond with a norm.[25] Shame is not only what an individual feels but also what he communicates to others and what others are feeling in response to his actions. Those who experience shame and talk about its significance and outcomes construct its content.[26] Because these agents engage with the effects of shame, they create its psychological and political value. To keep the psychological and political connected, I conceptualize the emotion of shame as a political intervention when it is mobilized to articulate a wrong such as "I feel inferior and you make me feel this way."

I opt to describe shame and humiliation as separate political emotions. Whereas shame is a feeling of inadequacy, humiliation underscores one's inferiority in harsh terms. It is an extreme manifestation of shame. When it is employed in political language, humiliation involves disgust, contempt, and even the exclusion of a person from humanity. I keep my usage of the word shame for feelings that are associated with the failure to fulfill a particular standard, and I use the term humiliation to describe a particular form of shame that is harsher. "I feel humiliated" describes an experience in which one not only feels deficient but also despised or contemptible.[27]

Also, although I investigate the political rhetoric of shaming, *physical* shaming and humiliation fall outside the scope of this study.[28] And because I do not locate sexuality exclusively in genital sex, I use the term *sexuality* to explore gestures, behaviors, and affective responses that are seen or felt as having a sexual component. For instance, J. S. Mill scholars have debated whether the friendship between Mill and Harriet Taylor had an overt sexual dimension.[29] What is—or is not—sexual is contested in feminist activism and scholarship.[30] My interest is not to provide or refute evidence about what counts as actual sex, but to analyze practices that undermine a traditional conception of sexuality.[31]

I also distinguish between shaming mobilized against those who oppose *the police* and shaming aimed at *the police*. When shaming is used to stigmatize subjects who disturb the order of domination, I consider it harmful and trace its effects on particular individuals and their behaviors.[32] For example, when certain insults are applied to sexual minorities, they function to shame and humiliate those who have sexual and gender practices that do not conform to a heteronormative standard.[33] On the other hand, when shaming is utilized against liberal politics, I see it as an effort to create a space for radical democratic politics. A different normative intention is in play when political elites fail to meet a particular democratic standard. Under such circumstances, shaming is used to hold them accountable to an ideal that they ignore.[34] I conceptualize shaming *the police* as a risky political practice that mobilizes the fundamental equality of those who are wronged.

What is Queer Genealogy?

I am utilizing the term *queer genealogy* to describe a method that, as Foucault argues, offers a permanent critique of our historical present.[35] This method is "a historical investigation into the events that have led us to constitute ourselves and to recognize ourselves as subjects of what we are doing, thinking, saying" (Foucault 1994: 315). Foucault's work is a study of historical processes that "constitute the normal" (Elden 2016: 24). The frames—or the *dispositifs* of normalization—produce what is intelligible and what is kept invisible or rendered monstrous. To expose the mechanisms of normalization, Foucault appeals to genealogy, which is "a tactic" that "once it has described these local discursivities, brings into play the desubjectified knowledges that have been released from them" (Foucault in Elden 2016: 30). Another term that Foucault (2003: 7) deploys to talk about the payoff of critiquing normalization is "disqualified" knowledges, which are forms of knowledge that have been traditionally dismissed as "nonconceptual knowledges, as insufficiently elaborated knowledges: naive knowledges, hierarchically inferior knowledges, knowledges that are below the required level of erudition and scientificity."

I put genealogy to work by treating the contemporary discourse about shame as a historical formation that needs to be interrogated. I open up a territory of historical inquiry in order to see where it is possible to transform the meaning of shame and to capture its novel political forms. In this study, I utilize the term *queer*, by which I understand like Cathy Cohen (1997: 438) a broader coalition of figures that have been excluded, to designate political subjects that seek to transform the basic fabric and dynamics of systems of oppression.[36] My hope is that the result of this interrogation is our ability to separate from "the contingencies of what we are, think or do" in relationship to shame, the possibility of no longer being, thinking, and acting this way (Foucault 1994: 316).

The method of this study is a queer genealogy because I identify modes of struggle against normalization, which have been rendered useless or irrelevant. I see my book as a project that embarks with unknowingness about the past to discover what is unheard of (Doan 2013: 4). My intention is *not* to trace queer beings at any given moment but to see how sexuality and shame operate and produce subjects and their actions. In doing queer historiography, I do not "detect" repetitions across time, nor touch on an already constituted past (Doan 2013: xii). Rather, I "conjur the past into existence" as a way to make history (Doan 2013: xii). The goal is to shift a prevalent understanding of an affect such as shame by transforming its current frame and meaning. This effort to historicize shame is similar to what, in sexuality studies, goes by the name of "queer critical history" (Doan 2013: xii). One version of this critical history is "ancestral genealogy," whose goal is to understand whether the homosexual is defined by acts or identities, or whether the homosexual is essential or socially constructed (Doan 2013: 14). But later iterations of this genealogical project move toward a "queer genealogy," which historicizes sexuality by tracing back the categories of our present to queer histories and "the process of their interrelations, their crossings, and, eventually, their unstable convergence in the present day" (Halperin 2002: 107).

Like Sam Chambers' method of analyzing "social formations," doing queer genealogy means seizing the changes in what we understand today as shame. Practicing queer genealogy presupposes that one analyzes the world as it is, so that this method will grasp "its terms of existence, its formation, its possible moments of transformation, and the limits that are placed upon them" (Chambers 2014: 18). Concerns about shame have their contingent and contextual emergence. They mobilize historical tropes that are considered effective and timely, and they advocate for different meanings about what constitutes shame. But the queer past does not merely present us with a description of historical actions. It also creates possibilities for imagining a different future that is critical of current understandings of politics.

In rejecting a normatively restrictive vision of shame, my goal here is to demonstrate the value of queer feminist practices. These practices are political interventions that challenge *the police order* because they disrupt established sex and gender norms. *The police*, as Rancière argued, is "an order of the visible and the sayable that sees that a particular activity is visible and another is not, that this speech is understood as discourse and another as noise" (1999: 29).

I elaborate on various practices that indicate how certain political actors offered a different partition of the visible, or to use John Stuart Mill's language, "part[ed] company with the opinion of the world." These political actors take forms of living and acting from the category of "noise" and make them intelligible. I include certain forms of shame that are associated with unconventional relationships, silence, humiliating language as *disqualified knowledges*. It is important to capture and analyze these particular forms of shame because they offer a "historical knowledge of struggles" (Foucault 2003: 8).[37]

My genealogy of queer practices starts from identifying three counter-figures that help denaturalize and transform current understandings of shame. I demarcate types of shame that have been invisible to political theorists because they have been obscured by a particular frame about emotions. In doing so, I learned from Foucault that shame should not primarily refer to the act of feeling shame but rather to the *dispositif* that structures this affect.[38] Foucault deployed the term *dispositif* in his history of sexuality to name "the structure within which individual instances of behavior, pieces of knowledge and acts of resistance find their place and their meaning" (Elden 2016: 54). In his analysis of the Victorians, he identified four figures of the *dispositif*, which produced a normalization of sexuality: the hysterical woman, the masturbating child, the Malthusian couple, and the perverse adult.[39] I conceptualize a contemporary liberal *dispositif* that normalizes sexuality and political activism, and I find this frame to derive from the assumption of an ontological order of exclusion. By "order of exclusion" I mean a liberal theory of discriminated minorities which claims that one knows who are excluded subjects because one knows their identity. According to this view, we already know that excluded members in politics are queers, ethnic minorities, women, and other stigmatized categories. However, this liberal order provides "a hierarchical ordering and allotment of roles that operate within a logic of domination" (Chambers 2013: 10). Like Chambers, I argue that when viewed through a Rancièrian lens, this liberal view is the order of *the police*. Like Foucault, I intend to show that shame is a problem at the heart of who we are in the present and deploy a genealogy of counter-figures to make a submerged problem visible.

The first counter-figure I use to challenge liberal political theory is *unconventional intimate practices*. The problem today is that our political lives are organized around the monogamous heterosexual model, which structures sexual and gender relationships in Western societies. It is shameful not to fit into this ideal. Unconventional intimate practices, however, *can* positively resignify actions that are considered immoral or illegitimate.[40] I analyze the emergence of queer tactics within the alleged nineteenth-century origins of modern Western feminism.[41] These tactics introduce us to how to interrupt the policing of alternative sexualities. Butler's tactic of resignification calls for a reformation of sexual norms so that alternative sexual and kinship arrangements can be recognized as important and vital. Resignifying transgressive relationships and sex slurs—and in particular resignifying terms such as *queer*—politicizes actions in a way that points to the reorganization of a given normative order.[42]

The second counter-figure is *disturbing silence*. Currently, it seems that any speech that challenges the silence about this heteronormative ideal is *always* perceived as brave and urgent. When the US government failed to recognize the AIDS crisis and its impact on gay communities, ACT UP devised the famous slogan "Silence is Death." Their political activism saved the lives of many queers, but it became associated with an injunction to speak against the silence regarding one's sexual practices. *Coming out* became the opposite of being silent in one's closet. Rather than perceiving silence as the opposite of queer feminist agency, I claim that often silence disturbs the order of the visible and produces the possibility of political disagreement. Silence works as an effective practice when it is used to generate a distinct space in which to experiment with living in transgressive sexual relationships.

The third counter-figure is *performative slur*. Political theorists produce various categories to distinguish between good and bad forms of shame, and so ignore the fact that shame functions primarily in its performative capacity. I argue that political theorists who reflect on shame suppress politics or get rid of "the scandal" that is inevitably brought about by the exercise of politics.[43] Instead of theorizing that feminist agency and humiliation (which is seen as "a bad type of shame") are opposed, I show that the performative slur has been a powerful and risky weapon for feminist activism.[44] It has been so when it undermined a given partition of roles and powers and suggested a different evaluation of what is visible and valuable.

In short, by gesturing toward a new queer political theory, this project identifies practices that shift our perception about how shame functions. I offer an alternative to policing, as it is today instantiated through current definitions of shame. Yet, why do I emphasize the role of practices in deploying queerness? Fiol-Matta showed that queerness could be appropriated by various state policies and interests, and it cannot function only as a counter-normative term (2002: 19). But with its discussion of *queer practices,* my book aims to capture a dimension of politics in which agents risk their positions to challenge the order of *the police.* This element of risk is central to political action where individuals put themselves in danger and oppose conventional norms. What I show is that Victorian activists articulated a site of contestation, or a "site of the irruption of what is underneath, below, of what in a culture has no right, or at least no possibility of expression" (Foucault 2010: 188). This site has to be enunciated not only by taking an antinormative position with regard to traditional sex and gender norms, but also by risking one's position and status in a particular hierarchy of power. The emergence of new political subjects is tied to practices where subjects challenge exclusionary norms by articulating their position of equality.

Queer Practices

This book is a contribution to debates in queer and feminist theory about the nature of agency. First, a new conception of queer political agency is needed that is disentangled from a liberal theory of politics.[45] Arguing against a liberal conception, I propose that queer practices emerge as a declaration of a wrong, are practices of disidentification from a given position in a hierarchy, and produce a stage for articulating a conflict. As interventions that destabilize a given order, they have the potential to oppose a liberal order. When one feels shame one is given an inferior position in a hierarchy. But feeling inferior troubles a taken-for-granted identity. It disturbs the idea that there is a recognized partition where one knows the subjects of discrimination and oppression. Shame has a visceral quality that is often expressed through a performative act, which produces a scene of struggle. Central to this concept of queer feminist agency is the Rancièrian idea that politics does not exist before it is articulated in a practice and has become a party to a disagreement. This interruption cannot be grasped in abstract terms, and it needs a genealogy. This is why a new conception of agency must draw on a historicized mode of thinking to focus on practices and activism.

Second, this disentanglement from liberalism needs to draw on resources provided by queer theory.[46] Robyn Wiegman (1999: 108) noted that throughout the 1990s academic feminism confronted the conflict between queer scholars who refused to accept the category of women as a foundational referent and other scholars who believed that such a critique is unproductive for, if not damaging to, feminism's public political voice.[47] The stakes were high for feminists, because the queer revisions of accepted notions of power, politics, and subjective agency powerfully contested the foundational assumptions of the activist feminist agenda.[48] At the heart of these disputes was the role of women in feminism. Queer thinkers such as Butler argue that "women" emerges as a political category in the terms of historical arguments and political questions. Likewise, feminism, as Joan Scott (1999: 31) emphasizes, needs to be primarily concerned with the production of the category of "women." But Martha Nussbaum, who is opposed to a version of feminism that shies away from the gains of liberal feminism, advocates a return to a feminism that is strongly grounded in the category of women as the subject of domination.[49] She calls for a return to the theory and activism of John Stuart Mill and Catharine MacKinnon, who fought to change social practices and laws. Butler, on the other hand, is a "professor of parody," who adopts a passive attitude toward gender discrimination and offers irresponsible politics that "collaborates with evil." Drag, subversion, and the acceptance of "humiliating structures" are corrupt forms of political agency, and they should be removed from the feminist political agenda.[50]

Nussbaum's polemical exchange with Butler shows why the project of feminist theory needs queer theory to be decoupled from its liberal underpinnings. As Ruth Abbey (2011: 1) claims, "Modern Western feminism grew up as a sister doctrine to liberalism." For most feminists, feminism has its source in liberalism, and figures such as Mary Wollstonecraft, Harriet Taylor, John Stuart Mill, and Susan B. Anthony are included in the canon as feminist liberals (Abbey 2011: 1). Because of this strong association between feminism and liberalism, Nussbaum holds Butler accountable for abandoning the liberal feminist commitment to the struggle for justice and equality for women. Although the term liberal includes values such as individual freedom, equality before the law, equal opportunity, moral equality, personal autonomy, consent to rule by those who rule, and freedom of conscience, Nussbaum focuses her critique of Butler on the poststructuralist understanding of power, which betrays the traditional rejection by liberal theorists of arbitrary and hierarchical power.[51] For Nussbaum, Butler's new and dangerous feminism

> instructs its members that there is little room for large-scale social change, and maybe no room at all. We are all, more or less, prisoners of the structures of power that have defined our identity as women; we

can never change those structures in a large-scale way, and we can never escape from them. (Nussbaum 1999)

Nussbaum's call to feminists is for a return to the liberal concept of agency—i.e., opposition to power—while Butler argues that the liberal concept of agency is defective and needs to be replaced. These two accounts of feminist agency have strong implications about what feminists should do and what strategies they need to pursue in their academic and activist lives. If Butler is right, and feminism can be decoupled from a liberal epistemology, what type of agency should be at the forefront of feminist theory?[52]

This book offers a theoretical framework that moves beyond a conception of agency rooted in known subjects of politics. I focus on prominent Victorian activists and thinkers such as John Stuart Mill and Josephine Butler, who are generally mobilized to justify the value of standard feminist agency, and seek to disentangle them from the prevailing liberal narrative. In this canonical story Mill is a liberal feminist, but I analyze Mill's political rhetoric and practices to broaden our view about his political interventions. I make the case for queerness in Mill's politics and focus on specific interventions that do not fit the standard view of his liberalism.[53] Mill is not the only nineteenth-century feminist who is seen as a liberal feminist. Josephine Butler was primarily analyzed as a liberal figure, with a focus on the tension between her feminism and liberalism (Caine 1992: 155–6; Frederickson 2008: 208).[54] Feminists involved in the sex wars in the 1980s deployed Josephine Butler to counteract the perceived dangers of an alternative, poststructuralist conception of agency.[55] Neither Mill nor Butler, however, have to be examined as they are primarily liberal feminists.[56]

To break away from a liberal feminist framework, Judith Butler offers two key tactics to advance a conception of queer feminist agency. First, Butler emphasizes the idea that feminist political action is not neutral to the power it opposes; it is shaped by the participants' involvement in relations of power. In Lisa Disch's formulation, Butler shows us that there "exists no standpoint of critique that is not sustained by and complicit with the forces it seeks to transform" (1999: 546).[57] Feminist agency emerges from the question of "how to take an oppositional relation to power that is, admittedly, implicated in the very power one opposes" (Butler 1997a: 17).[58] When Butler argues that "called by an injurious term, I come into social being," she does not endorse passivity, as Nussbaum assumes. Rather, she points to a political predicament that allows for turning a term of oppression against *the police*. For Butler, change cannot come merely from opposing humiliating structure, but from modifying and transforming structures of power that are already "humiliating."[59]

The second tactic is that shame is not only inhibiting action, but also as produces it. While Nussbaum holds primarily a negative view of shame and its potential for politics, Butler is interested in harnessing shame's capacity to prompt political resistance. Butler argues that queer subjects are produced through shaming and insult, which suggests that resignifying the term *queer* offers a strategy for resisting politically oppressive norms (1993: 172). Instead of accepting *queer* as a slur, *queer* can be resignified and transformed into a disruptive gesture. "The politicization of abjection" is an attempt to "rewrite the history of the term" and force a different meaning upon it (1993: xxviii–xxix). This tactic allows an injurious term to be occupied, resisted, and modified by giving it an alternative connotation: "Precisely because such terms [*queer*] have been produced and constrained within such regimes, they ought to be repeated in directions that reverse and displace their originating aims" (1993: 83).

Although asserting oneself as queer risks a repetition of injury, the performative act of affirming queerness opens up new possibilities for agency. Butler warns us that the uses of queer are context dependent and cannot constitute a plan of action with specific requirements, but she also claims that queer can serve as a tool for transforming conventional politics.

Political Theory and *The Police*

I use Rancière's understanding of politics to distinguish between two theoretical camps that engage with the use and value of shame. The thesis that I start with is that policing is the activity that seeks to predetermine the field of politics, and it does so in the name of a certain purity (Chambers 2013: 60). Policing is the activity of demarcating the visible, and it aims to demarcate between the proper and improper uses of politics. In contrast, a democratic logic politicizes demarcations and blurs and displaces the borders of politics. It seeks to politicize impurity by enacting the scandal of being excluded from a field of visibility.

A caveat is in order before I make my demarcation of theoretical factions. If particular thinkers are involved in policing shame, that does not make them the embodiment of *the police*, as opposed to, let us say, a second group of theorists that would be the queer anti-police wing. If politics is impure, there is no given identity of the police. Politics is about practices in which sides are taken and a political conflict is enacted. In ontological terms, thinkers associated with queer theory can be *the police*, and theorists associated with liberalism can challenge the order of hierarchy and inequality. This is an important point that I want to get across by genealogically unmooring a group of nineteenth-century thinkers from liberalism. My assumption that there are no fixed theoretical groups shows why this demarcation is contingent on the goals of this specific argument. Theorists do no align easily in only one category. Thinkers such as Jill Locke (2016: 47–72), whom I challenge because of her understanding of shame as a disciplinary affect, have developed sophisticated accounts of "unashamed citizenship," in which she draws on the unruly and anti-disciplinary practices of the Cynics.[60] In turn, queer theorists such as Brown and Butler have engaged in their own practice of policing by demarcating between what is proper and what is improper in politics.[61]

In this section my argument is simply that certain political theorists—associated with a liberal orientation—seek to police the category of shame on the basis of ideals such as autonomy and respect. By developing *constructive* and *respectful* strategies of deploying shame, political theorists reject other forms of shame that are considered illegitimate, such as *primitive* or *stigmatizing* shame.[62] For Nussbaum, shame, particularly *primitive shame*, is an emotion that is troubling because it threatens the equality and autonomy of human beings. While Nussbaum sees guilt as "potentially creative," shame, "at least shame of the primitive sort, is a threat to all possibility of morality and community, and indeed to a creative inner life" (Nussbaum 2001: 218).[63] However, Nussbaum also recognizes forms of shame that do not possess the same dangerous content as primitive shame. *Constructive* shame does well what *primitive* shame fails to produce. *Constructive shame* is an emotion that is productive for citizens in liberal democracies, because it reinforces vulnerability, generates inclusion, and highlights people's interdependence and mutual responsibilities (2004: 213). The invitation to feel shame is normatively good when it is "non-insulting, non-humiliating, and noncoercive" (2004: 214).

Because she believes that constructive shame can be useful to respond to democratic dysfunctions, Nussbaum finds it useful for liberal democratic thought.

Like Nussbaum, albeit with important distinctions, Christina Tarnopolsky (2010) also argues that shame can be constructive and positive. Drawing primarily on *Gorgias*, she argues that respectful Platonic shame produced a "salutary" but "painful, perplexing and discomforting" recognition of the inadequacy of the self—a recognition that was beneficial for democratic norms. When Socrates shamed his interlocutors, he wanted to show them that they do not correspond with a beneficial normative standard.[64] Tarnopolsky, too, argues that shaming is a positive practice for feminist and democratic politics. For instance, non-governmental organizations such as Human Rights Watch should shame regimes that carry out torture or stigmatize and punish unwed mothers who have AIDS (2010: 2). She draws the line at humiliation, however, since, unlike shaming, humiliation could lead to horrific events such as the abuses perpetrated against Iraqi prisoners at the Abu Ghraib prison (2010: 1). To humiliate is to show contempt and disgust for the person in question, and to profess the belief that that person is not human; the humiliating judgment is likely to be "self-shattering" and "to involve a global assessment of the self as completely unworthy" (2010: 156).[65]

The problem with this liberal understanding of shame is that it demarcates between the normatively good and bad without taking into account power and its hierarchies. In turn, queer feminist theorists are concerned that many normative proposals strengthen inequalities of power, rather than dismantling them.[66] For instance, political action that appeals to state and courts of law is problematic because it tends to enhance state regulation.[67] Rather than utilizing the power of the state, queer thinkers praise the importance of agonism in politics, as well as what Brown (1995: 27) calls "the possibilities of indeterminacy, ambiguity and struggle for resignification and repositioning."[68] Queer feminist theorists contribute to a wider understanding of agency by taking seriously one's involvement in a complicated power dynamic. They call for a better understanding of the contextual consequences of various interventions and interrogate the production of identities such as *women, gays, queers* and subjects of oppression. And while queer feminist theorists do not categorically endorse the feminist use of silence, slurs, and humiliation in feminist rhetoric, they seek to understand what is excluded from mainstream feminist discourse and to politicize gestures and actions that are considered "excluded" or "illegible."

One of the things that queer feminist theorists urge us to rethink is the value of *silence in counter-normative relationships*. When Nussbaum (2010: 141–2) discusses John Stuart Mill's political positions, she argues that Mill had a strong conservative side because he was silent on the topic of sexual experimentation and did not consider alternatives to monogamous and heterosexual forms of family organization. In contrast, queer thinkers criticize the assumption that speech always reflects an oppositional stance.[69] They also ask us to consider that humiliation and coercion are not only opposed to queer feminist agency but that they *constitute* queer feminist rhetoric and action.[70] Indeed, *humiliating rhetoric* shapes their vocabulary and interventions.[71] Foucault understands the value of humiliating situations that challenge traditional norms about sexuality. In his discussion of Cynic practices of freedom, Foucault identifies humiliation as a systematic use of dishonor.[72] In this sense, slurs could become queer practices in specific contexts. Butler shows that by resignifying slurs, these slurs can be used by feminists in a positive manner to respond to words that injure and produce harm. For example, the term queer has been used as "a paralyzing slur" and "an interpellation of pathologized sexuality" (1993: 169).[73] Because one's resistance to power cannot take shape outside of the possibilities that are offered by power (including its definition of words), to fight shame one must resignify the shameful terms that are used against oneself.[74]

In this book I genealogically investigate the deployment of shame in the nineteenth century to challenge a current articulation of *the police*—that is, the liberal feminist view of agency. I benefit from an important feminist body of literature that has investigated and criticized Mill's work and activism.[75] Various feminist scholars (Okin 1979; Eisenstein 1981; Ring 1985; Di Stefano 1989) have analyzed the flaws in Mill's political theory, which are associated with his liberal feminism, but my intention in this study is not to examine Mill's limitations as a liberal feminist.[76] The feminist perspective implicitly assumes that Mill is relevant primarily because of his liberal conceptions about gender and freedom. Di Stefano (1989) and Zerilli (1994) notwithstanding, feminists do not investigate Mill's work from the standpoint of queer feminist theory.

I want to change the standpoint of the analysis. Nussbaum, in a surprising move, suggested that Mill could be a valuable resource for queer feminists, only to immediately shut the door on this possibility.[77] I take her invitation seriously, but my aim is to challenge the boundaries that liberal feminists deploy in interpreting canonical figures. Rather than typecasting Mill as liberal feminist, I seek to explore the importance of his interventions for a new conception of political agency. Feminists influenced by poststructuralism (Di Stefano 1989; Zerilli 1994), like liberal feminists, demonstrate the limitations of Mill's account of sexual difference and political freedom. Here I do not seek to emphasize Mill's limitations as a theorist, but rather to understand his contribution to grasping queer forms of politics that disturb *the police*. I do not make a case for a queer Mill or Mill the queer theorist, however, because I am interested in queering as a political intervention.[78] Jon Simons (1995: 116) suggests a productive direction of research when he notes that Mill's *experiments in living* can "translate into Foucauldian vocabulary as aesthetics of the self."[79] What I intend to do is to show that elements of Mill's rhetoric and life point toward a queer political theory, and that these elements need to be decoupled from a liberal framework.

This study challenges the conventional narrative by making visible parts of Mill's life that are left unseen.[80] First, I offer an account of Mill's less known relationship with the intellectual radicalism of English feminism in the 1830s and between 1865 and 1872. I explore Mill's radical positions as a young journalist and contrast his attitude toward sex and gender discrimination during the Contagious Diseases (CD) Acts debates with other radical voices in the women's movement. Second, I shift the attention of political theorists from the interpretation of ideas to Mill's practices. A stronger conception of queer feminist agency can emerge from an investigation of practices that were previously left unexplored.[81] Thus can political theorists interested in Mill's liberalism not only learn the value of his radical interventions but also modify their perceptions about agency. The concept of *practices* does not require the assumption of an agent who is in full control of his or her actions, nor does it ask one to interpret the agent's actions as deriving from a non-changing self.[82] Scholars of modern liberalism can learn from this study that not only is Mill's explicit political theory important, but also his actions as a historical agent involved in contradictory and surprising acts.

In order to highlight these interventions, I de-naturalize gestures and practices that are considered normal. As Chambers (2013: 66) claimed, while "the social order is already being naturalized," this work of naturalization, "of passing off as natural that which can only be conventional," is the work of policing.[83] In this sense, my recourse of the exceptions, the bizarre, and the strange is not merely to relativize claims about the conventional understanding of shame. Like Butler, I believe that the exception, "that which falls 'outside,'" gives us a way of understanding what is taken for granted in our perception of politics (1999: 149). This is why shame is productive—it generates actions that are traditionally considered outside of politics and relegated to the margins of scholarship.[84]

In the next section, I explain how the views of nineteenth-century Anglo-American feminists urge us to take seriously a politicized, queer view of shame.

Why Nineteenth-Century Feminists?

If politics happens on the terrain of *the police*, then a strategic field of contestation is "the origin" of liberal feminist theory. To dismantle *the police*, I argue that we need a genealogy of the activism of "the precursors" of liberal feminism. When Nussbaum challenged the "new feminism" of Butler, she accused hip feminists of abandoning the engaged politics of John Stuart Mill and Catharine MacKinnon. Queer feminists have extensively responded to Catharine MacKinnon's work on hate speech and pornography and explained that MacKinnon's theory and legislative proposals have serious conceptual and political flaws (Brown 1995; Butler 1997b), but these queer feminists *have* overlooked the work and thought of nineteenth-century feminists such as Mill, whom liberal feminists have widely referenced to justify their positions. To abandon the "classical liberal-humanist formulation" of power (Butler 1997a: 17), queer feminists must rethink agency at its alleged roots. Therefore, the project of politicizing feminist agency beyond liberal theory requires an analysis not only of contemporary scholars such as MacKinnon but also of nineteenth-century activists and theorists who have been incorporated into the feminist canon.

The standard view of political agency—one that derives from the classical account of liberal feminism in the nineteenth century—emphasizes the battle for political vote and representation, the need for economic empowerment, and the fight against domestic violence.[85]

But queer feminists can re-examine their view of agency by paying attention to the distinct unconventional forms of political action that emerged alongside classical forms of nineteenth-century activism and by embracing the work of historians who emphasize the radical side of Victorian feminists.[86] Instead of uncritically accepting the standard narrative, queer feminists can open up to novel political interventions of the first wave feminists. A conception of queer practices that emphasizes agency's formation within power relations and the role of equality in challenging the order of *the police* offers a new lens through which to perceive the contribution of nineteenth-century activists.

Moreover, I turn to Victorian activists because, rather than buttressing the claims of liberal feminists about the significance of the state and the law for responding to injustice, they often support Butler's call for "non-state-centered forms of agency and resistance" or "non-juridical forms of opposition" (1997b: 19, 23–4).[87] According to Butler, fighting hate speech with rights claims and establishing same-sex marriage rights "may actually do less to enhance individual freedom than to increase state power."[88] Drawing on Butler's suggestions about "non-state centered" action such as resignification, I locate the potential for creative and novel interventions in the nineteenth-century activists' responses to shame.[89] The activists' rhetoric and practices offer a guide to theorists who are committed to a project of radical democracy.[90]

Nineteenth-century activists criticized those who used political power to marginalize women and the poor. They also raised awareness of the social subordination of women and advocated for the adoption of better policies for women, "prostitutes," and the working class. They used the rhetoric of shame to challenge the social hypocrisy of the upper class elites in both England and the United States. Yet they also used unconventional tactics to challenge politics that promoted inequality. Some of the nineteenth-century activists did not hesitate to humiliate their political opponents, when it was risky to attack the power elite. Others, like Mill and Woodhull, lived in unconventional relationships, which challenged the assumption that people have to live according to a heteronormative standard. Some of them resignified slurs into affirmative descriptions of identity and intellectual contribution. Some, including Mill, suggested that silence is an effective strategy when one's sexuality is used against oneself to diminish one's reputation. These feminists point to a concept of queer feminist agency, which troubles a standard view of liberal agency.

My primary contribution in this study is to offer a genealogical alternative to the standard perception about liberal feminist precursors, but I also offer a comparative study of several feminists who previously have not been analyzed as a unit.[91] This study began as an analysis of Mill's theoretical and practical relationship to shame, but it evolved into a study of early queer feminist strategies. In this group I integrated Mill, the feminist critics from the *Monthly Repository*, the British feminist Josephine Butler, and the US feminist "black sheep" Victoria Woodhull. These feminists do not comprise a coherent group or a single feminist network. Rather, they have in common a particular mode of political contestation that is, I argue, at odds with the contemporary perception of feminist agency.[92] My initial impulse was to challenge Nussbaum's (2010: 142) reading of Mill's work as being "not queer enough." This impulse is still an important part of this book, at least in the book's explicit claim that liberal feminists fail to understand the significance of unconventional political activism.

The critics I draw upon illustrate the complex intellectual architecture of radical dissent in the nineteenth century. Mill was perceived as an intellectual star of the English feminist movement in the second half of the nineteenth century.[93] His book *The Subjection of Women* (1869) criticized the patriarchal social and legal norms of Victorian England, called women's subordination evil, and advocated for women's open access to employment. Mill campaigned for women's rights, women's suffrage, and equal access to education, and proposed an amendment that would have given unmarried women the right to vote. As I discuss the role of performative rhetoric of *The Subjection of Women*, I examine Mill's relationship to feminism with regard to several key times in his life. Like Mill, Josephine Butler was one of the most prominent advocates for women's rights in Victorian England. She was actively involved in rescue work amongst prostitutes, established her own House of Rest for sick and dying women, advocated for the opening of university degrees to women, and became the fiercest opponent of the CD Acts. Also, I examine the queer practices of Victoria Woodhull, who was an important American activist who used Mill's advocacy of free speech to unsettle accepted notions of women's sexuality. Unlike the English feminists, Woodhull took strong public positions about the value of political and sexual revolution. Woodhull is key to this project because she is an example of a feminist who not only performed but also theorized about interventions that moved away from the conventional narrative of feminist action.[94]

The Structure of the Book

This study is organized in three parts. In the first part, titled *Shame and Queer Political Theory*, I introduce the scope, goals, and methodology of the book. While the first chapter is a theoretical introduction to the argument, Chapter 2 shows how the concept of queer practices helps us rethink nineteenth-century feminist activism. I draw on Butler's theory of performativity but I argue that shame needs a stronger conceptualization that captures its disruptive function in relationship to the *police*. Rancière's concepts of "subjectivation" and "literarity" help me draw out the antagonistic role of queer practices. In this new conception of shame, Mill's unconventional relationship with Harriet Taylor, his silences and humiliating rhetoric become queer interventions that interrupt Victorian sexual norms.

In Part II, *Counter-Figures*, I deploy three tropes as devices to flesh out how to do queer genealogy. First, the counter-figure of *disruptive silence* is important because it challenges the practice of speaking out as the normalization of activism. To do this, in Chapter 3 I challenge Martha Nussbaum's theory of shame (and her argument against the value of silence). I examine the early stage of Mill's relationship with Harriet Taylor, discuss Mill's relationship with a group of radical Unitarians, and analyze his interventions in the context of conservative critiques of sex radicalism. I use Rancière's (1999: 2) distinction between "speech" and "groan" and Brown's (2005: 89) argument that silence offers a "shelter" against the judgment of public opinion to argue that Mill's silences contest the demand to always speak out against oppression.

Second, the counter-figure of *performative slurs* has the potential of opening up radical democratic interventions when it makes visible subjects who previously had no part in politics. To show this, I respond in Chapter 4 to scholars who believe that humiliation is illegitimate as a political strategy (Nussbaum 2004: 139; Tarnopolsky 2010:156). I distinguish between two types of rhetorical interventions. A first use of humiliating rhetoric produces new political subjects, while a second becomes a way for *the police* to control who is visible in the public space. To highlight its first use, I show that during debates about the Contagious Diseases (CD) Acts in England, feminists' radical rhetoric resignified exclusionary political conventions such as prostitution laws and prohibitions against voting. To explain a second use of performative slurs, I analyze Mill's rhetoric against a group of radical feminists. Because Mill wanted to achieve political enfranchisement, he policed radical activists and practices, and diminished the force of the women's movement.

Third, the counter-figure of *unconventional relationships* functions as a line of escape from oppressive norms about sexuality. By drawing on Rancière's concept of line of escape and Butler's mode of dispossession, I investigate in Chapter 5 the actions of a nineteenth-century US feminist radical, Victoria Woodhull. Woodhull's strategy was a line of escape from a certain progressive activism, which policed the capacity to imagine sexual relationships outside monogamy. Her actions show that sex dissenters can create reveries that produce a theatrical disorder of the senses. When shame dispossess, it interrupts what is proper in sexuality and produces a space for dreaming about novel forms of intimate life.

In part III, *Queering Shame*, I reflect upon the possibilities unleashed by exciting scholarship in queer political theory. I discuss the future of queer political thinking by insisting that the act of interpretation has to draw on how one becomes both irritated by and surprised by scholarly arguments. As an affective practice, irritation offers the incentive to challenge what is already known while the surprise opens up a new territory for investigation. To enact my interpretative method, I critically engage with the work of Eve Sedgwick, Leo Bersani, José Esteban Muñoz, and Lauren Berlant to argue that queer practices can articulate an equality-oriented vision of politics.

Notes

1. I locate my book in a flourishing feminist and queer literature about shame and politics. For "the affective turn," which represents a vibrant research agenda in social sciences and humanities, see Cvetkovich (2003); Brennan (2004); Ahmed (2004); Hemmings (2005); Gordon (2007); Love (2007); Muñoz (2009); Berlant (2011); Locke (2016).
2. To describe the theoretical orientation of thinkers such as Judith Butler, Wendy Brown, and Eve Kosofsky Sedgwick, I will use the term queer feminists. By *nineteenth century feminists, first wave feminists* and *early feminists*, I identify activists and scholars such as John Stuart Mill, the radicals at the *Monthly Repository*, Josephine Butler and Victoria Woodhull. Mill, the radicals, and Butler were English Victorians and Woodhull

was an American activist and free love advocate. The term Victorian refers to a period of time in British history, but also in American history, between the early 1830s and the beginning of the twentieth century. I follow scholars who date the beginning of this period as starting with the Reform Act of 1832 in England.
3. While in this study I will use terms such as emotions, affects, and feelings as synonymous, psychologists and queer theorists distinguish between affect as the visceral portion of emotion and emotion as the rational, processed feeling. While I believe that the distinction between affect and emotion has value in particular contexts, I generally use the term emotion to describe reactions associated with shame.
4. I will use the italicized term *police* to talk about Rancière's understanding of the police. When I mean the police as the institution of control and punishment, I use the term without the italics. Like Rancière, I utilize the distinction between politics/*the police* as polemical intervention in queer feminist theory, as well as to rethink our perception of the history of political thought (see how Rancière sees his own mode of writing theory in Chambers 2013: 33).
5. Drabinski (2012: 125) suggests that shame, in relationship to anti-black politics, is "a critical site of analysis as both diagnosis (we must understand the affective life produced by anti-black racism and how deeply it is written into the psyche) and transformative resistance (the confrontation with shame is a moment of transforming subjectivity and the future, as well as a moment of retrieval of forgotten elements of black history)." Like him, I seek to understand the life of shame in both dimensions, but what I take from Rancière is a reflection about the potential of shame to be disruptive.
6. I use the term genealogy in the sense that Foucault used it. See the section entitled "What is Queer Genealogy?" for an explanation of the term.
7. See Rancière (1999: 11): "politics exists when the natural order of domination is interrupted by the institution of a part of those who have no part."
8. For a deeper understanding of the relationship between queer theory and feminist theory, see the special issue of *Foucault Studies* (September 2013) on Foucault and feminism.
9. As he points out in *The Birth of Politics* (2008), Foucault begins his historical work by a study of practices that are not a reflection of traditional categories of academic research such as the state, the people, civil society, the madness, the pervert and so forth. Instead of "deducing concrete phenomena from universals," he seeks to "start with concrete practices" and to bypass these "universal" categories of thought. In *The Hermeneutics of the Subject* (2005), Foucault allies these practices with the ancient notion of the care of the self, by which one works on one's

habits, comportment, relationships and abilities so that one mitigates the threat of being dominated and of dominating others. See McWhorter (2013: 71–2) for this point about Foucault. Also, Valdez (2016: 18) develops an insightful distinction between genuine practices of freedom and "practices of the self that are unreflective responses to systems of government."

10. Queer theory is a field of poststructuralist critical theory that emerged in the 1990s in US academia, particularly in women's studies, LGBT theory and literary criticism. Influenced by the work of scholars such as Judith Butler, Eve Kosofsky Sedgwick, and Michael Warner, queer thinkers criticized the idea that sexual and gender categories are "natural," "essential," and "fixed."

11. For some queer theorists, the political potential of resignification lies in its capacity to generate performative moments "in which a subject—a person, a collective—asserts a right or entitlement to a livable life when no such prior authorization exists" (Butler 2004a: 224).

12. Butler's theories have been "enormously influential" for challenging the assumptions of the politics of identity, particularly in the context of the feminist and LGBT movements (Lloyd 1999: 1). Butler finds a powerful political potential in this possibility of repetition and resignification of norms. Butler formulated her concept of performativity to stress that gender is not an expression of what one is, but of what one does. To perform is to produce or enact that which one names through repetition. Butler, opposed to the conception that gender is an eternal essence that precedes social and linguistic norms, argued that gender is produced through various performative gestures (Lloyd 1999: 197). *Straight* and *queer* are not fixed categories because they do not "identify" or "represent" particular groups of subjects. Rather, gender expression is fluid and open, which creates possibilities for citing and repeating norms differently.

13. Queer theorists analyze and theorize the performativity of affects. Like Sedgwick, Butler gives affects a central role in her analysis of political power. She believes that affects "became not just the basis, but the very stuff of ideation and of critique" (2009: 34). For Butler, particular affective responses, such as guilt and mourning, "call into question the taken-for-granted character" of various interpretative frames of politics; they provide "the affective conditions" for social critique (2009: 34). Her theory of performativity decenters action from a model of individualistic, rational choice. Because individuals are not entirely sovereign over their actions, human agency has a powerful unconscious component. When we act politically, "it is already within a set of norms that are acting upon us, and in ways that we cannot always know about" (2009: xi). Performativity "is a process that implies being

acted on in ways we do not always fully understand, and of acting, in political consequential ways" (2009: xii). Because performativity contains in its repetition the potential for political action, resignification is an effect of our capacity for performativity. Neither fully intentional, nor unconscious, resignification is a strategy for politicizing forms of actions that are excluded as "abjected" and for tracing the history of their effects and impact.

14. Bersani saw shame as a primary component in why sex has value when it is "anticommunal, antiegalitarian, antinurturing, antiloving" (2009: 22).
15. Homonormativity is a critical concept in queer studies that claims that a certain organization of homosexuality—manifested in the gay mainstream—has become normalizing. See Dean (2009: 9) and Lisa Duggan (2003).
16. While Martha Nussbaum embraces the label "liberal feminist," I assume that Christina Tarnopolsky would not define her politics as liberal. However, I argue that Tarnopolsky theorizes ideal types of shame that restrict the deployment of uglier types of political action such as humiliation.
17. In her (2011) book *The Return of Feminist Liberalism*, Ruth Abbey explores the thought of major liberal feminists such as Martha Nussbaum, Susan Okin, and Jean Hampton, yet ignores any alternatives to standard feminist interventions.
18. By identity politics, Wendy Brown understands the process by which certain cultural and social identities function politically by being kept separated from a critique of capitalism. She suggests that feminism, as identity politics, was strongly tied to the politics of *ressentiment*, that is, to the politics of using pain and insults as responses to exclusion (1995: 70–1). However, Brown raises the possibility of achieving a "radically democratic political culture" that would allow the expression of pain in the public space in order to transform and reconfigure cultural practices (1995: 75).
19. Like Queer Nation's chant "We're here! We're Queer! Get used to it!," for Chambers (2013: 159) a political moment appears when a wrong has been made visible so that an order of equality has been asserted.
20. Differently put, if Chambers does not show how *politics* functions today in relationship to the past, Brown fails to theorize that *politics* also operates in identitarian terms. For Brown, politicized identities seem to always produce political impotence (1993: 406). Compare that with Susan Bickford's (1997: 126–7) claim that identity politics is an important part of democratic politics. I thank Inés Valdez Tappatá for this reference.
21. See also Joan Scott's understanding of critical history: "It's using history to critically engage the way taken-for-granted concepts are used in the present," in Watson (2011: 110).

22. I borrow this formulation from Chambers (2013: 20), who argues that "the political subject can never be the bearer of politics, since the subject emerges by way of, through, and as articulated above, *after* politics."
23. Many feminist theorists conceptualize shame as a negative feeling that produces a diminishing "global assessment" about one's self (Manion 2002: 21; Locke 2007: 149). As such, shame is especially likely to be "normatively distorted," and, along with disgust, is "unreliable" as a guide to "public practices" (Nussbaum, 2004: 13–14).
24. Bernard Williams's book *Shame and Necessity*, represents a groundbreaking work in political theory that explores the meaning and ramifications of shame in Greek thought. For Williams, shame is "essentially interactive" and it serves "to bond as much as to divide" (1993: 81).
25. Sociologists and feminist theorists theorize the role of shame as a response to social norms. Goffman (1963: 8–10) shows that shame derives from the constant demand people put upon themselves to fulfill a social and political ideal. Lorde (2009: 203) claims that "the mythical norm"—the white, thin, male, heterosexual, young, Christian, financially secure individual—holds a normative, hegemonic power over the Western world. Whereas Goffman and Lorde analyze the impact of shame on the construction of social identity (Goffman) and black female identity (Lorde), I investigate queer practices that are designed to counteract the damaging effects of shame.
26. Rather than conceptualizing shame as an emotion with a specific content, I assume that its meaning derives from interaction with other emotions and affects, especially affects such as fear, silence, and humiliation. When the Homeric hero Ajax stirs his companions by appealing to their sense of shame, the shame mobilized as a "battle cry" is also a form of fear (Williams 1993: 79). Other theorists of emotions, including scholars in political theory, agree with Williams's understanding of the complex character of shame. Sara Ahmed (2004: 90–2) investigated the relational nature of emotions and theorized their "stickiness." Emotions attach themselves to objects; they stick to them and define their meaning and value. Psychologist Gershen Kaufman claims that shame generates silence under particular conditions, because shame is an affect that causes the self to hide (2004: 194).
27. Although I treat shame and humiliation as distinct emotions, I see them as forming part of a continuum. They are not completely separate emotions. Shame and humiliation describe bodily reactions and feelings that overlap significantly. When one feels that one is mortified or humiliated, shame is a central part of that emotion. Sometimes shaming can be perceived as humiliation, or a humiliating attitude as shaming, according to a particular context. For the purposes of this study, I use shame to describe feelings that are moderately hurtful and humiliation for feelings that are perceived as extreme.

28. Ian Gibson's (1978) study of corporal punishment and shame in Victorian England analyzes the role of flagellation in British public schools. For him, shame and humiliation are primarily physical acts that were undertaken to enforce disciplinary rules.
29. See, for instance, Rossi (1970) and Nussbaum (2010), who both offer their interpretations about whether and when Mill and Harriet Taylor had sex.
30. Mill's relationship with Harriet Taylor had a sexual component. Not only did they mention erotic gestures in their letters, but also friends and acquaintances saw their relationship as sexual. Various Victorians, including Mill's father and friends, felt that their unconventional arrangement was transgressive and hard to agree with.
31. I draw both upon the agents' perception of their actions and a public discourse that describes specific gestures and relationships as sexual. Thus I focus upon the relationship between the actors' understandings of their actions and the impact of these descriptions on their life.
32. The term queer has operated as a practice whose purpose is to shame its subject (Butler 1993: 172). Slut shaming is another strategy to shame minorities who do not sexually fit a standard (SlutWalk Toronto website, 2012). Similarly, words such as nigger and cunt have been used as humiliating terms intended to underscore the superiority of a white male political agent.
33. By *heteronormative standard*, I mean a convention that claims that sexual and gender practices should conform to a monogamous relationship between a man and a woman. Heteronormative standards deem practices that do not correspond to this norm to be illegitimate. Warner (1993: xxi–xxv) coined the term *heteronormativity* to argue that queer politics is not only a call for inclusion of sexual minorities but also a political project of imaging new forms of life and relationships. Butler (1999: 6, 47) utilized the term "heterosexual matrix" to criticize the same standard that privileges a particular normative life.
34. In the 1970s, feminist and gay/lesbian activists put sexual issues on the public agenda and argued strongly about the importance of intimate life. Progressive social movements have tried to cut the link between sexuality and shame, and have contested conservative social practices and laws that opposed abortion, contraceptive rights, nonmonogamous sex and sex between same-sex couples. Conservatives, on the other hand, used shame against the liberalization of sexual and intimate relationships (Stein 2006: 2).
35. For a methodological presentation of genealogy in political theory, see Koopman (2013) and May (1993).
36. For Cohen (1997), these figures are "punks, bulldaggers, and welfare queens."

37. By *struggles*, Foucault meant a conflict between marginal and official knowledge, whereby marginal knowledge challenges the hierarchy and privileges associated with official knowledge. He believed that the reconstruction of such knowledges through the genealogical method led to "the meticulous rediscovery of struggles and the raw memory of fights" (2003: 8).
38. See Foucault's insight that "we must not refer a history of sexuality to the agency of sex; but rather show how sex is historically subordinate to sexuality" (Foucault in Elden 2016: 61).
39. See Koopman's description of genealogies as concerned with submerged problems (2013: 1–13).
40. Recent attempts to legalize gay and lesbian marriages challenge the hegemony of the heterosexual monogamy. Yet, the downside of a contemporary progressive effort to promote lesbian and gay marriage is that it renders "illegitimate and abject" sexual arrangements that do not comply with marriage (Butler 2004a: 5).
41. See Lloyd's (2008: 92) critique that "Butler fails to engage adequately with the historicity of the social, that is, with the historical practices that constitute the social." While I agree with Lloyd, my work shows that Butler's theory can be productive for illuminating historical and psychological dynamics of queer feminist activism.
42. These politicizing tactics can address and transform shame about sexuality. Resignification is not only a practice of changing the meaning of a word but also a practice that produces "greater possibilities of life" (Butler 2004a: 223). It implies that "a subject—a person, a collective—asserts a right or entitlement to a livable life when no such prior authorization exists" (Butler 2004a: 224). Although the black South Africans did not have the right to vote, they went to the polling booths and showed with their gesture that the so-called democratic process was exclusionary (Butler 2004a: 224). By assuming their right to vote, they expanded the meaning of concepts such as inclusion and democracy.
43. For politics as a scandalous intervention, see Rancière (1999: xii).
44. Various scholars hold Butler accountable for what they consider an ethical, apolitical turn in her recent work. For Jodi Dean (2008: 110), Butler offers a set of responses to "contemporary fundamentalisms" by eschewing "condemnation and conviction." Like Dean, Honig (2013: 45–8) asserts that Butler's work embraces a non-political stance in *Precarious Life*, which also abandons an image of Antigone as "divisive" and "political."
45. Like Arditi (2007: 1), I am interested in looking at "a grey zone of phenomena where one is tempted to suspend the qualifier 'liberal' when describing politics, or at least where it is difficult to assert unambiguously that what happens within it is governed by a liberal code alone."

46. See also Chambers (2013: 157–71).
47. While scholars such as Judith Butler, Joan Scott and Denise Riley claimed that feminists needed to open up the category of women by analyzing its historical emergence and exclusions, other scholars, such as Martha Nussbaum, Susan Bordo, and Susan Gubar, argued that this theoretical focus hinders the political aims of feminism (Wiegman 1999: 108). For a discussion of the theoretical assumptions that underpin the debate, see Zerilli (2005: 1–31).
48. In this context, Nussbaum attacked Butler in a famous polemical piece in *The New Republic* (1999) titled "The Professor of Parody" for collaborating with "evil" and abandoning practical politics, while Wendy Brown responded in an equally famous piece titled "The Impossibility of Women Studies" (1997), where she argued that feminism's institutionalization within the academy is probably an "error."
49. For Nussbaum, Butler's theory endorses political "quietism," focuses on drag and cross-dressing as "paradigm of feminist resistance," and supports amoral anarchist politics. It also solidifies a tragic tendency in feminism to ignore "public commitments" and the material conditions of women's lives. For another critique of Butler's abandonment of Marxist politics, see Fraser (1998).
50. Nussbaum's intention is to offer a version of agency that rejects queer insights about power and calls for a return to old-style liberal feminist politics. Nussbaum (1999) says that poststructuralist feminist theory à la Butler claims that one can not "escape the humiliating structures without ceasing to be," so Butler "prefers the sexy acts of parodic subversion to any lasting material or institutional change." Another problem she sees with Butler's feminism is its acceptance—and even enjoyment—of sadomasochism, since according to Butler, "We all eroticize the power structures that oppress us, and can thus find sexual pleasure only within their confines."
51. See Abbey (2011: 1) for a list of key liberal feminist assumptions.
52. Prominent political theorists such as Bonnie Honig (1993) and Linda Zerilli (2005, 2008) stress the importance of rethinking agency in political theory. Zerilli (2005: 12) claims that "agency is the paramount problem for feminism after identity politics." Like Zerilli, Honig (1993: 2) draws on Hannah Arendt's concept of action to argue that major thinkers such as Kant, Rawls, and Sandel contribute to the "displacement of politics." In her later work (2013: 183), Honig calls for an interpretative reading of classical political texts (such as *Antigone*) in order to "exhibit the benefits of a more agonistic, conspiratorial, and political (that is, less moralistic, less heroic, less sentimental) approach to texts."
53. See, for instance, the title of Susan Okin's chapter, "John Stuart Mill, Liberal Feminist," in her *Women in Western Political Thought* (1979).

54. For Caine (1992: 155–6), "While liberalism provided the framework for Butler's social and political approach," it was not helpful for addressing questions about sexuality and desire in Josephine Butler's work. Butler struggled with the conflict between liberal principles and women's sexuality, yet she was not able to resolve this tension–"except by resort to religion."
55. While Nussbaum mobilized Mill to reject Judith Butler's understanding of feminist agency, Josephine Butler was deployed in the so-called sex wars in feminist theory to denounce prostitution and pornography as "female sexual slavery" (Barry 1979; Jeffreys 1997). By arguing against a queer perspective on sexuality, Jeffreys (1997: 8–9) used Josephine Butler to reject attempts to a narrow feminist perspective on prostitution and pornography, which sees such phenomena as sexual oppression. Lorna Bracewell urged me to think about Sheila Jeffreys' work in relationship to Josephine Butler, and I thank her for this.
56. Burton (1998) criticized Josephine Butler's liberal feminism, which led her to justify British imperialism by appealing to arguments against slavery and the subordination of women. Butler's rhetoric about war reminds us "how easily political discourses can mobilize violence – feminist discourses included—when they are motivated by the kind of liberal protectionist ethos that requires persistent 'states of injury' for its own legitimation" (Burton 1998: 356).
57. Butler criticizes the fatalistic view that all agency is corrupted; for fatalists, nothing is to be done if one participates in power structures. In Butler's view, because people are implicated in the power one opposes, their actions are neither "already" domesticated, nor articulated according to a "set" of generalized assumptions about what one should do. As such, one cannot accept the naivety of "some classical liberal-humanist formulation," to which agency is *always* opposed to power (1997a: 17).
58. Anne Marie Smith (2008: 90) locates the importance of Butler's reconceptualization of agency in her attempt to offer an answer to a critical dilemma: "With her Foucauldian approach to political theory, Butler consistently addresses a question that has become absolutely crucial in our contemporary conditions: how can contemporary progressive social movements successfully negotiate the insidious lures of the institutions that give rise to the movements' formation and political practice but threaten even the most promising campaigns with colonisation and self-betrayal at the same time?"
59. See also Bonnie Honig's (2013: 48) concise rendition of Butler's project: "This has been Butler's project throughout her work, to identify openings for resignification, iteration, subversion, to press for the aberrant repetition of norms, insisting on their weak dependence on the acts of

subscription that others take as a sign of the norm's dominance and power."
60. Jill Locke's book (2016) is an important contribution to describing how shame has been mobilized against the vulnerable and the poor. In a Rancièrian manner, she shows that "the death of shame" has been used to stifle popular unrest and alternative sexual practices. Unlike her, however, in this book I see shame not as a disciplinary affect but as a resource for queer and democratic activism.
61. See Brown's (1993: 394–5) attack on identity politics, which, in her view, derives from *ressentiment*, as well as Butler's (2004b: 17–18) condemnation of violence as a political practice.
62. Nussbaum's (2001, 2004) studies on the value of emotions represented a significant breakthrough. She analyzed particular objects (feelings, bodily movements, passions) that have previously been overlooked and left unexamined. Nussbaum's argument is that emotions are not the opposite of rational judgments; on the contrary, emotions are "suffused with intelligence and discernment" and constitute important moral and political judgments (2001: 1–3). Although Nussbaum is enthusiastic about the value of love and compassion for understanding moral and political life, she is also concerned with the use of disgust, envy, and shame in liberal democracies—particularly at the level of legal norms.
63. In Nussbaum's view, *primitive shame*, which is closely related to "the demand of perfection and the consequent inability to tolerate any lack of control or imperfection," is a specific form of shame that is dangerous to democratic thought (2001: 345–50). Shame is a barrier to compassion (2001: 344). Because of its narcissistic quality, shame could lead to misogyny and extreme forms of prejudice such as Nazi ideology. To underscore shame's dangerous capacity, she draws on Klaus Theweleit's (1989) studies analyzing the masculine omnipotence of German paramilitary troops (*Freikorps*), as well as on Elisabeth Young-Bruehl's (1996) argument that sexism derives from a psychological inability to accept one's dependence on one's mother.
64. Socrates' use of shaming introduces a gap or wedge into their narcissistic self-image. Because in imperialistic Athens citizens were shameless hedonists, Socrates shamed them and launched a powerful debate that challenged their conventional assumptions. Plato's model of respectful shame suggests that we should use perplexity "to open up rather than foreclose discussions about the kinds of democratic polities or selves that we might now want to become" (Tarnopolsky 2010: 196).
65. The Athenians humiliated others by calling them "barbarians," and this imperialistic attitude led to Athens' collapse, which, for Tarnopolsky, is evidence of the danger of humiliation (2010: 166).

66. In legal theory, Catharine MacKinnon's argument about pornography promoted a binary and heterosexual understanding of gender (Brown 1995: 88–9). Many interventions of the LGBTQ international associations enforced particular norms about who and what is gay (Massad 2007: 160–91). As a result, the human rights discourse about non-Western gay people is a function of the "racism" of the global gay left and its acceptance of Islamophobic rhetoric (Puar 2007: x–xi).
67. See Butler (1997b: 23), for whom feminist strategies to "expand the scope of obscenity" or including speech as "discriminatory conduct" tend to potentially empower the state to "invoke such precedents against the very social movements that pushed for their acceptance as legal doctrine." Like Butler, Brown (1995: 28) is worried "about the transformation of the instrumental function of the law into a political end, and about bartering political freedom for legal protection."
68. A vision of feminist action grounded in legal action and state interventions has important risks for queer theorists. This kind of action reifies the identities of the injured and the injurers as "social positions," casts the law and the state as "neutral arbiters of injury" and injured individuals as needing protection by such institutions, and seeks "the revenge of punishment" (Brown 1995: 27). While queer thinkers do not reject anti-discrimination laws in general, they show that such feminist actions are problematic and suggest innovative ways of opposing conservative views and laws.
69. Brown (1997: 136) interrogates the value of "compulsory discursivity," by which certain narratives offer specific forms of resistance. Silence about one's experiences is not automatically a sign of conservatism but rather can represent "resistance to regulatory discourse" (Brown 2005: 89). She worries that the practice of confessions—the compulsive putting into public discourse of hidden or private experiences, the "catalogues of sexual pleasures" and "litanies of sexual abuse," the "chronicles" of eating disorders and "the diaries of gay parenting"—empty the private life into public domain.
70. In Butler's view, the act of becoming a subject presupposes a strong relationship to "passionate attachments" like guilt and humiliation. Drawing on Althusser, she suggests that one becomes a subject when one is "interpellated" (1997a: 5–9). For example, imagine that a police officer hails a passer-by, and the passer-by turns and recognizes the authority of the police. In her usage of the word, *humiliation* indicates the feelings of subordination to, or dependence on, the powers of others. Such rejection of humiliation—of being dependent on, and subordinated to, others—is an important part of the formation of human subjectivity. Butler explains the sense of humiliation that adults feel when they are confronted with the earliest objects of their love (parents, guardians, siblings) by a foreclosure,

or by a refusal to feel again the ties to their old love objects (1997a: 7). Yet the term humiliation has an ambivalent value in her work. While Butler sees humiliation as a physical and illegitimate attack on a person's bodily integrity, she also deploys the term *humiliation* to point to larger psychological processes that constitute human subjectivity (1997a: 8–9). Within humiliating situations, a response to injurious language constitutes "an insurrectionary moment."

71. Words are going to injure. Performative gestures such as Robert Mapplethorpe's art or the language of rap used by African American artists, albeit offensive to many people, have significant value (Butler 1997b: 22).

72. To acquire *adoxia* (a bad reputation) the Cynic had to be insulted, despised, and humiliated by others. This dishonor is sought after by the Cynics because they train themselves "in resistance to everything to do with opinions, beliefs, and conventions" (Foucault 2010: 261). In addition to cultivating indifference to harmful circumstances, seeking out humiliating situations offers this advantage: it allows one to "turn the situation around" and "take back the control of it" (Foucault 2010: 261). In Foucault's example, Diogenes was eating in the public square and treated as a dog by passers-by. Diogenes used that situation to reverse the power dynamic by saying "But you too are dogs, since only dogs form a circle around a dog which is eating" (2010: 261). In another context, Diogenes pushed this scandalous technique to piss on his guests and prove that he was a real dog. For Foucault, the Cynics viewed their practices and mode of life as an essential condition of truth-telling.

73. The resignification of the word queer shows that injurious social discourses can be transformed, but such strategy does not guarantee that the insult or the pain associated with slurs is eliminated, nor can resignification be easily transformed into a tactic that advances the interests of those who are perceived as sexually deviant. Butler criticizes the idea that one could call oneself queer without that act being shaped by history or by previous meanings of what queer is (1993: 173). The resignification of shame takes meanings according to various contextual discursive practices. In one context, the term queer is used by a younger generation who want to resist the institutionalized politics of the lesbian and gay movement; in another context, it marks a discourse of a white feminist movement that fails to address how the term queer is deployed in non-white communities; in others, it mobilized activism or signaled a false unity between men and women (Butler 1997b: 174). Although the meaning of queer is contested and multiple, it represents in many contexts a strong feminist strategy to respond to sexual injustice.

74. Resignification builds on Butler's larger theory about the linguistic potential of various words. She believes that words have specific meanings that vary according to context. Terms such as *feminism* or *universal* have their meaning "reified" in the sense that they become associated with a single, fixed meaning. But by relying on an established meaning, one runs the risk of stalling the meaning of a term "within the bounds of established conventions," naturalizing its exclusions, and pre-empting the possibility of its radicalization (Butler 1997b: 90).
75. See Annas (1977); Kamm (1977); Okin (1979); Eisenstein (1981); Ring (1985); Di Stefano (1989); Urbinati (1991); Donner (1992); Zerilli (1994); Smith (2001); Nussbaum (2004, 2010); Stafford (2004).
76. Okin (1979: 228) faults Mill for not criticizing the traditional division of labor within the family; Eisenstein (1981: 115) argues that Mill's feminism (and Harriet Taylor's) is classist and constrained by "the ideology of liberal individualism"; Ring (1985: 41) believes that Mill's theoretical flaws are generated by his liberal commitment to "empirical validation"; and Di Stefano (1989: 167) claims that Mill's liberal feminism "collapses on the terrain of *difference*," because of his problematic account of the m(other) in his work.
77. For Nussbaum, Mill "turns out to have significant affinities with the 'queer' feminism of followers of Michel Foucault" (2010: 130). Yet, because she wants to justify a liberal feminist position, Mill has the best "insights" without "the worst excesses" (2010: 130).
78. However, the project of finding gay, lesbian, feminist, and queer precursors in political theory is important and potentially radical. Like Doan (2013: x), I find that genealogical methods stem from both a gay and lesbian historiography, as well as from queering these histories.
79. Simons argues that both Mill and Foucault wanted people to have the freedom "to fashion their lives as they wanted" and "resist the models of subjectivity that society tries to impose on them" (1995: 117).
80. Mill's key significance for political theorists derives from his role in liberal political thought. Major liberal scholars such as Isaiah Berlin (2002) and John Rawls (2005) used Mill to articulate innovative theoretical contributions such as the distinction between positive and negative liberty and a theory of political liberalism. Berlin's (2002: 174–8) discussion of Mill's concept of freedom gives him the theoretical basis for conceptualizing "negative liberty." Rawls (2005: 78) formulates his political liberalism in opposition with the "comprehensive liberalism" of thinkers such as Mill and Kant.
81. These practices of freedom "counter the persisting tendencies toward sexist domination" and "become central to the project of creating and maintaining selves able to exercise freedom" (McWhorter 2013: 71).

Because Foucault was sensitive to the impact of shame within contemporary societies, he valued the freedom to invent new ways of living and relationality (Sawicki 2013: 87).
82. Rather than a rational choice actor, Butler calls for thinking about the agent as "driven by passions it can not fully consciously ground or know" (2013: 4).
83. Rancière (1999: 17) thinks that politics, as opposed to *the police*, is a rare occurrence: "Politics does not always happen—it actually happens very little or rarely."
84. Not only queer feminists, but also political theorists such as James Tully focus on the theoretical value of practices. In Tully's view, an emphasis on practices reveals how political power is deployed in particular historical contexts and how practices become "the locus of contest and negotiation" (2009: 16). Instead of understanding a political agent only as a theorist, the investigation of practices serves as a guide to understanding political theory as a specific political intervention. Another advantage of this focus on practices is that it points not only toward political theory as an interpretative method, but also toward a "specific genre of critique" concerned with contemporary politics (2009: 16).
85. Prominent accounts of woman's suffrage emphasize the liberal character of feminist dissent in the US women's movement (Marilley 1996: 2–3). In this account, woman suffragists introduced "liberal feminist dissent" into a larger movement for equal rights and opportunities by demanding equal rights and the vote for women (Marilley 1996: 2).
86. Other scholars complicate a traditional feminist account which strongly embraces a liberal feminist view of political action. For Joannou and Purvis (1998: 1), the English women's movement deployed militant political action, such as "heckling politicians, window smashing raids, setting fire to pillar boxes, planting bombs in empty buildings, and attacking art treasures."
87. The historical persons that I analyze, such as the Unitarian radicals, Josephine Butler, Mill in the 1830s and Victoria Woodhull, were primarily activists and citizens concerned about gender inequality. Yet, because I also draw on Mill's activity as a member of the parliament, my study explores not only activism, but also legislative politics. I discuss the contrast between the position of an activist and that of a politician with regard to the women's movement in Chapter 3.
88. For this point, see Zivi (2008: 159).
89. See Zivi's (2008: 157) observation that "given Butler's critique of traditional social movements strategies and her call for somewhat unusual political practices of drag, parody and insurrectionary speech, it is not surprising that she has failed to win over many who see themselves committed to progressive politics."

90. As Brown and Halley (2002: 8–9) noted, in American politics, contemporary egalitarian and emancipatory efforts such as the women's movement and the LGBT movement modeled their strategies after the civil rights tactics. Because of its success, the civil rights movement is regarded as providing the standard narrative for Leftist politics. This particular project, however, is deeply associated with a liberal legalistic discourse, where rights are "paradigmatic in any understanding of the justice-seeking legal resources of the state" (2002: 9). Brown and Halley call for a different political project, one "not fully saturated by legalistic constraints and aims" (2002: 20).
91. Caine (1997: 108–12) discussed Mill and Butler's relationship with feminism, while Gleadle (1998) and Mineka (1944) explored Mill's relationship with the Unitarians at the *Monthly Repository*.
92. The label "radical" is sometimes deployed to qualify these thinkers as provocative and relevant to a wide audience. Nussbaum (2010: 143) claims that Mill's thought was "radical," while others have claimed that Unitarian thinkers, or Josephine Butler, or Victoria Woodhull were radical intellectuals. Mineka (1944) and Gleadle (1998) use the term radical to refer to Unitarians such as W. J. Fox and Adams; for Josephine Butler's radicalism, see Jane Jordan's claim that she was radical because she raised her children to believe "in women's intellectual and social equality with men, and in the right of the working people to full political representation" (Jordan and Sharp 2003a: 1); for Woodhull's sexual and political radicalism, see Frisken (2004: 20).
93. For Mill's less prominent role in the women's movement, see Caine (1992: 33–4). In particular, see her observation that while important activists such as Frances Power Cobbe, Josephine Butler, Emily Davies, and Millicent Gareth Fawcett "acknowledged Mill's importance for the women's movement," "none of them regarded him as a leader" (1992: 34).
94. Because of her support of free love and her involvement in radical politics, Woodhull became a marginal figure in many accounts of nineteenth-century women's rights. Liberal feminist reformers such as Susan B. Anthony and Elisabeth C. Stanton saw her as a threat to the women's movement (Carpenter 2010: xi). She was the first person to print Karl Marx's Communist Manifesto in the United States, gave speeches that explained the value of free love, and advocated a more equal distribution of wealth and legal rights for women. She became the first woman stockbroker on Wall Street and the first woman to run for president of the United States (Carpenter 2010: 1).

Chapter 2
How to do Queer Genealogy
with J. S. Mill

In *The Psychic Life of Power*, Judith Butler claims that her work challenges a common assumption in liberal thought that one simply needs to oppose political power in order to become liberated. She analyzes the social and psychological formation of the subject and argues, in a Foucauldian vein, that power is not just "what we oppose but also, in a strong sense, what we depend on for our existence and what we harbor and preserve in the beings we are" (1997a: 2). Differently put, for Butler we become political subjects as we become subjected and subordinated to social and political dominant power.[1]

Her argument has strong implications for a theory of political agency. Rather than perceiving political action only as refusing conventional political norms, as in, for instance, Rosa Parks's refusal to sit in the back of the bus in 1955 in Montgomery, Alabama, we can understand Parks's actions as generated by a set of conditions that preceded her intervention. Parks's actions had an enduring impact because they came from a woman who was perceived as having integrity and honesty. Her image as a hardworking black person helped the cause of black civic activism. Had she been seen as lazy and dishonest, the impact of her gesture of civil disobedience would have been different. Rosa Parks's act of resistance was a performative intervention. It was enabled by conventional racial assumptions even as she contested such assumptions and disrupted the normative order of Southern racism. Parks did not oppose racial discrimination in a vacuum; ideological and racial conditions provided the circumstances for her to act as a decent black woman and to contest the racist definitions of blackness. Her disruptive intervention was made possible by norms that constituted her as a viable political subject.

Power, in Butler's understanding of the term, is constituted by a constitutive tension. Political agency—and the possibility of an emancipatory politics—is inherently marked by a double bind. On the one hand, we are formed by power because power offers the condition of the subject's possibility and articulates its formation. Without previous conventions about social and linguistic existence, the subject would not exist. When thinking about the formation of identities such as gay and black, Butler points out that the formation of such identities depends on a history of shaming and exclusion:

> One need only consider the way in which the history of having been called an injurious name is embodied, how the words enter the limbs, craft the gesture, bend the spine. One need only consider how racial and gendered slurs live and thrive in and as the flesh of the addressee, and how these slurs accumulate over time, dissimulating their history, taking on the semblance of the natural, configuring and restricting the *doxa* that counts as "reality." (1997b: 159)

On the other hand, shaming is not only the opposite of political resistance, but it also shapes the prospects of opposition to racist and homophobic practices. Because slurs enter "one's limbs" and "bend the spine," they are not toxic parts that are easily disposable. They deeply constitute one's subjectivity and possibilities for political action.

The concept of performativity points toward an innovative politics that moves away from the liberal vision of agency. Unlike liberal agency, which traditionally assumes that agency equals opposition to power, Butler's queer agency draws from, and opposes, "the power by which it is compelled" (1997a: 82).[2] While power shapes one's actions, political agency is not determined by the power that previously enabled its articulation. Political agency exceeds the power by which one's actions are made possible. When agency diverges from its previous conditions of possibility, agency becomes "the assumption of a purpose *unintended* by power, one that could not have been derived logically and historically, that operates in a relation of contingency and reversal to the power that makes it possible, to which it nevertheless belongs" (1997a: 15).

Butler's concept of performative action offers a unique meaning for political agency, because it illuminates interventions that transform the established conventions from within. These acts of resignification destabilize norms by opening them up to new meanings. Although performative interventions are deeply implicated in the conventions that make them possible, at the same time, they change these conventions during their new iteration. For Butler, human agency is deeply connected to signification.[3] To signify is to establish the terms of intelligibility and meaning. Signification is a practice based on repetition. To *resignify* is to offer a different meaning to a practice, so that the terms that are traditionally accepted become differently articulated.[4] Rosa Parks's gesture of sitting in the front section of the bus challenged segregationist conventions in the South (Butler 1997b: 147). By sitting there, she claimed a right for which she had no authorization.[5] Her gesture resignified the convention that produced racial segregation.

Yet Butler's theory of performativity has serious limits. As Heather Love points out, Butler's project "retains a faith in the possibility of transforming the base material of social abjection into the gold of political agency" (Love 2007:18). More importantly, Butler's theory seems to be unable to provide an account of how contemporary social order functions (Chambers 2014: 12).[6] Because her theory seems to have embraced basic liberal assumptions, it is harder to see this body of work as a theoretical tool that can denaturalize categories critical theorists take for granted in their work (Chambers 2014: 80). Currently, Butler's theory does not appear to be a threat to the liberal mainstream consensus.[7] Also, as I show in this book, Butler's performativity does not seriously engage with historical practices that are considered abject, such as illicit relationships, silence, and the use of shame and humiliation.[8] By contrast, queer genealogy can illuminate the use of performativity in its historical context and so allow queer feminist theory to broaden its understanding of political action.

Unlike Butler's recent theoretical work, queer genealogy and Rancière's work can help illuminate nineteenth-century feminists' political interventions. First, I conceptualize queer practices as performative acts, in the sense that Butler understands "the political promise of the performative:"

> I would insist that the speech act, as a rite of institution, is one whose contexts are never fully determined in advance, and that the possibility for the speech act to take on a non-ordinary meaning, to function in contexts where it has not belonged, is precisely the political promise of the performative ... (1997b: 161)

For Butler, performatives act as political interventions because they unsettle and resignify a previous norm, but in my deployment of queer practices, I take seriously the embeddedness of performatives in their historical context. Second, queer practices do not represent political subjects but produce subjects of politics. By *subjectivation* Rancière means a series of actions "not previously identifiable within a given field of experience" but which reconfigure this field in new ways (1999: 35). This process of becoming a subject involves the enunciation of a wrong, the dis-identification from "the naturalness of a place," and the "opening up of a subject space" where new subjects can be counted (1999: 36).[9]

In the following chapters I demonstrate that the experience and life of a major nineteenth-century feminist, J. S. Mill—and his activity as a politician and public intellectual—offer an important conceptual map to begin thinking about expanding queer feminist agency. In this chapter, I explore Mill's actions and responses that utilize shame as a queer practice. Mill lived in a society where being a male feminist and having unconventional intimate relationships was considered shameful. But Mill did not merely live in shame; he also deployed shame-based tactics to respond to his alleged political transgressions.

In the first section I explain how Mill's relationship with Harriet Taylor challenged traditional Victorian norms. In the second section I focus on Mill's silences and illuminate their performative dimension. And in the third section I demonstrate how Mill used humiliating language that was seen as inappropriate and uncivilized.

How to "Part Company with the World"

John Stuart Mill argued, like Butler, that shaming has dangerous social effects, and he responded to disciplinary power by engaging in risky practices.[10] The dimension of risk is key in these interventions because challenging power inequalities presupposes the presence of what Foucault calls a position of "danger."[11] These practices have a significant performative dimension, not unlike Rosa Parks's refusal to go to the back of the bus. But these lived moments are not always planned and calculated. They can surprise not only the addressee of the speaker but the speaker himself. Neither knows what he will say or do. Mill's "parting company with the world" was an intervention that was unexpected and that interrupted an order in which the speaker has a certain position and expectations about what it is proper to do and say. By interrupting this order, queer practices disturb inequalities of power and introduce an equal position for those who are considered illegible.

Mill understood that a fundamental ambivalence undergirds the use of shame in politics. On the one hand, Mill was concerned with the disciplinary use of shame, which damaged people's lives. Mill saw that when people are exposed to social shame, they can be excluded from social activities, lose their financial resources, and face the prospect of leading an unhappy life. The fear of shame was an important deterring power and like Butler, Mill understood that shame is a political tool of coercion that can "bend the spine" (Butler 1997b: 59). The power of shame could "render life miserable" and "exclude [one] from social intercourse" (*CW* X: 417). The public opinion produced "terrors" through the "fear of shame," and "many murders have been committed" in order to prevent disclosures of secrets (*CW* X: 417). On the other hand, Mill also argued that one was justified in shaming individuals who are self-destructive. Although he was concerned about the dangers of one's exposure to public shame, he defended political shaming as long as it was not exercised by the state.[12] It seems that for Mill shame was both dangerous and potentially useful for achieving normatively good goals.

I do not want to make sense of Mill's ambivalence by solving it, and I do not want to show that the conflict can be erased if we better understand, let us say, another part of Mill's work. Rather, I am more interested in how this ambivalence about shame can produce certain interventions. In this regard, I appeal to queer studies and its long engagement with the question of antinormative relationships and shame. Specifically, in queer studies shame and antinormative relationships have been seen as an important location to imagine the possibility of new sexual and affective intimacy.[13] Foucault argues that the classical institutions of intimacy such as family and marriage are disturbed by "the formation of new alliances and the tying together of unforeseen lines of force" (1994: 136).[14] Queer feminist thinkers develop Foucault's insight and demand a reorganization of sexual norms to generate a better life for those who live sexually and affectively outside the marriage bond. When people who live in these intimate arrangements generate "sustaining webs of relationships," this leads to "a 'breakdown' of traditional kinship that displaces the presumption that biological and sexual relations structure kinship centrally" (Butler 2004a: 26). "Sexuality outside the field of monogamy" may open us to "a different sense of community" (Butler 2004a: 26).[15] Also, relationships outside of marriage "disrupt what has become settled knowledge and knowable reality" (2004a: 27). By this process of interruption, the norms themselves can be open to resignification and alter the negative component of what is abnormal or transgressive.

John Stuart Mill and Harriet Taylor, two nineteenth-century feminists who lived in an unconventional relationship for nineteen years, offer a powerful example of a queer practice, and I see its value in its contestation of established sexual norms. Because Harriet Taylor was a married woman while she was intimately involved with Mill, they faced disciplinary shame and the prospect of social exclusion. They both found their intimacy hard to navigate because of the shame associated with adultery. At the beginning of his relationship with Harriet, Mill felt that he had "parted company with the world" (*CW* XII: 149); his relationship had the potential to make him "obscure and insignificant" (Packe 1954: 154). While they acted as though their relationship was outside the authorized discourse about sexuality, their experiment in living became functional in time. They exemplified Butler's claim that a performative gesture is a crucial part not only of a subject's formation but also of the "ongoing political contestation and reformulation of the subject" (1997a: 159). These two feminists opened up the notion of intimacy beyond the options that were traditionally offered to Victorians, such as marriage and family.

Many Victorians saw relationships outside heterosexual marriage as highly transgressive and morally problematic. The gender of those who transgressed traditional sexual norms was significant in such assessments. When Frances Cobbe, an important Victorian feminist, social critic, and political activist, reviewed Mill's *The Subjection of Women*, she expressed her concerns that the institution of marriage required the state's intervention to function properly. Taking the ideal of marriage as a "sort of glorified friendship," Cobbe argued that the happily married couple should find the same easiness and pleasure that other friends find in their relationships (Pyle 1995: 66–7). While it might seem peculiar to us that a Victorian writer would offer as a standard of mutual understanding and love relationships between friends and siblings, Sharon Marcus (2007) showed that love relationships between female couples in Victorian time were publicly acknowledged and valued. Many female couples enjoyed "a right to privacy associated with marriage and the public privileges accorded to female friendships:" for instance, Victorian feminists like Emily Faithfull and Frances Power Cobbe publicly described their relationships with female lovers and were not severely penalized for their bonds (Marcus 2007: 51). Yet while "a woman could enjoy, without guilt, the pleasures of toying with another woman's affections," adulterous relationships, as well as relationships where women showed desire and sexual interest, were harshly condemned (Marcus 2007: 59).[16]

Mill, like Cobbe, lived in a transgressive relationship with his partner and future wife, Harriet Taylor. When Harriet and John Taylor were a married couple, Mill was romantically involved with Harriet, saw her regularly, and worked together with her as a writing partner on various projects. Mill was in a relationship in which he felt—and was—marginalized for that relationship. Theorists of sexual marginality describe such experiences as queer.[17] As Halperin points out, queer is a position that is available to anyone on the margins:

> "Queer," then, demarcates not a positivity but a positionality vis-à-vis the normative—a positionality that is not restricted to lesbians and gay men but is in fact available to anyone who is or who feels marginalized because of his or her sexual practices: it could include some married couples without children, for example, or even (who knows?) some married couples *with* children—with, perhaps, *very naughty* children. (1995: 62)

However, Mill had queer experiences not only because of his relationship with Harriet Taylor but also because of the various ways in which his personal and public life was shaped by shame. Mill had a sense of identity consistently tuned to the note of shame, which remains for queers "the most important mediator of identity" (Sedgwick 2009: 60–1). Like Sedgwick, Butler locates shame at the center of queer experience. She notes that the term "queer" has been used to produce a subject through "shaming interpellation" (1993: 172). The force of its performative draws on "the repeated invocation" by which it became linked to accusation, pathologization, and insult. Queer, for Butler, operates as a "deformation" of one of the strongest gestures that organizes social relations, namely the "I pronounce you . . ." of the marriage ceremony (1993: 172). Queer opposes the heterosexualization of the social bond by resisting its imperative. Queer encompasses the multiplication of forms of relationality that operate beyond marriage. It becomes a shaming taboo that draws its capacity for political resistance and opposition from the strength of the norm of marriage. As a term and as a practice, *queer* not only opposes marriage but draws its power from the conditions of the intense heterosexualization of social relations. Both Sedgwick (2009: 58–9) and Butler (1993: 174) give an account of how queer subjectivity emerges from experiences that do not conform to traditional standards about sexuality, gender, social class, ability, or age.

Mill's sexual "deviance" became a weapon for some of his opponents who attacked his reputation. He was criticized not only because of his liberal progressive ideas (such as advocating birth control) but also because he was involved in a long-term relationship with a married woman. Abraham Hayward argued that because Mill fell in love with a married woman, he advocated unlimited liberty of divorce in *The Examiner* (Mineka 1972: 5). Hayward's claim was false, because Mill did not publish arguments about the unlimited liberty of divorce, but the intention of the attack was merely to portray Mill as an immoral person. His relationship with Harriet was a particularly vulnerable spot for him, since in the eyes of Victorian public morality, adultery was perceived as a major sexual transgression.

In the obituary that *The Times* published on the day Mill died, Hayward portrayed Mill as a radical who promoted extreme ideas with regard to gender and sex relationships (Mineka 1972: 3–4). In this infamous obituary, Hayward, who was one of Mill's harshest critics, mentioned Mill's association with the early birth control movement and wrote that "he must have been a boy in years when a foolish scheme for carrying out the Malthusian principle brought him under the lash of the satirist" (Mineka 1972: 3). He then reproduced a part of a poem by Thomas Moore, who ridiculed Mill for distributing birth control pamphlets:

> There are two Mr. Mills, too, whom those who like reading
> What's vastly unreadable, call very clever;
> And whereas Mill senior makes war on *good* breeding,
> Mill junior makes war on all *breeding* whatever. (Mineka 1972: 3)

Mill was seventeen when he distributed handbills that advocated the use of contraceptives to working class people in London. His courage in participating in a highly performative event such as distributing "obscene" material severely qualifies Martha Nussbaum's dismissive remark on his radical politics.[18] The handbills described in vivid and explicit detail how to prevent pregnancy. Of one method, he writes, "It consists of a piece of sponge, about an inch square, being placed in the vagina previous to coition, and afterwards withdrawn by means of a double twisted thread, or bobbin, attached to it" (*The Republican* 1825: 562). Mill was arrested for obscenity, because he attempted "to corrupt the purity of English womanhood" (Packe 1954: 57). He was condemned to fourteen days in prison, but was released after a day or two for good conduct (Packe 1954: 57).[19]

More importantly, Mill's relationship with Harriet Taylor was a performative intervention that unsettled the rules of intimacy in Victorian times. In the summer of 1830, Mill was twenty-four years old and, according to Carlyle, was "a slender, rather tall and elegant youth, with a small clear Roman-nosed face, two small earnestly-smiling eyes; modest, remarkably gifted with precision of utterance, enthusiastic, yet lucid, calm . . ." (quoted in Reeves 2008: 81). Mill took an active part in the numerous *salons* that sprang up across London. Mr. and Mrs. John Taylor invited him for a dinner in the company of other brilliant, radical minds. John Taylor was a wealthy pharmacist, a supporter of radical causes, and a patron of political refugees. Harriet was a smart, beautiful woman who was interested in literature, music, and the political emancipation of women.

John Stuart Mill and Harriet Taylor fell in love and began the complicated process of negotiating their relationship while trying to protect the other people involved in their lives (in particular, John Taylor and Harriet's children). Harriet told John Taylor about her feelings for Mill, and her husband initially did not agree to them seeing each other. But in the autumn of 1832, the three people involved in the affair settled for a *modus vivendi* (Reeves 2008: 83). Mill lived with his family in Vicarage Place, Kensington, and was permitted to dine with Harriet at her house when John Taylor went out to his club. Later, Taylor bought a house for Harriet in Kent. He visited her for the occasional weekend, and Mill was there for the majority of the others (Reeves 2008: 84).

Harriet Taylor, John Taylor, and John Stuart Mill settled for an agreement in which the husband had some protection from destructive gossip, Harriet kept both men in her life, and John Stuart Mill was allowed to work and spend time with his friend. Until the agreement between the three was reached, Harriet and Mill had many important conversations about how to face social shame. They were both anxious about their positions in English society. Mill faced a brilliant future as a moral philosopher and was vulnerable to "the touch of scandal" (Packe 1954: 138). Harriet had three children to consider and was also very fond of her husband and grateful for his kindness (Packe 1954: 138). John Taylor was very upset that Harriet had fallen in love with Mill, and advised her "to renounce sight" (Packe 1954: 139). Mill's family—James Mill, in particular—disapproved of their relationship (Reeves 2008: 90).[20] Harriet proposed to Mill that she should remain married to John Taylor even as she was intimate with Mill. However, Mill was possessed by doubts and anxiety about such an arrangement. Harriet tried to convince him to compromise on his desire that she would be entirely his. She encouraged him to put less "strength" into resisting her and to trust her judgment:

> It is false that "your strength is not equal to the circumstances in which you have placed" yourself.—It is quite another thing to be guided by a judgment on which you can rely and which is better placed for judgment than yourself. (Packe 1954: 144)

Harriet urged Mill not to submit to the social pressure of conventional norms but to follow their desires and pursue an unpredictable path. Mill was not entirely convinced that he would wholeheartedly accept such an agreement. Writing to his friend W. J. Fox, Mill shared his anxiety about challenging "the opinion of the world":

> she is like herself: if she is ever out of spirits it is always something amiss in me that is the cause—it is now—it is because she sees that what ought to be much easier to me than to her is in reality more difficult—costs harder struggle—to part company with the opinion of the world, and with my former modes of doing good—however, thank Heaven, she does not doubt that I can do it. (Packe 1954: 144)

The young philosopher noted that although Harriet was in a difficult position because she had family responsibilities, it was harder for him to get rid of his fears. He felt that "parting company with the opinion of the world" would be a very difficult and costly process. Mill already knew in 1832 that a transgressive life would require important sacrifices. In her letters to John Taylor, Harriet explained the state of her feelings and her commitment to keep J. S. Mill in her life. She and Mill went through "so much suffering and so much effort" to achieve a reasonable compromise. These troubles and pain were worth it for Mill because "for us even so the gain is great" (Packe 1954: 146).

Harriet Taylor and Mill's early views on marriage were at odds with conservative views on human sexuality. They opposed Victorian norms of respectability, which made it hard for them to be together in public. Because their relationship was seen as illegitimate, they both confronted shaming and social rejection. Mill complained to Harriet that the experiment made him feel "quite miserable" (Packe 1954: 150). As Packe claimed, he feared that "the multitudes," or vulgar people, would not understand their motives and take their arrangement as a justification for immorality. Harriet fought back, however, and wanted to preserve the arrangement that brought "much happiness." Responding to Mill, who suggested that their actions were immoral in the eyes of the "wise and good," she argued that "the wise and good" are themselves hypocrites (Packe 1954: 150–1). For her, people who hold to strong dichotomies between morality and vice are "insincere" and unable to understand that "occasional hard necessity" requires exceptional actions. She said that she knew how much Mill feared the "opinion" of the public, but she could never understand why he dreaded the opinion of "fools." After Harriet was able to have her own place in the country, Mill was able to spend weekends with her and became less concerned about the arrangement (Packe 1954: 152). Harriet was relatively content with a plan that allowed her to have both men in her life. A divorce would have required an Act of Parliament and was difficult to obtain. As they wrote to each other in private letters, they believed that marriage was an institution that should be dissolvable at the wish of either party.

Mill and Harriet Taylor's feelings of shame and anxiety were provoked at social events. Packe described a soiree at Mrs. Butler's when what he calls a "disaster" happened (1954: 152). Most of the guests were already assembled when Mill stood in the spacious door with Harriet Taylor on his arm. People gossiped mercilessly about their relationship: "a half-audible titter ran swiftly across the room" (1954: 152). Roebuck, who was one of Mill's closest friends, warned him that he would bring ridicule on himself by entertaining such company. Mill was very hurt by his friend's advice and decided to end his friendship. Subjected to this public shaming, Mill wrote to Harriet that he feared obscurity as an intellectual and writer. Unlike married people, whose arrangements do not involve an inherent social price, Mill's agreement with Harriet was costly and involved social shame, the disapproval of Mill's family, and the loss of close friends.

Rather than being paralyzed by the fear of their transgressions, Mill and Harriet Taylor used these concerns to generate a strong intimate relationship. Their performative intervention was either met with skepticism or directly condemned, but they showed that they could transform their fear into a resource for intimacy. Shame was a critical—and versatile—emotion in this process. On the one hand, their shame led to many anxious exchanges between the two friends, who were concerned about the consequences of their actions. They struggled with painful feelings and depression, and they faced rejection from their families. On the other hand, such anxiety had a productive dimension because it created the possibility of imagining new ways of living in intimacy. Harriet opened Mill up to the possibility that "violations of conventions" could be performed by "persons otherwise loveable and admirable" (*CW* I: 141). Out of this ambivalence and anxiety, Harriet and Mill produced queer interventions such as their decision to show themselves publicly as a couple.

Neither Mill nor Harriet Taylor wanted to live in an intimate arrangement that involved a third party. They were both surprised by their relationship and could make sense of it only as it was happening. They were both astonished by this new context in which intimacy was no longer defined exclusively as a married couple's intimacy. Their position within the heteronormative Victorian order is not unique, however. Queer studies with a Victorian focus describe the position of many subjects who lived an antinormative life (Cocks 2010: 1–11). In this regard, queer scholars follow Foucault's injunction that the problem is not to discover in oneself the truth of one's sex but to use one's sexuality to generate a multiplicity of new relationships. This emphasis on relational novelty in generating alternative lifestyles is key to queer politics. But, as Butler explains, to resignify a sexual practice that is considered shameful is not "an easy task." For her, the goal of a more inclusive life is "to compel the terms of modernity to embrace those they have traditionally excluded, and to know that such an embrace cannot be easy" (1997b: 160–1). This acceptance of new terms of living is neither simple assimilation nor accommodation of what has been excluded. Rather, sexuality outside heteronormativity "establishes for that time an unknown future, one that can only produce anxiety in those who seek to patrol its conventional boundaries" (1997b: 161).

Mill and Harriet Taylor's relationship was an intervention that challenged *the police*, by which I mean the order of roles and positions shaped by heteronormative assumptions about sex and intimacy. Their relationship would have been impossible if they had given in to others' assumptions about proper sexuality, but they were able to navigate hostile social conventions and imagine a viable existence. The risk and the appeal of their agreement is that they transformed a shameful situation into a creative lifestyle. Mill and Harriet Taylor's intervention suggests that resignifying the shame associated with adultery can expand the definition of what counts as a "livable life" (Butler 2004a: 224). Like drag, which for Butler operates as a practice of showing that gender is performative, Mill and Harriet Taylor's arrangement denaturalized the ideal of monogamous heterosexuality.[21] Mill and Harriet Taylor's arrangement represents a form of alliance that provides an historical example of a livable life of deviance.

But this arrangement also produced, in a Rancièrian understanding, an alliance of two individuals who showed that politics is not merely *logos*. *The police* seek to keep a clear separation between what is speakable and what is not, between what is deemed intelligible *logos* versus what is unintelligible speech. When it is instantiated as a queer intervention, politics becomes not only the capacity to utilize a conventional use of the language but also the ability to make the unintelligible speak and to inaugurate a new "partition of the sensible."[22] Mill and Taylor's arrangement made possible a new articulation of two people occupying a public space. They "conduct[ed] themselves like beings with names" so that they could imagine a new stage of politics (Rancière 1999: 24). This stage did not exist before Mill and Taylor chose to live intimately, and, like Rancièrian plebs who spoke when they should not have, the stage was created by this new intimate arrangement.[23] Mill and Harriet Taylor became political subjects when they acted as lovers at the soiree that Packe described as disastrous. By creating a new scene for what was, until then, unintelligible—a public relationship at odds with sexual respectability—Mill and Taylor disrupted a politics organized according to a rigid partition of what was visible.

Mill in Drag, Shame and Silence

While my argument thus far is that shame as a political gesture can be mobilized against *the police*, here I want to show that shame can generate an interruption in liberal politics when it manifests as silence. First, I distinguish between two types of silence. Silence can be a non-response to a public accusation, but it can also be an embodied and performative reaction to political shame. We can find an example of the first type in an aggressive anti-women's rights political campaign that targeted Mill. Victorian journals represented him as a transgressive cross-dresser, but Mill did not respond to this public scorn. This silence is not yet what Rancière calls politics, or an interruption that "stops the current" (1999: 13). For an example of silence that disturbs *the police*, I offer one of Mill's performances as an orator in Westminster. This performative intervention upset the norms of conventional political discourses and introduced the potential for a new dynamic in an actual conflict in the British Parliament.

I focus here on silence as a weapon against *the police* because an important area of scholarship in political theory works primarily with Aristotle's emphasis on speech as defining political activity.[24] But instead of exclusively celebrating speech, deliberation, and political arguments as the substance of politics, we should recognize those deployments of silence that show that we should abandon the distinction between *logos*, which is intelligible human speech, and what animals have in common, which is pleasure and suffering.[25] My intention is to criticize this distinction, and I show that silence can be a moment of shame and suffering that disturbs liberal politics. Of course, not all silences function in similar ways, and like drag, there is silence that is produced by disciplinary power and silence that potentially disturbs *the police*.

Drag is a weapon that not only subverts what Butler calls the "heterosexual matrix" but also reinforces particular gender norms and even humiliates sex dissenters. Drag is not merely a practice that opens up new ways of perception; it can also be used to shame and humiliate politically. Martha Nussbaum, in her attack on Judith Butler's theory, *The Professor of Parody*, claims that Butler proposes drag and cross-dressing as a paradigm of feminist resistance. Butler's intention in *Gender Trouble* (1999), however, was different. Butler argues that cultural practices of drag, cross-dressing, and butch/femmes identities undermine a fixed notion of gender identity (1999: 186–7). Drag is *not* an example of feminist resistance that challenges conventional norms. Rather, it represents the possibility of a change in perception. It shows that "natural" gender is in fact constructed. Drag gives us a different meaning for what we take for granted as "given" or "real" in terms of gendered bodies. Such interventions resignify the fixed conception of gender. They put the reality of gender into crisis, so that "it becomes unclear how to distinguish the real from the unreal" (Butler 1999: xiv).

Mill was a fierce feminist who, as a public intellectual and parliamentarian, criticized the social and legal norms of nineteenth-century England. During 1866–7, the Tories, Mill's conservative enemies, were particularly worried about the Reform Bill proposed by Liberals, a Bill that would extend the right to vote to the urban, male, working class in England and Wales. Mill supported the Reform Bill as a member of Parliament. He also led the Jamaica Committee, which counted among its members Charles Darwin and Thomas Huxley, and which publicly condemned the Jamaican governor for killing and flogging black peasants.

Mill's speeches embodied aggressive progressive politics, and his political opponents met such speeches with derision. Mill was attacked not only in political meetings but also in the public press, for example in satirical journals such as *Punch* and *Judy*. Articles that appeared in *Judy* were part of a larger conservative hostility to his feminism. Mill was familiar with these journals, as he showed in a letter to Harriet Taylor (CW XIV: 373). However, he neither commented on nor responded to their attacks. He did not consider it appropriate to react to these political efforts to humiliate him. He chose to ignore them.

In a cartoon published in *Judy* one year before the publication of *The Subjection of Women* (Figure 2.1), Mill is ridiculed for losing his parliamentary seat. He is represented in women's clothes and invited to join the group of women who sit outside the room where political decisions are made. In the caricature, the winner of the election, Conservative W. H. Smith, takes Mill's chair and shows him out. Mill holds a fan and seems annoyed that his dress is stuck under the chair. In the corner, Edward John Eyre, the governor of Jamaica and one of Mill's political opponents, contemplates Mill's ejection from Westminster. Mill is portrayed as emotional, offended, and sexual, whereas Smith and R. W. Grosvenor, a Liberal who was elected in the same parliamentary race, appear manly and in control. As Grosvenor studies his wine and Smith displays the courtesy of a gentleman, Mill is represented as being angry and in drag. His naked shoulder suggests sexuality, as opposed to the proper, asexual attitude of the men in the cartoon.

In *Judy*'s political imagery, Mill is an angry, sexual cross-dresser who is excluded from the gentlemen's club. The message of this cartoon seems quite straightforward. In publishing this satire, *Judy*'s intention was to shame and humiliate Mill. His defeat was associated with his campaign for women's rights and his opposition to Governor Eyre's brutal racist policies in Jamaica. Mill was ridiculed for losing; the place for losers was in the company of women, outside the center of power. What is significant about this particular attack is the intention of the cartoon to sexually shame Mill. Dressed as a woman, he was represented as powerless and not manly enough to sit at the table of the powerful. His overt sexuality was depicted in contrast with the lack of sexuality of the other men in the picture. Because a dress on a man was a symbol of lost authority, Mill "in drag" marked his transition from statesman to regular citizen, stripped of his power to oppose colonial and sexist social practices.[26] *Judy*'s strategy in shaming Mill was to reverse British feminists' demand for power and voting rights. Women feminists at the time demanded power by dressing up as men, but the tabloid ridiculed Mill by dressing him as a woman.

JUDY, OR THE LONDON SERIO-COMIC JOURNAL.—Nov. 25, 1868.

Figure 2.1: "Miss Mill joins the ladies" (*Judy*, November 25, 1868: 46–7) (photo courtesy of Indiana University Libraries)

In response to what they perceived as a reversal of the natural roles of men and women in society, *Judy*'s strategy was to shame Mill by representing him as an excluded, powerless female. Mill wanted to empower women and Jamaicans, people who had traditionally been stigmatized and left out of British politics, and Mill "in drag" had to be punished for crossing gender and sexual norms. *Judy*'s sarcastic description of Mill's life sought to reinforce the assumption that Mill's scholarship and talent for argumentation had been exaggerated. These exceptional gifts were, they argued, the result of an experiment conducted by an insane philosopher, James Mill. In a mocking tone, *Judy* expressed anxiety about the fact that Mill's life and work contested the values of decency and respectability in Victorian England. Mill's politics and philosophical attitudes unsettled traditional views about gender identity, which aimed at preserving clear dichotomies between concepts such as masculinity vs. femininity and reason vs. emotion. Mill was criticized elsewhere in the Victorian press, as well. *Punch*, the masculine tabloid version of *Judy*, attacked and humiliated Mill for various reasons. After Mill's death, they published an obituary in which they ironically pointed out that it is "strange" that Mill's mind, "high and calm and clear," shrank to "nought" ("Mill" 1873a: 216). They implied that he was "grinded" with knowledge by his father, while his mother, in "presenting her spouse with an heir," brought "grist to the Mill" ("Mill and Miller" 1873b: 222).

Judy's cartoon was not unique in representing Mill in drag—or Mill in a dress. Like the first cartoon, the second (Figure 2.1) portrays his failure to become a "powder-mill"—or a catalyst—for the women's movement. With a flirtatious air of casualness, he holds an umbrella with one hand and his skirt with the other. His naked leg, like his naked shoulder in the first image, signals his exposure to erotic encounters. While it is not at the center of the caricature, Mill's sexuality is an important part of the cartoon. Mill is ridiculed here not only as a gender-bending feminist but also as a person who has used his sexuality to provoke and incite. The content of the article is more explicit about *Judy*'s attempt to sexually shame Mill. *Judy* used controversies within the feminist movement to claim that some feminists considered him a "muff." "Muff" at the time was a slang word for vagina (Green 1998: 250). *Judy* humiliated Mill through an indirect accusation, and like women who are called "sluts" and sexual minorities who are shamed as "queer" in contemporary politics, Mill was considered deficient. *Judy* also attacked Mill's reluctance to campaign for his seat by labeling him "a little crotchety" and "Quixotic." Both

Figure 2.2: Mill "in drag" (*Judy*, 24 July 1867: 156) (photo courtesy of Indiana University Libraries)

"crotchety" and "Quixotic" implied that Mill was outside the norm, and that he was freakish in some aspects of his life and philosophical arguments. *Judy* reacted to what the Victorian tabloid perceived as a "revolution" in gender norms. Mill the freak, Mill the muff, and Mill the cross-dresser was *Judy*'s attempt to construct a shameful identity for the feminist philosopher.

Yet, under different circumstances, Mill's silence introduced a break in the conventional tradition of doing politics. Leslie Stephen's account of Mill's oratory shows how his shame functioned so as to destabilize the order of *the police*. As Stephen notes, when Mill advocated various kinds of radical progressive politics in Westminster, his political adversaries received Mill's speeches with strong opposition. His ideas "were specially irritating to the rows of stolid country gentlemen who began by listening curiously to so strange an animal as a philosopher, and discovered before long that the animal's hide could be pierced by scornful laughter" (Stephen 1968: 72). As opposed to the human who masters the *logos*, Mill is here a strange animal whose shelter is penetrated by ridicule.

Rancière observed that politics of a superior kind, which is achieved in the family and the city state, emerges from the opposition between speech and the groan. The groan, or the speech of the animal, seeks to capture a wrong, or the beginning of what counts as politics. The division of what can be seen and articulated as politics is "marked precisely in the logos that separates the discursive articulation of a grievance from the phonic articulation of a groan" (Rancière 1999: 2). The speech of Mill the orator does not fully embody what Rancière calls a teleological logic, by which pain fully becomes justice (1999: 2). Stephen observes the stark contrast between Mill, a man with a "slight frail figure," and the rows of "stolid country gentlemen." Adding to this image, Packe remarks that conservatives taunted Mill in different ways during his speeches, particularly "by reading up and quoting at him fragments from his own work" (1954: 454). One can imagine the tension and political agitation that shaped Mill's political environment and picture Mill being harassed by opponents who interrupted him by reading out loud passages from his writings. Written speech is deployed to repress spoken word, as spoken word has the quality of being not yet *logos*, or not *yet* a true and just partition of goods and power. But Mill is not here the representative of discursive speech; on the contrary, he embodies a different humanity, or better said, a strange animality, which opposes the logic that sees the groan as an inferior type of politics. The unarticulated animal speech is the speech that is not counted as politics.

Mill's image to his contemporaries is one of a very articulate and rational intellectual. As opposed to the image of Mill as a "utilitarian" cold thinker, Stephen describes Mill as a very passionate man deeply involved with progressive ideas (1968: 71–3). In his parliamentarian interventions, Mill was neither "the saint of rationalism" of the Utilitarians, nor the "forensic giant" and "embodiment of pure passionless reason" that his political adversaries, the Tories, had been afraid of (Packe 1954: 452). Stephen portrays Mill as an irritable person, enthusiastically involved in heated debates, who employed emotions in his rhetoric. Mill also had moments of withdrawal—or of losing his train of thought. In Westminster, the MPs saw:

> a slight frail figure, trembling with nervous irritability. He poured out a series of perfectly formed sentences with an extraordinary rapidity suggestive of learning by heart; and when he lost the thread of his discourse closed his eyes for two or three minutes till, after regaining his composure, he could take again his parable. Although his oratory was defective, he was clearly speaking with intense feeling and was exceedingly sensitive to the reception by his audience. (Stephen 1968: 72)

As witness to Mill's actual performance as parliamentarian, Stephen offers an image of an emotional person deeply engaged in political conflicts.

The silence that Leslie Stephen points to is breathtaking. Why did Mill close his eyes? Why was he silent for a couple of minutes during his speech?[27] Mill's silence indicates an experience of withdrawal, similar to what Sedgwick describes as failure of contact or a "disruptive moment" (2009: 50). In Sedgwick's account, the feeling that one lacks the recognition of others triggers shame. The activist involved in feminist reforms is particularly at risk because he or she makes her or his personality available to injury (2009: 51). In his account of the event, Stephen suggests that Mill's withdrawal was caused by the Tories' reception of his speech. Exposed to the judgment of his political peers, Mill hid by closing his eyes and tried to regain his composure. In this moment of averting his gaze and offering himself a moment of pause, Mill responded to shame with silence.

Although silence and the act of closing one's eyes are generally seen as a *negative* outcome of shame, Mill's silence introduced a break in the liberal political routine. Mill's silence was constituted by the linguistic and political field that had previously established the rules of political engagement. The rule in Westminster was that speakers must not pause in the middle of their discourses. Within Butler's theory of performativity, the value of silence consists in expanding the notion of what is allowed as political behavior. Mill's silence during his political speech was an assertion of a right to a different practice, a behavior for which no clear convention was in place. It represented a break in the flow of normal politics. It unsettled the convention that politics should be exclusively a rational discourse organized around "the forceless force of the better argument" (Habermas 1999: 332). Mill's silence shows that one can creatively intervene in a particular political setting by disrupting the conventions of the day. The aim of such an intervention was to offer the speaker a space of protection— a safe space within the rhetoric of aggression and shaming.

Moreover, Mill's gesture of closing his eyes shows that human agency is not fully intentional, because it is in many ways beyond one's control. Butler challenges the idea that speech is necessarily under the control of the speaker. Her main concern in *Excitable Speech* is to show that speech should not be construed as identical to deed, as what Austin calls an illocutionary act. An illocutionary act is one in which, in saying something, one is doing something. Butler's insistence that speech and conduct are not identical is intended to "lend support for the role of non-juridical forms of opposition, ways of restaging and resignifying speech in contexts that exceed those determined by the law" (Butler 1997b: 23). Her move is to dislocate the speech act from a sovereign subject, who is imagined as always responsible and in full control of the words he or she uses. In contrast with such a sovereign speaker, the value of the performative for Butler is that it is "always in some ways out of our control" (1997b: 15).[28]

Mill's silence constituted a performative intervention in the context of political discourses in the British Parliament. Leslie Stephen, the narrator of this scene, opts to give us a picture in which Mill behaved like an "emotional" politician with "defective oratory." From the standpoint of queer theory, however, Mill's silence is a political moment because that shame is not a "toxic" part of a group or individual identity that needs to be "excised" but rather is integral to the formation of identity and available for "metamorphosis, reframing, refiguration, and transfiguration" (Sedgwick 2009: 60). When he was exposed to shaming, silence served him to provide what Brown calls a "shelter" from the violence of norm-regulating behavior (2005: 86). In a Rancièrian understanding, this silence is a democratic moment and its function is similar to the groan's. Like the sound of an animal, Mill's silence was a break from *the police* and showed the "gap" between the act of speaking and "the ethical harmony of rules" (1999: 101). This silence points to the possibility that democracy is neither the parliamentary system, nor the legitimate State, nor the state of the social (1999: 99). The democratic moment was the transformation of Mill as a political subject, when he became "a strange animal" with "a defective oratory" whose hide was "pierced by scornful laugher."

In this section I distinguished between non-responsive silence and silence as an embodied performativity to highlight the democratic value of disturbing silences. Like drag, which is an intervention aimed at unsettling the assumption about the natural character of gender, and like Rosa Parks's gesture of refusing to sit in the back of the bus, Mill's act of closing his eyes rejected established conventions. This act was made possible because of rules that delineated what was conceivable in a political setting. Mill's silence was beyond his conscious control, and it shows in a Rancièrian sense why democracy is not a set of institutions but a disruption of what represents a particular order of politics. By behaving like "a strange animal" and a "defective orator," Mill introduced a new order of equality that destabilized the idea of democratic expertise and authority. Like "an interlocution that undermines the very situation of the interlocution," Mill's silence exposes the opposition between two orders, an egalitarian order and the order of *the police* (Rancière 1999: 100). This moment of equality is not liberal politics. In contrast, like a groan, or a sound that does not fit into the speakable politics, Mill's silence interrupted the conventions of the British Parliament.

"Barbarians" and "Lunatics": Harsh Language and Mill's Rhetoric

In the third section, I claim that the rhetoric of shame and humiliation is a radical element of queer practices. Unlike political theorists such as Nussbaum and Tarnopolsky, who argue that humiliation is an illegitimate democratic practice, I argue that the performative slur is a key tactic that can be mobilized for queer feminist goals. Here I conceptualize slurs as a practice of excess, which is expressed from a position of risk with the aim of conveying a position of equality. It is similar to what Rancière calls "literarity." Rancière indicated that writing, an excess of words, "goes places it should not go, including into the hands of those who should not . . . wield it" (Chambers 2013: 116). Humiliating rhetoric is in this sense literature because it disrupts the proper use of *logos*. Like unconventional relationships and disrupting silences, humiliating rhetoric is a practice of excess because it disrupts "a logic of the proper" (Chambers 2013: 116). This excessive irruption of speech leads to a disagreement, so that "literature" does not exist without a political conflict. No disagreement without excessive speech, to paraphrase Chambers' formula "no disagreement without literature" (2013: 117).

But in addition to theorizing humiliating rhetoric as a practice of literature—when our speaking thwarts efforts to privilege speech—I want to think about this practice in conjunction with Butler's theory of resignification. I undertake a genealogical interpretation of practices in nineteenth-century England in an effort to locate "time-spaces" in which the order of *the police* is disrupted by humiliating rhetoric. Butler's intention in her work is to politicize bodies and actions that are associated with the "abject" and to assert the value of those whose lives are perceived as "unlivable" (1993: 3). By theorizing the performativity of specific practices and acts, Butler offers a conceptual framework that focuses on the contextual value of political actions. According to her theory, specific contingent actions have value because they resignify previous conventions about political power. Drag is useful for articulating a critique of the natural character of gender. Rosa Parks's actions show the possibility of transforming racist conventions that are prevalent in political life. Like drag and civil disobedience, shaming and humiliating are practices of excess that draw attention to political exclusions. They highlight the inequalities of power that are in place to ensure that certain categories of subjects do not have access to legal and social resources.

Butler's theory about the use of violent language urges us "to attend" to particular goals and contexts of injurious language. She asks us to focus not on the content of language but on its rhetorical intention and effects. Against a liberal conception that bans the use of humiliation in any circumstances, Butler claims that autonomy in speech—and the responsibility of the speaker—is conditioned by "a radical and originary dependency on a language" that is shaped by exclusions. Butler defended the importance of speech acts that are constructed as injurious, such as Robert Mapplethorpe's photography, the practices of coming out, and explicit sex education (1997b: 22). Offensive terms that are part of politics "precede and occasion the utterance by which they are enacted" (1997b: 27). That is, humiliating and shaming language precedes a given speech act. The direct consequence of this precedence is that the responsibility of the speaker is to negotiate "the legacies of usage that constrain and enable the speaker's speech" (27).[29] But rather than thinking about excluded subjects as already existing, or political exclusions as *always* heteronormative, I want to push the theory of resignification in a Rancièrian direction. In this way we will consider the practice of exclusions as producing subjects, and not merely representing categories of politics such as gay, queer, or workers. If disagreement produces politics, then arguing that certain subjects are inferior from a certain standpoint is a political intervention. The rhetoric of humiliation is, however, risky politics when it targets the powerful, and excessive when it seeks to disrupt the proper order of politics.

Mill's insulting words were performative interventions, which challenged an order that rejected women, working class people, and colonial subjects. At times, Mill was driven by an excessive need to disrupt the boundaries of civility. Mill not only employed shame to demonstrate that people who opposed gender equality were wrong; he also used humiliating rhetoric to portray opponents as inferior and worthy of contempt. Dubbing them "ruffians," "barbarians," "stupid," and people who posses "a degraded state of mind," Mill argued that people who did not share his progressive values should be corrected and chastised. Mill did not explicitly claim that humiliating language was a legitimate political tool, but he deployed humiliation in his rhetorical interventions.[30]

Mill's strategy was to use the liberal language of individual rights to justify individual injuries, that is, injuries that affect only the individual who generates them.[31] For Mill, the right to injure oneself should be protected from public opinion and the regulation of the state.[32] Unlike Mill, Butler did not conceptualize injuries as individual harms. While Mill appeals to "constructive injuries" to defend particular behaviors, Butler claims that injuries need to be produced by both social norms and individuals. Butler's emphasis is on a person's capacity to act such that a particular conventional norm could become more inclusive of "deviants" and sexual minorities. She claims that appealing to laws to distinguish what is and what is not obscene is problematic. Although she argues that the state should have the power to decide what is injurious in specific cases, she is worried about "the noxious results" that emerge from the intervention of the courts. Courts can declare obscene the art of Mapplethorpe and defend threats of violence as "free speech" (Butler 1997b: 52–62). Rather than appealing to the state as an impartial arbiter of what is pornographic and offensive, Butler wants to leave that judgment to agents who struggle in political conflicts.

Humiliating rhetoric can be a demand to rethink the conventions that organize political actions. Mill's use of harsh language shows that a certain excess of words can challenge *the police*. In his logic, Mill employed various strategic rhetorical figures to respond to the humiliating force of male power, which had been sanctioned by centuries of physical and political domination.[33] He criticized those who treated women as inferior, attacked the legal system for discriminating against women, and used many kinds of slurs to respond to the harm done to women. He argued that his opponents' opinions were "barbaric" and suggested that those who voted against gender equality encouraged rape and domestic violence (Rossi 1970: 126, 176). He argued that individuals who oppose enfranchisement lack several important human characteristics; they are "ruffians" and need to be chastised. Writing with Harriet Taylor for the *Morning Chronicle* about domestic violence, Mill was horrified by the lack of legislative measures to protect women (CW XXV: 103–5). He called for increased severity of penalties with regard to violence against children and women.[34] Denouncing the tyranny of the "ruffians" who abuse their spouses, he argued that it was a "deep disgrace" that the government had done nothing to protect women (CW XXV: 105).[35] In calling the government a disgrace, Mill was not merely exposing the government as inferior and worthy of contempt—he was trying to mobilize the British state to pass laws for reducing domestic abuse and increase punishment for men who abuse women.[36]

Mill used harsh language to condemn the courts for facilitating social injustice. He wrote about the suicide of a woman, Sarah Brown, who was seduced by a man and deprived of her child (CW XXIV: 177–9). The man who seduced Sarah Brown, whom Mill called "the creature called a 'gentleman,'" did not have any legal rights over the child. According to Mill, the primary obligations and responsibilities for children belonged to the mother. But in many cases male judges were inclined to favor men in their decisions. Sarah Brown killed herself because she was afraid that the courts were going to favor her seducer. Mill claimed that, because it did not offer Sarah Brown the possibility of just reparation, the justice system did not pass the standards by which it held itself accountable (CW XXIV: 179). Brown knew that her man would get only a month or two of imprisonment for violating the law. Mill linked Sarah Brown's suicide with the failure of the justice system and shamed the government for its inclination to protect men. Because of the bias within the legal system, women had stopped trusting a legal system ruled by men.

Mill and Harriet Taylor's newspaper articles about women's social and legal predicament are not unique in using a harsh tone. Mill sustained an active correspondence with many English, French, and American feminist activists. In this correspondence, he argued that the government should be embarrassed into taking action to protect women's lives, and that shaming should be an important part of a feminist's strategy to promote social justice. In his letter to French feminist activist Julie-Victoire Daubie, who published a book about the plight of poor women in France, Mill expressed his appreciation of this work "of great value," which "must have been very painful to write" (CW XVII: 163). He believed that Daubie's book would make many educated people "ashamed of their culpable inaction in the face of evils so frightful and injustices so monstrous" (CW XVII: 163). Mill was acutely aware of the importance of shaming the educated class so that they would take active measures to fight women's social subordination.

Mill felt that women's enfranchisement was "the most important of all political improvements now under public discussion" (CW XVII: 342) and supported the use of shame to fight for the women's cause. As a member of Parliament, he fought for women's enfranchisement between 1865 and 1868, but without being able to win the right for women to vote. Mill thought that conservatives would vote for the enfranchisement because Benjamin Disraeli, the leader of the Tory party, had signaled possible support for such a cause (Reeves 2008: 447).[37] But Mill knew that any victory for the women's cause had to be won both at the level of society and in Parliament. He advocated a strategy of "propagandizing in a quiet way, by lectures and otherwise" to win the battle of public opinion (Reeves 2008: 446). In 1866, in a letter to Caroline E. Liddell, who promoted the representation of women in Parliament, Mill argued that feminists like Liddell should shame members of Parliament as a strategy for gaining representation:

> I am glad to be able to say that I know several members of Parliament who wish to grant the franchise without distinctions of sex, but I know many more who would be ashamed to refuse it if it were quietly and steadily demanded by women themselves. (CW XVI: 168)

He explained that men who want to change unfair laws are met with the objection that the ladies themselves see "no hardship" in the state of the current legislation (CW XVI: 168). Since he had been accused by his critics of wanting to emancipate people who did not desire their own emancipation, he felt that women should be much more active in asking for voting rights. He told Liddell that women who desired equality needed to engage in a concentrated effort to reach their goals by using shame. They should not be ashamed of being "strong-minded," because strength of mind is "one of the noblest gifts" and "the best measure of the degree of efficiency of working in the cause of truth" (CW XVI: 168).

Mill not only shamed but insulted his political adversaries. His use of insults became the focus of political debates in Westminster when he called the Tories "stupid." During Mill's tenure in Parliament between 1865 and 1868, Sir John Pakington, one of the Conservative MPs who was ideologically opposed to Mill's politics, asked him to explain his comment that the Conservatives were the stupidest party in the state (Packe 1954: 454). Mill, who was sometimes unable to "conceal his contempt or keep his temper" in the face of the Tories' humiliating reactions (Stephen 1968: 72), replied that he did not mean to say that Conservatives are stupid but that stupid people are generally Conservative (Packe 1954: 454).

Mill's classic feminist manifesto, *The Subjection of Women*, employed many performative insults. Mill claimed that the opponents of women's rights cling to "barbarisms" (Rossi 1970: 126); that the adoption of a system of inequality was "never" the result of "deliberation" and "forethought" (Rossi 1970: 129); and that women's "dependence" on men is a result of a "primitive state of slavery" (Rossi 1970: 130). One of the most frequent rhetorical tropes in his work was the contrast between a historical state in which inequality and unchecked power were taken for granted, and a more progressive state in which power is controlled by various institutions and social norms. The historical state is opposed to "civilization," because it (i.e., the historical state) represents a "system of privilege and enforced subjection," which has "its yoke tightly on the necks of those who are kept down by it" (Rossi 1970: 137). Men who have power over women want more than mere obedience. They want "not a forced slave but a willing one," a "favourite"; and so men "put everything in practice to enslave [women's] minds" (Rossi 1970: 141).[38] Mill wanted to humiliate men for their desire to keep women slaves and for relying on fear to maintain control.[39] The implication of Mill's argument was that one was complicit with obsolete institutions of human degradation by not responding with disgust and indignation to their harmful effects.

A conservative man who read Mill's pamphlet would see himself portrayed as "barbaric," an apologist of slavery, an opponent of moral progress, and a person with a "degraded state of mind." Frances Power Cobbe, a leading Victorian suffragette and social reformer, understood very well the harsh rhetoric embedded in Mill's *The Subjection of Women*. She knew that Mill and his "daring" argument against the roots of women's oppression were going to be viciously attacked and abused. She anticipated "a fierce simoom of prejudice" and believed that only a miracle would prevent him from being "blown upon with a vengeance" (Pyle 1995: 56).

Mill did become a target for people who did not appreciate the value of freethinking. Cobbe articulated potential objections to Mill from a conservative position: "We always knew he was a dangerous free thinker (we hear them say), but truly this new doctrine outherods Herod. Where are we drifting, when such subversive ideas can be unblushingly enunciated by a man of reputation?" (Pyle 1995: 54). Cobbe knew that the conservatives would utilize shame to indict Mill because they would feel that he had articulated a shameless and "subversive" doctrine. Mill's opponents would believe that a proper gentlemen and public person would feel shame for advocating social and legal equality for women, but Mill, a reputable philosopher, had stated his destabilizing ideas "unblushingly." Cobbe thought that Mill would be exposed not merely to shame but to humiliation. His opponents would generate an "avalanche of sarcasms and rebukes and jokes" to ridicule him and downplay his political argument (Pyle 1995: 56).[40]

Butler's theory of resignification helps us understand how humiliating rhetoric, such as the shaming, harsh words that Mill used in his political activism, can disrupt conventions about civility in liberal politics.[41] Butler argues that progressive resignification has a positive impact when it produces radical democratic transformations. The norms that justify this transformation are not derived from the act of resignification but from its context and political practices. Resignification works differently according to different normative intentions. Like Rosa Parks's actions, the rhetoric of feminists such as Mill sought to extend norms that sustained viable life to disenfranchised communities. But more importantly, it shows that an excessive use of tone and feelings, or what Rancière calls "literarity," produces a political stage, on which subjects who were not speaking before can make themselves heard. The use of slurs and fighting words can be understood as "a politics of literarity," as channeling the force that can threaten the police order.

To conclude, performative slurs are important because they show that the process of becoming a political subject involves the abandonment of neutral, civil language. Aggressive, harsh language does not aim to represent politics but to bring political subjects into disagreement. In a Rancièrian mode of thinking, political subjectivation is not the recognition of categories of identity but the disruption of these categories. The order of *the police* cannot be dismantled from the position of an existing social class. To think of "the poor" or "women" as an already given category is to ascribe to the order of *the police*. Mill and Taylor were not advancing arguments from the position of the poor nor of women but from the position of a new political subject that sought to fight against social injustice. The "poor," or "women," or any new category of political conflict does not exist before a political claim has been made. Similarly, we can think about the use of harsh rhetoric as having value not simply because it challenges liberal and civilized discourse but because it makes this intervention in spaces and places were it is considered forbidden. The irruption of what is considered forbidden, particularly when subjects who are not supposed to utter this rhetoric appropriate it, is a practice of disrupting *the police*.

Conclusion

In *Proletarian Nights*, Rancière tells us that in the nineteenth century the order of *the police* was interrupted by working class people when they appropriated the power reserved for the other—the middle and upper class individuals. He argues that

> a worker who had never learned how to write and yet tried to compose verses to suit the taste of his times was perhaps more of a danger to the prevailing ideological order than a worker who performed revolutionary songs. (Rancière 2012: xxvii)

This appropriation of what is not supposed to be said or thought is an irruption of the order of equality. These intolerable practices disturbed the established conventions about what people can and should do.

In this chapter I appealed to Rancière's work to theorize practices that emerge from shame to disturb a given order of normativity. I followed Rancière's thought that *the police* are an order that allocates "ways of doing, ways of being, and ways of saying" (1999: 29). In this sense, policing is not a disciplining of bodies so much as a configuration of occupations and the property of the spaces in which these occupations appear (1999: 29). I showed that Mill's queer practices, such as his relationship with Harriet Taylor, his performative silence in Westminster, and his use of humiliating rhetoric disrupted the order of *the police*. Butler's theory of performativity captures the political potential of "twisting" norms so that these interventions expose and rework power hierarchies. Yet a theory of performativity does not go far enough in drawing on the contrast between politics and *the police*. Rancière's philosophy provides a sharper point of critique by capturing disturbing interventions that defy social hierarchy and the order of the proper. Like the workers who moved at the borders between classes, Mill's practices blurred the boundaries between what was respectable and what was shameful. These interventions resignified traditional conventions and produced a new political progressive stage on which alternative relationships, performative silence, and slurs acquired a positive meaning.

In the second part of the book I conceptualize three counter-figures that challenge a current perception of shame in political theory. The next chapter focuses on the value of performative silences with regard to sexuality and illuminates silences that break with a liberal political order. Mill was politically associated with a group of radical Unitarians who presented a radical critique of marriage and gender in their journal titled *The Monthly Repository*. I draw on Mill's practices and reflections about unconventional intimacy to argue that liberal feminist theory polices shame. To do so, I revisit Nussbaum's claims about Mill's conservatism and his silences, and show why Mill's disturbing silences were an interruption of *the police* order.

Notes

1. Butler valorizes the moment when a subject "asserts a right or entitlement to a livable life when no such prior authorization exists, when no clearly enabling convention is in place" (2004a: 224).
2. See also Mahmood's (2005: 5–25) argument about the opposition between liberal and poststructuralist agency.

3. For the distinction between signification and resignification, Butler draws on J. L. Austin's theory of the performative use of language in *How To Do Things with Words*. Both signification and resignification are practices that derive from a performative use of language. Against a theory of representation which believed that the meaning of a word is represented by its content, Austin argued that words not only represent reality, but also produce particular meanings. In this sense, to say "I proclaim you man and wife" is a performative action that does what it says it does. In addition to the function of representation, language has an important performative dimension based on the idea that speaking is a practice with its own effects.
4. Political theorists such as James Tully (2009: 55) mobilize the possibility of "re-description" of various words and practices against a reified vision of language. Like resignification, to redescribe means to use a word in its "deviant" meaning, without offering a rule for justifying such practice. By drawing on Wittgenstein, Tully argues that words acquire different meanings in different language games, which can not be subsumed by a general rule (2009: 55).
5. Butler articulates her theory of resistance and performative action in *Gender Trouble*, where she draws on her example of drag queens to theorize about the performative dimension of gender. She elaborates her theory in *Excitable Speech* in response to feminist arguments about censorship. She claims that the strategy to ban pornography and hate speech advocated throughout the 1980s and 1990s by feminists and critical theorists such as Catharine MacKinnon and Mari Matsuda had important limitations. For these thinkers, the only way to secure substantive equality and respect for all citizens is to censor "injurious language." Yet, Butler believes that speech is outside the control of its users and that feminists should respond to political injuries by avoiding the power of the state. In her view, the *redeployment* of a slur could undermine its insulting meaning. To produce "insurrectionary speech" means to open up new contexts for understanding words and practices and give such terms new meanings.
6. Chambers' notion of social formation has a broader scope than queer genealogy. While my specific project wants to change the meaning of shame, Chambers addresses larger questions such as: "how a social order is put together, what it must do to stay together, and how to work required to stay together transforms the very regime that it simultaneously maintains" (2014: 12).
7. See also footnote 42, Chapter 1, which presents key critical objections to Butler's theory of politics.
8. For an argument that Butler avoids theorizing the political value of negative emotions, see also Popa (2015: 250–1).

9. In this sense Rosa Parks not only resignified the previous norm about blackness and politics but became a political subject that introduced an order of equality where previously there was a racialized distribution of power. As a queer practice, Rosa Parks's interrupted the logic of a given distribution of power and roles.
10. Because people are imperfect, Mill believed that we need different opinions and engage in "new and original" experiments in living and welcomed challenges to received truths (CW XVIII: 282).
11. See Alison Ross (2008: 62). Foucault's criterion for fearless speech is "his sincerity," which means that the speaker "says something dangerous—different from what the majority believes" (2008: 62).
12. Mill, however, did not explicitly theorize his reactions to shame. In an essay titled *The Utility of Religion* published posthumously in 1874, he worried about the high costs of social shame. Shame is not only an individual emotion, but also an emotion that has powerful social consequences. When it is deployed by the public opinion, it drastically undermines people's quality of life: "The fear of shame, the dread of ill repute or of being disliked and hated are the direct and simple forms of its [public opinion] deterring power. But the deterring force of the unfavorable sentiments of mankind does not consist solely in the painfulness of knowing oneself to be the object of those sentiments; it includes all the penalties which they can inflict; exclusion from social intercourse and from the innumerable good offices which human beings require from one another; the forfeiture of all that is called success in life; often the great diminution and total loss of means of subsistence; positive ill offices of various kinds, sufficient to rend life miserable and reaching in some states of society as far as actual persecution to death" (CW X: 417).
13. Queer scholars have strongly responded to Michel Foucault's insight that "our problem today" is "to work on ourselves and invent a manner of being that is still improbable" (1994: 137). Foucault claimed that what upsets traditional gender norms is not a sexual act that does not conform to the law, such as the homosexual act of two young men "getting each other off in a quarter of an hour" (1994: 136). The actual trouble about a homosexual way of life is that it generates unease.
14. Because individuals imagine new relationships that contradict institutional codes, these new relations undermine conventional norms and introduce love "where there is supposed to be only law, rule and habit" (1994: 137). For Foucault, homosexuality is an historical occasion to reopen affective and relational virtualities not because of the "intrinsic qualities of the homosexual," but because of the transgressive nature of such intimate relationships.

15. This "derealization" of human intimacy negates "the reality and truth to the relations at issue" (2004a: 27). The danger for Butler is that such unconventional arrangements and relationships are denied reality.
16. Although Cobbe kept her relationship with her partner mostly private, she clearly indicated in her published work that Mary Lloyd and she shared a special intimate relationship (Marcus 2007: 53). John Stuart Mill, along with Charles Darwin and William Gladstone, were part of Cobbe's social network, and recognized Cobbe and Lloyd as a conjugal unit and invited them as a pair to social gatherings (Marcus 2007: 51).
17. Foucault thought that the work of imagining new relational rights would permit "all possible types of relations to exist and not to be prevented, blocked, or annulled by impoverished relational institutions" (Halperin 1995: 82).
18. See Nussbaum's statement: "Mill is the last person whom one would associate with the street theater of Act Up or any other public manifestation of 'queer radicalism'" (2010: 141).
19. Mill never talked about his arrest, especially because the reputation of a public person was central to one's power and visibility. Although Mill distributed handbills that advocated safe sexual intercourse, Hayward accused him of promoting a radical sexual pamphlet about the necessity of equal sexual relationships called *Every Woman's Book, or What is Love?* By associating him with Carlile, the intention of Hayward was to describe Mill as a sex radical who advocated immoral views about sexuality.
20. As Packe argues, James Mill's radicalism, unlike his son, did not carry into everyday life. The father told his son that interfering in the affairs of another man is interference in the rights of property, and is similar to "coveting his ox or his ass" (Packe 1954: 139).
21. Drag and camp are effective forms of undermining heteronormative understandings of gender and sexuality. Butler's drag performances have the potential of showing that social norms privilege heteronormativity. Halperin describes camp, that is, "parody, exaggeration, amplification, theatricalization, and literalization of normally tacit codes of conduct," as a form of cultural resistance (Halperin 1995: 29; Butler 1999: 188–90). The goal of such movement is to "rework and revise the social organization of friendship, sexual contacts and community to produce non-state-centered form of support and alliance, because marriage, given its historical weight, becomes an 'option' only by extending itself as a norm (and thus foreclosing options), one that also extends property relations and renders the social forms for sexuality more conservative" (Butler 2004a: 109).
22. Like Chambers (2013: 183, note 3), I do not think that the Rancièrian phrase "partage of the sensible" has a right rendition in English, and thus, for instrumental reasons, I use the above translation.

23. See Rancière (1999: 23).
24. For the large literature on speech and deliberation as central to democratic politics, see only Gutmann and Thompson (1996) and Elster (1998).
25. See Rancière's (1999: 1–4) discussion of the famous passage about *zoon politikon* in Book I of Aristotle's *Politics*.
26. Since a man dressed in women's clothes was a mark of loss and disempowerment, in Victorian times, for women, men's clothes represented a strategy of empowerment. Mill's advocacy of women's rights and his role in the British feminist movement were very important for Victorian gender and sexual dissenters. In his essay "Women since 1860" George Bernard Shaw describes Mill's influence on women's public display of their gender: "the followers of John Stuart Mill and Henry Fawcett cut their hair short; put on men's stiff collars and cravats; wore waistcoats and shirtfronts and watchchains; and made themselves mannish above the waist whilst remaining quakerish below it" (Shaw in Lenker 2001: 111).
27. For psychotherapists such as Gershen Kaufman, the affective source of silence is shame, "which is the affect that causes the self to hide" (2004: 194).
28. Felman argues that the speech act, as the act of speaking body, "is always to some extent unknowing about what it performs, that it always says something that it does not intend, and that it is not the emblem of mastery or control that it sometimes purports to be" (quoted in Butler 1997b: 9). Mill's reaction points out the limit of the intentionality of the speech act and shows that agency is beyond the control of the speaker.
29. Butler argues that senator Helms's conservative speech about banning Robert Mapplethorpe's work shares with Andrea Dworkin's ban on pornography a normative effort to define sexuality (2004a: 183). These efforts of both conservative politicians and feminist theorists mobilized particular conceptions of what was sexually acceptable and what was legitimate to fantasize. Both Helms and Dworkin's efforts to legislate an acceptable type of sexual behavior fail to eliminate "injurious language." Instead of purging sexual humiliation from public spaces, they used offensive words and "pornographic" representations in their attacks on obscene representations.
30. For Mill, to feel humiliated and injured did not necessarily represent a political weakness. These affective responses could instead lead to political awareness and mobilization. He claimed that the feeling of "humiliation" is positive if it leads to action and the arousal of "political energies of the constituency" (*CW* XVI: 489).
31. In *On Liberty*, one of the aims of Mill's famous essay was to justify a strong distinction between self-regarding actions and actions that harm the interests of others. He was worried that society could intervene through laws to regulate the life of individuals and sought to identify

a sphere—self-regarding actions—that would provide a buffer against social interventions. For "the sake of the greater good of human freedom," he defended what he calls a "constructive injury"—or an injury that neither hurts society nor inflicts hurt "to any assignable individual except himself" (CW XVIII: 283).

32. For Mill, the injuries that one does to oneself, such as "constructive injuries," were a necessary part of human life. Mill argued that "gambling, or drunkenness, or incontinence, or idleness, or uncleanness" were harmful to the self-destructive individual and to intimate others (CW XVIII: 282). Most—if not all of our actions—are both affecting oneself and others. Such actions were to be permitted because human beings have the right to be self-destructive and because social interventions are often either wrong or propose the wrong intervention. While society should not have laws regulating "constructive injuries," Mill allowed for interventions on behavior such as persuasion, disgust, contempt, and avoidance. Unlike socially sanctioned penalties, which are enforced by political institutions, he believed that shaming and contempt in relationships are permitted. In his view, because some people have better taste, they should be contemptuous and disgusted by other people's behavior and choices (CW XVIII: 279). Because people with "superior taste" feel disgust over "lowness and depravation of taste," shaming is legitimate when it is directed at self-destructive behavior.

33. Many Victorians—not only Victorian feminists and progressives—believed that the existing laws and social practices were shameful and humiliating to women. Margaret Oliphant asserted that "the phraseology of the law" about women conveys "a stinging sense of humiliation and insult" (Pyle 1995: 116). Anne Mozley, who vehemently attacked Mill's *The Subjection of Women*, believed that administrators of the English law did not adequately punished domestic abuse and "no one can be other than ashamed" by their leniency (Pyle 1995: 102).

34. See Mill's argument: "there ought to be severer penalties for killing or ill-treating a wife or child than for killing or ill-treating, in similar manner, any other person" (CW XXV: 105).

35. In their reading of police reports, Mill and Harriet Taylor seem to take for granted the record of the police without questioning its authority and partiality. First, Mill seems to ignore that overpopulation was caused by factors such as demolition of houses, dock developments, the building of warehouses and offices, and plans of urban improvement. Second, while he seems to put himself on the side of the victims, he advocates for serious penalties when it comes to poor laborers who have large families and not many time resources to invest in raising children. Third, he overlooks the social and political conditions of producing poverty and overcrowded spaces in the heart of London. For a

critique of how Victorian intellectuals responded to gentrification in London, see Jones 2014.

36. In a letter to George Grey, Mill protested against a law that regulated the sale of arsenic and discriminated against women. Mill argued that discriminatory laws are "an insult to every woman in the country," are "a return to barbarous ages," and "degrade" women (*CW* XIV: 87). He told his friend, John Cairnes, that he was "ashamed" of the state of public opinion with regard to slavery in England (*CW* XV: 219). The conduct of the Governor of Jamaica provoked "a deepest indignation" and "humiliation" in Mill (*CW* XVI: 393). He thought that the actions of Governor Eyre are "abhorrent" and worthy of "contempt" because he tortured and killed many people (*CW* XVI: 393–4). He felt humiliated by the thought that people who read his work would doubt his commitment to "chastising" the Governor for his deeds (*CW* XVI: 394). He would have been "ashamed of [his] country" if he was not convinced that the "majority of the English nation does desire judicial enquiry" into such events (*CW* XVI: 394). Mill's strong reactions to Eyre's violent crimes had led him to open a judicial inquiry in the Parliament.

37. He believed that the members of Parliament who did not support the enfranchisement could be persuaded to change their mind. His political interventions helped progressive causes, which were generally advocated by the Liberal Party. He also believed that the cause of women could be appealing to the Conservative Party, the Tories. The petition that Mill submitted to the House of Commons in 1866 about the women's right to vote was surprisingly backed by prominent conservative figures such as Disraeli and Salisbury and rejected by Gladstone and Queen Victoria (Pyle 1995: ix).

38. In Mill's view, people who oppose legal and social equality between men and women opposed the "slow process of modern history" by which barriers to equality "have since been wearing away" (Rossi 1970: 174). They were hostile to a "new order of things," where justice would be "the primary virtue" (Rossi 1970: 174). They resisted what an intellectual elite has discovered or felt as "the futurity of the species." The observer who understood the legal slavery of women and their physical subjection to men's will should feel "disgust and indignation" at the institutions who led a "depraved state of human mind" (Rossi 1970: 176).

39. In his effort to prove his point, Mill inaccurately claimed that the condition of wives in England was even worse than the condition of female slaves in America. Unlike the female slave in the United States, who was protected by the law, an English man could legally rape his wife (Rossi 1970: 160). Mill's belief that laws protected American slaves from rape, however, was mistaken.

40. Cobbe had good reasons to worry about a conservative backlash. Anne Mozley, an essayist and journal editor, published in *Blackwood's Magazine* a review of *The Subjection of Women* in which she compared Mill's arguments with those of "the lunatic who proved logically that all the rest of the world was insane" (Pyle 1995: 89). Mozley portrayed Mill as a subversive philosopher who unjustly castigated women. She argued that his work derived from his feelings of shame and disgust toward women (Pyle 1995: 90).
41. Butler notices that both Right and Left modern politicians use resignification for their goals (2004a: 223). Butler argues that resignification is a political practice that is not automatically progressive (2004a: 223).

PART II
COUNTER-FIGURES

Chapter 3
Disturbing Silence: Mill and the Radicals at the *Monthly Repository*

> So: why is Mill, so 'queer' in some ways, not queer enough? One could try to say that *Subjection* is already such a shocking word, and Mill is already so aware that he might not get a hearing (see pp. 1–3), that he avoids making it more shocking by tying his critique to radical changes in the family. This may be a sufficient explanation for the text's silences, and in that case they would be merely pragmatic and superficial silences. I believe, however, that they may well lie deeper. Despite his radicalism, Mill was in many ways a rather conservative man.
>
> (Nussbaum 2010: 142)

Writing about Mill's *The Subjection of Women,* Martha Nussbaum expresses her disappointment that the book lacks a theoretical chapter exploring "new rules" for marriages, alternative life styles and "experiments in living" (2010: 143). Although Mill was queer because he condemned the tyranny of the social norms over eccentric individuals, Nussbaum believes he was not "queer enough" because he was silent about many experiments that were going on at the time. Like many feminists (Annas 1977; Okin 1979; Eisenstein 1981), Nussbaum claims that the argument of *The Subjection of Women* is not radical enough. Mill's reluctance to ask men to participate in child rearing and his failure to imagine women's work opportunities stemmed from his conservatism. Mill was silent on radical gender projects because he shared a deep attachment to "the orderly forms of Victorian life" (Nussbaum 2010: 142).

In this chapter, I propose to rethink Nussbaum's assumption about the inherent conservatism in the philosopher's silences. Nussbaum is not unique in thinking that silence, as opposed to speaking out, is a conservative gesture.[1] Here I utilize the counter-figure of disturbing silence to contest the demand to always speak out about sexual injustices. This figure reconceptualizes shame as an interruption of norms instead of constituting a stand-in for an undemocratic disciplinary affect. Disturbing silence is the first trope that I deploy to change a contemporary view about shame as negative and restrictive. To further this genealogical project, I argue that disturbing silences open up a space to live a life that unsettles normalized sexuality. To flesh out this point, I analyze silences as performative actions that contested disciplinary assumptions about sexuality in Victorian England and focus on Mill's reactions to the *Fox Affair* in 1834, when he was a young writer for various progressive journals.

By suggesting that Mill's silences are an expression of conservatism, Nussbaum employs the strong dichotomy between speech and silence that queer thinkers criticize. A queer theoretical perspective challenges Nussbaum's suggestion that silences are inadequate interventions in politics. For queer theory, Foucault opened a distinctive manner of perceiving silences when he argued that silences are integral to what is speakable in public.[2] Sedgwick drew on Foucault to argue that silence around the "closet" is a performance that "accrues" in relation "to the discourse that surrounds and differentially constitutes it" (1990: 3). In the *Epistemology of the Closet*, her intention was to show that silence could become as "pointed" and "performative" as speech (1990: 4). When writing about homoerotic experiences around the last decade of the nineteenth century in England, Cocks saw "the closet" as both "resisting and making use of secrets" (2003: 158). Silence, rather than being a disgraceful expression of fear, is considered a method of "resisting condemnatory accounts of homosexual desire" (2003: 158). Like Sedgwick, Butler (2013: 86–7) suggests that silence could offer an important "political promise" because of its capacity for performativity.[3] Yet a performative silence is not unsettling when it does not interrupt *the police*. I deploy Rancière's work to show that queer performativity needs a stronger understanding of the scandalous and disruptive force of silences.[4]

I trace Nussbaum's argument about silence to her typology of shame, which distinguishes between a legitimate (*constructive shaming*) and an illegitimate use of shaming (*primitive shaming*) (2004: 209–17).[5] This typology reinforces a strong dichotomy between shame that is articulated in speech, which is democratic and inclusive of others, and shame that is negative when it is silent and experienced as painful. Yet the belief that silence and speech are opposites is, for Brown, "a conceit underlying most contemporary discourse about censorship and silence" (2005: 83).⁶ First, silence could be useful because it keeps valuable objects and experiences from public circulation and scrutiny (Brown 2005: 95). The danger in talking incessantly about private experiences is that it re-enacts the condition of marginalized people, whose life remains without a "room of one's own"—or without a domain of creativity free from public surveillance (Brown 2005: 95). Second, silence is effective in protecting the lives of those who live sexually and affectively outside the marriage bond. As Butler claimed, sexuality outside "the field of monogamy" could enlarge the possibilities for a "livable life" (2004a: 27). Unconventional relationships can transform conventional norms about intimacy and resignify the shame associated with sexual transgressions.

This chapter not only offers insights into feminist and queer arguments about the role of shame and silence in politics, but also helps in illuminating the relationship between Mill and a group of radical Unitarians feminists between 1831 and 1834. Scholarly contributions such as Kathryn Gleadle's *The Early Feminists: Radical Unitarians and the Emergence of the Women's Rights Movement, 1831–51* (1998) and Francis Mineka's *The Dissidence of Dissent: The Monthly Repository, 1806–1838* (1944) clarified the relationship between Mill and this group, who strongly advocated a feminist agenda in England in the 1830s. In particular, Gleadle showed the importance of the group for English Victorian feminism and persuasively demonstrated that the radical Unitarian coterie, born from W. J. Fox's ministry at South Place Chapel in Finsbury, London, became a strong "breeding-ground for feminist ideas and discussions, with the *Monthly Repository* acting as a much-needed platform" (1998: 5). But, unlike Gleadle and Mineka, I focus on the radical Unitarians and Mill's performative use of shame and their responses to public shaming. Between 1831 and 1834, W. J. Fox, the mentor of the radicals, Eliza Flower, J. S. Mill and Harriet Taylor had unconventional intimate relationships. W. J. Fox had to face the prospect of a public sexual scandal. The politics of radical Unitarians came to represent "immorality and profligacy" to a number of Victorian intellectuals such as Thomas Carlyle and Harriet Martineau, who strongly disagreed with their sexual politics (Gleadle 1998: 35). Mill and Fox's unconventional relationships, however, offer us important historical examples of feminists who responded to public shaming.

Mill's disturbing silence is also important because it shows that unconventional relationships were at odds with a certain sexual respectability in 1830s London—and as such, these relationships challenged *the police*. As Mason shows, sexual moralism was a widespread ideology that controlled sexual behavior and shaped middle class opinion (1994a: 139–40). Prostitution, courtesanship, and concubinage were associated with poverty and low morals (Mason 1994a: 73). In particular, elite workers, or what was called "labour aristocracies," had to show strictness and orderliness in moral behavior (Mason 1994a: 148). Mill and Taylor were in an illicit relationship according to the standards of middle class respectability, but they were willing to live it. In this sense, their queer practice produced a different partition of what counted as sexually visible. Like Rancière's workers who refused to become "workers" as it was expected from them, Mill and Taylor's queer practice functioned as a migrant who moved at the border between classes. Their relationship disturbed the established division of sexual labor and showed that this order is arbitrary and therefore changeable. Rancière (2011: 197) noted that:

> Perhaps the truly dangerous classes are not so much the uncivilized ones thought to undermine society from below, but rather the migrants who move at the borders between classes, individuals and groups who develop capabilities within themselves which are useless for the improvement of their material lives and which in fact are liable to make them despise material concerns.

For Rancière, in his analysis of the workers in nineteenth-century France, these migrants propagated a cultural disruption which sought to undermine the established social order. But these figures also refused the call from elite workers to show better moral attitudes, which sought to police spaces of exchange between classes. If the workers' policed role was to work during the day and sleep at night, their conquest of the night showed their capacity for political emancipation. In a similar vein, rather than looking at silences as reactionary gestures, I see silences as enabling and producing the potential for new queer relationships.

Unitarian Radicals and Performativity

In an article published in 1833 in the April issue of the *Monthly Repository*, the journal of the young English radicals, W. B. Adams made one of the strongest arguments against marriage that was heard at the time. It anticipated in its description of the oppression of women John Stuart Mill's radical feminist manifesto, *The

Subjection of Women (1869), yet it made much stronger claims about divorce and sexuality than Mill's pamphlet. Adams, who wrote under the pen name Junius Redivivus, argued that the prohibition of divorce leads to immorality. Because women could not get divorced, they were pushed into vices such as alcohol and prostitution (Adams 1833: 227–8).[7] Adams was not only radical because he suggested that marriage should be a civil contract, which could be dissolved by either party, but also because he argued that women's chastity—the central core of early Victorian sexual politics—enslaved women (1833: 227).

While Adams's radical arguments were bold and piercing, his strong anti-marriage position was articulated under a pseudonym. Adams's arguments were powerful because they were public and could be accepted or rejected by any citizen. In addition to their public character, they were effective because they were deployed under the protection of a secret name, which provided a reasonable degree of security for the author. His pen name functioned as an epistemological "closet" which protected him—at least to some extent—from public outrage. Because reputation in Victorian England was key to the reception of one's work, writers often chose anonymity when they articulated controversial opinions. Adams's choice to hide his name was deeply connected to the impudence of his arguments. Rather than an accident in his rhetoric, anonymity made possible his attack on conventional gender norms. As Foucault claimed, what one does not say—in Adams's case, he hides his name—is "integral" to the rhetorical strategies in his argument. Adams's epistemological closet shows that silence was not only the negative other of a radical speech act, but that it constituted the possibility of its articulation. It shows that silence and speech do not function only as opposite pairs, but that they are mutually producing each other in particular contexts.

Adams utilized various rhetorical tropes to contest social arrangements such as marriage. He transformed the meaning of marriage from a term that designated a respectable institution to a term that symbolized negative practices, such as slavery and prostitution. His intention was to shame the men, the primary readers of the journal, so they would understand their role in women's subordination. In Adams's argument, men sought women because they wanted slaves. Yet, they did not only want slaves, but also prostitutes (1833: 217). In Adams's sociological analysis, marriage was in an institution heavily involved in oppression because of its social ramifications. Women were passive agents within marriages; marriages were business contracts; and women were sold on a marriage market like prostitutes. Adams argued his case to the readers of the *Monthly Repository* with provocative sentences:

> Disguise it as we will, under the fine sounding names of 'honourable alliance,' 'excellent match,' and other specious terms which have been invented to make interest look like affection, the marriage which is entered into by a female for the consideration of wealth or station, is at best but prostitution clothed in the robes of sanctity. (Adams 1833: 218–19)

Instead of accepting traditional words that were used to glorify the institution of marriage ("excellent match"), Adams proposed that the institution should be regarded as prostitution. In doing so, he resignified the social meaning of marriage. His rhetorical gesture turned an institution associated with respectability into its opposite.

The aim of such an inversion of values was to show that traditional political institutions were perpetuating a system of gender oppression. Adams's performative intervention emphasized the inequalities of early Victorian society. Women were seduced, abandoned, and their hearts became "hardened" and "selfish" because they lived under atrocious conditions. Because children were raised by servants, women grew within an environment where they secretly hated their husbands for treating them as inferior animals (Adams 1833: 219). Not only women were prostitutes, but an entire system of domination was in place where children had to live in families where women and men were at war. While Adams claimed that the process of gender formation was underpinned by oppressive practices, he also intended to show that oppression works through sexual norms. He argued that women were "sensual toys" (Adams 1833: 217–18). The word "toy" signaled the inferior status of women, while the word "sensual" showed that women's inferiority was sexual. "Sensual toy" was part of Adams's intention to locate gender discrimination in sexuality and use such exposure to shame men. In doing so, he utilized the resources that were available to him through language.

Rather than understanding agency as an act of an individual opposing power, Butler argues that we need to conceptualize it as a performative act under conditions which are shaped by power. Butler's argument shows that Adams utilized a language that was already shaped by gender assumptions, such as the idea that women are inferior. Adams did not deploy his critique outside of a language that was not tainted by women's oppression. On the contrary, he mobilized the political and linguistic resources that were part of the Victorian self-understanding. Yet, he did not use these linguistic resources uncritically, because he wanted to make them tools of his critique. Because women were kept in shame by a system of organized oppression, he articulated his opposition by appealing to words that marked women's sexual inferiority. He utilized them to unsettle a system of gender inequality that generated them in the first place.

In addition to offering new meanings to linguistic expressions such as marriage and sensual toys, Adams rejected the idea that women should be sexually pure. Although his pamphlet was far from being a manifesto about sexual liberation, Adams did not shy away from attacking the requirement of women's chastity:

> But we must go altogether to the root of evil. Women must be made morally the equal of man. Hitherto, precisely after the custom of the Turks, whom we abuse, we have required of women but one virtue—chastity. The woman who has studiously preserved this virtue, has been allowed to indulge in other vices, almost with impunity, and those vices have been the result of retaining her in domestic slavery. (Adams 1833: 227)[8]

By arguing that chastity was at the core of women's exploitation, Adams wanted to show that oppressive norms about sexuality organize particular social practices.

His attack on chastity was not unique in the 1830s Victorian England. Robert Owen challenged a traditional notion of sexuality by undermining the idea that chastity designated a practice of sexual abstinence. For him, chastity was intimacy with "affection," while prostitution was "sex without affection" (*CW* XXI: 45). Likewise, by deploying Owen's definition, Mill and Harriet Taylor gestured toward their opposition to a conventional understanding of sexuality.[9] For the two friends and lovers, chastity was "sexual intercourse with affection" while prostitution was "sexual intercourse without affection" (*CW* XXI: 105, 467).[10]

W. B. Adams, the social critic from the *Monthly Repository* who used Victorian language to weaken women's subordination, was a philosophical radical. He was closely associated with the editor of the magazine and Unitarian minister, W. J. Fox, and with the up-and-coming intellectual star of English intelligentsia, John Stuart Mill. Like Mill, Fox, and Harriet Martineau, Adams was a part of group of thinkers who were disillusioned with the politics of the Whigs and proposed new radical liberal reforms. Like Adams, Fox criticized the condition of oppression of women and supported radical views of women's oppression (Mineka 1944: 234–47, 262). The radicals criticized the Whigs for their timid liberal reforms because they wanted the full extension of the suffrage, a secular educational system, the abolition of the death penalty, the abolition of slavery, and civil and criminal reforms (Mineka 1944: 261). Their social views, and particularly their views related to the condition of women, marriage, and divorce laws, are among the most advanced at the time and the source of the most damning criticism (Mineka 1944: 260). The radicals' key argument was not only that marriage is an institution of inequality, but also that the institution could be reformed. Because women needed to be liberated from their oppression, Adams called for changes in marriage and divorce laws.[11] Taking issue with the state of marriage laws, Adams argued that the prohibition of divorce does in fact lead to immorality, "illicit intercourse," and children being born outside the wedlock. To respond to shameful practices that are generated by an unjust institution, he advocated legalizing divorce as a solution to women's oppression. His conclusion was that women could be liberated. In fact, actual examples of women who have judgment and knowledge pave the way to a better and more fulfilling life.

John Stuart Mill was associated with thinkers such as W. B. Adams and W. J. Fox, who developed "a powerful, social and political critique of modern society, and women's role within it" (Gleadle 1998: 6). In the same issue of the *Monthly Repository* that published "On the condition of women in England," Mill strongly praised Adams's work. For Mill, Junius Redivivus was the embodiment of a radical spirit, because for him unaccountable power was a source of oppression (*CW* I: 318). Mill celebrated his radicalism because he opposed racial, religious, class and gender inequalities of power:

> Our author is a radical in the best sense of the term, that is, he is an enemy to all institutions and all usages which deliver over any portion of the species, unprotected, to the tender mercies of any other portion; whether the sacrifice be of blacks to whites, of Catholics to Protestants, of the community at large to lords and boroughmongers, of the middle and working classes to the higher, of the working classes to the middle, or (a surer test of genuine high-minded radicalism than all the rest) of women to men. (*CW* I: 318)

The English radicals lived in an era that saw the passing of the Reform Bill (1832), which was seen as the first stage of dismantling an entrenched system of hierarchy and of handing over power to the bourgeoisie. Although the Whigs extended the right to vote, they deplored universal suffrage and did not want women to vote. The radicals were exceptional because they were calling for serious and deep progressive reforms in gender relations. Unlike traditional Unitarians, the radicals began to hold strong views on marriage and divorce and such arguments are prominent between 1831 and 1834. In their politics, the Unitarians were traditionally more advanced on social issues, yet their efforts were primarily confined to educating women. Before the 1830s, the Unitarians believed, like many other social reformers, that if women were better educated, improvement in their social condition was bound to follow (Mineka 1944: 284).

The critiques of marriage and the advocacy of divorce that were part of the *Monthly Repository* in the years 1831–4 were strong and unprecedented. Fox and Adams supported the idea that a marriage contract should be regarded as a civil transaction. The magistrate, argued Fox, should be "the only person known to the law in the formation of the marriage contract" (Mineka 1944: 288). Like Adams's pamphlet, Fox claimed that the indissoluble character of marriage leads to unhappiness, and more specifically, to prostitution. Because women are not free to act as responsible agents, they become enslaved in amoral marriages (Fox quoted by Mineka 1944: 288).

The *Monthly Repository* was strongly attacked for its position on marriage and divorce. The problem was that the journal was primarily a religious journal that articulated the doctrine of the Unitarians, a very liberal branch of Christianity historically practiced by thinkers such as John Locke and Mary Wollstonecraft. In 1831, the *Monthly Repository,* however, was an almost secular journal. W. J. Fox, a minister who had taken over the editorship of the journal, transformed it from a religious to a secular magazine. Yet this change was hardly welcomed by older Unitarians. They were particularly unhappy with the journal's new views on marriage and divorce. Because the *Repository* advocated divorce, one of the strongest taboos of English morality was openly attacked. A leading minister of the denomination, Lant Carpenter, criticized the *Repository* as presenting "a very exaggerated as well as degrading picture, calculated to give an unjust and baneful view of the state of society" (Mineka 1944: 256). Because of Adams's extreme views, Carpenter argued, the journal could not be read to "a circle of female friends" or given to a mixed company (Mineka 1944: 256). As with subsequent attacks on *The Subjection of Women* by conservative thinkers, the accusation was that the feminists promoted shameless ideas that would embarrass women.

The feminist radicals challenged conventional norms about gender relationships in England. Butler's theory of resignification provides a robust conceptual framework that allows us to grasp the politics of opposition of this group. Because an account of political resistance that *only* opposes power is conceptually naive, possibilities of resistance and opposition are shaped by a previous complicity with power. One is subordinated to power before one is able to intervene in its deployment, and one uses a language that is already tainted by unjust social norms. Radicals such as Adams mobilized the words and the language of his contemporaries to pursue his critique of gender normativity. Adams's attack on women's subordination and his critique of the unequal power relations between men and women represented a powerful argument that was intended to shed light on oppressive institutions and practices. He resignified several words that designated major social institutions with the intention of opening a new space for rethinking gender and political power.

Beyond Liberal Shame

In this section I claim that Nussbaum's concept of constructive shame fails to grasp the radicals' interventions in their articles for the *Monthly Repository*. Notwithstanding their appeal to *constructive shame*, the radicals used shame performatively to account for women's inequality. Fox sought to transform the meaning of the word marriage from a *religious engagement* to *civil transaction*. He also used strong rhetorical tropes, such as "men are slave owners," to shed light on the inequality of social practices and institutions in Victorian England. Like Fox, Mill articulated a strong critique of gender by resignifing the term marriage. He claimed that marriage was an institution built on slavery and domination. He believed that men were benefiting from an inherently unjust system. He understood, as Butler noted, that the task of his feminist work was to "compel" the political establishment "to embrace those who have been traditionally excluded" (1997b: 161). Mill knew that such "embrace" could not be easy, because it could "wrack and unsettle the polity that makes such an embrace" (Butler 1997b: 161). The task of resignifying particular social institutions was not only a matter of articulating particular rhetorical tropes, but also of crafting public arguments which would be effective for specific audiences.

Some of the radicals' strategies correspond to Nussbaum's (2004: 212–13) model of *constructive shame*. They believed that English men and women could reform themselves if they were to feel ashamed about the existing state of the affairs between men and women. By describing inequalities within marriages, as well as their impact on educational and religious practices, they intended to mobilize their audience to promote social and legal changes. Taking issue with the argument that women could not be educated, Fox argued that just as the large population shamed the upper class to gain voting rights, women could shame men into achieving intellectual progress (1832: 640). Fox and Adams believed that their English audience needed to feel shame about the fact that women were not treated equally. Since women were left in utter dependence, they could never "be treated as independent parties, making a fair and equal contract for mutual benefit" (Fox 1832: 641). The radicals invited their audience to examine their intimate relationships and feel shame for what they found there. They wanted to shame their audience by bringing them close to the lives of those to whom they thought themselves superior. Women who died under shameful circumstances, either by suicide or domestic abuse, were seen as unfortunate, unlucky, and reckless. The radicals showed it was not only working class or uneducated women who were affected by structural oppression, but that women of good condition could also be driven to death by bad marriages and abusive husbands.

However, Nussbaum's model of *constructive shame* cannot entirely capture the variety of the radicals' rhetorical interventions. The radicals wanted to resignify particular social institutions such as marriage and divorce. For Fox, key to his public interventions was his attempt to argue that marriage should be seen primarily as a civil contract rather than a religious contract. The goal of the Dissenters—the radical Unitarians who supported the transformation of marriage into a civil arrangement—was to change the meaning of an institution that was defined by the Church. For him, marriage as a religious practice was:

> one of the worst miseries which priestcraft and aristocracy have combined to inflict upon mankind, that the Dissenters are pledging themselves to endeavour to remedy. If they can induce the legislature to adopt the theory that the marriage contract is 'a common, in distinction from a religious engagement, should be regarded by the law as merely a civil transaction,' . . . they will do enough towards social reformation and the diffusion of social enjoyment. (1833b: 139)

Because Fox's intention was to shift the meaning of marriage, he intended to convince his readers to see the positive transformations that he anticipated. Marriage was for him "a political and social anomaly." He also claimed that marriage was shaped by larger norms about femininity and masculinity. Not only marriage, but social norms about gender needed to change, because social practices restrained women's capacities and potential for physical strength (1832: 639). He considered Victorian gender educational practices "the great evil" of his time (1832: 640). While men were educated for various professions and educations, women were "only educated to get married" (1832: 640). For Fox, this was an education of "irremediable dependence upon the other half" (1832: 640). Yet, women's condition could change. The transformation of marriage into a civil transaction was an important step toward "social reformation and the diffusion of social enjoyment." The radicals argued that if particular institutions were to change, then their contemporaries could achieve social progress.

Like Adams, Fox utilized strong rhetorical tropes to shame his audience. He claimed that under prevailing conditions women were "slaves," "toys," and "fools." His intention was to shock his audience into recognizing the damaging ramifications of corrupted social institutions such as marriage. By using inferior terms to designate women, his goal was to critique the conventional meaning of femininity. Rather than accepting that submission and willingness to obey are positive qualities, he argued that these attitudes led to strong inferiority and inequality:

> Under the present order of things, a large proportion of them must remain as they are, fools to be cajoled, toys to be sported with, slaves to be commanded, and in ignorant pride that they are so, boasting that they know nothing . . . (1832: 641)

Butler argues that one of the problems with racial and gendered slurs is that they "accumulate over time, dissimulating their history, taking on the semblance of the natural, configuring and restricting the 'doxa' that counts as reality" (1997b: 159). By using terms such as "toys" and "slaves," Fox wanted to reveal the "injurious" nature of the process of acquiring a female gender. Because he wanted to de-naturalize what was accepted as natural, Fox deployed words which marked women's subordination to re-articulate the meaning of femininity. His performative deployment of slurs was part of a larger attempt to contest the social and political norms of Victorian England. Because women were acquiring a gender that accorded with the traditional notions about the nature of women, they were molded in particular ways. Yet, Fox's critique of gender norms not only shows what Butler calls a process of social formation, but also marks "the ongoing political contestation and reformulation of the subject as well" (1997b: 160). His use of injurious language—women are "fools," "toys," and "slaves"—was mobilized to make social oppression visible, to contest gender inequality, and to transform the meaning of womanhood. His use of the performative was not only an analysis of social conditions, but it represented a practice that aimed at rearticulating women's subjectivity (Butler 1997b: 159).

In "A Victim," Fox's strategy of using shame corresponds with Nussbaum's "constructive shame." By using the story of Methabel Wesley (Hetty), the sister of the founder of Methodism, John Wesley, he intended to "knock hard at some unfeeling hearts" (1833a: 164). In Fox's narrative, Hetty died because of women's oppression. By arguing that social norms led to Hetty's death, Fox deployed shame to make his point. Because he understood that emotions were very powerful motivational agents for action, he wanted shame to generate frustration with the social conditions of women. He called emotion "the angel that comes and troubles the thick stagnation of the thinking pool, and gives it the power of healing" (1833a: 165). The privileged could learn and be changed by the stories of the oppressed (1833a: 165). He called such a strategy of using powerful stories of injustice "turning emotion to good account" (1833a: 165). A political strategy of deploying shame should be pragmatic, like the ability of a practical engineer. The social reformer should find "a full flowing steam," gave a blessing "on its beauty" and "puts up a corn or cotton-mill" (1833a: 165). By describing Hetty's childhood as a young girl victimized by her parents, this story was Fox's "flowing steam" (1833a: 166–8). The *constructive* component of shame was revealed in Fox's attempt to mobilize and use his audience's emotions.

However, Fox did not only utilize *constructive shame* in his political argument, but also used shame performatively. Fox appealed to a strategy that Butler called the "de-officialization of the performative," or its "expropriation from non-ordinary means" (1997b: 160). In *Excitable Speech*, Butler theorizes the strategy of counter-acting "hate speech"—or responding to hate speech by re-appropriating terms employed to injure and produce pain. Such strategy is to re-appropriate a term to "configure a different future" (Butler 1997b: 160). She did not only theorize about responses to hate speech, but also offered a larger strategy to re-appropriate conventional political concepts to include women, people of color, people who have been excluded along class lines or those who have a different colonial background. Justice, freedom, and equality are words that "may come to embrace" interests and subjects who have been excluded from their jurisdiction (Butler 1997b: 160).

Fox intended to re-articulate the meaning of marriage in Victorian England because he wanted to de-couple it from oppressive social practices and norms. Marriage generated pain in Hetty's life because it was "an immorality" (1833a: 177). Hetty's marriage coerced her into a "sexual companionship where mutual affection was impossible." The aim of Fox's strategy was to prove that for women like Hetty, "there ought to be redress, open and honourable redress" (1833a: 177). Such possibilities of justice could be achieved by changing the institution of marriage. Fox wanted to make marriage a civil transaction, so that women's lives should not be forced to have lives that were similar to Hetty's. He "expropriated" a conventional meaning of marriage so that the civil transaction could become a political tool for obtaining better social conditions for men and women. His "counter-hegemonic" move was to resignify the meaning of marriage to imagine a better future for those whose lives were deeply affected by social oppression. Also, Fox's mobilized the language of moral impurity to argue that marriage was a coercive and cruel social institution.[12] In his argument, Hetty would have been happier if she had committed adultery. In such a case, "she might have been liberated from an enforced and intolerable bond, and even have entered on a new state" (1833a: 177). By arguing that adultery is preferable to marriage, Fox advocated what Butler called "the scandalous impure."[13]

This endorsement of the scandalous was not left without response. The *British Magazine* published a rebuttal of Fox's argument and claimed that Fox misread the characters involved in Hetty's story. The conservative critic was upset that the radicals at the *Monthly Repository* were too bold and honest in their support of divorce and sexual affairs. Fox's system of morality, he said, was "base and degraded" (1833: 468). While Fox shamed his readers to generate an empathetic response to the condition of the underprivileged, the *British Magazine* reacted by arguing that Fox's opinion was shameful and should be heard "with indignation" (1833: 468). Fox's justification of adultery intended to show that actions that are perceived as immoral could represent a legitimate route for married women. Performative actions do not only resignify conventional institutions, but also suggest possible actions that challenge the idea that the marriage contract defines moral norms. Hetty's hypothetical adultery becomes moral, since it would have liberated her from slavery. Fox's performative resignification of adultery points toward resources that early feminists have found in the value of sexual "impurity."

Like Fox and Adams, Mill deployed shame strategically in *The Subjection of Women*. Mill understood that shame functioned as a strong inspiration for political action. When he explained the benefits of extending the suffrage to women to his contemporaries, he praised the influence of mothers on young men's characters. In such context, he drew on Greek literature to argue that *aidôs* (shame) was a powerful "motive of action in the great Hector" (Rossi 1970: 223).[14] Like the radicals in the early 1830s, Mill wanted to resignify the conventional meaning of marriage. He believed that marriage represented an instrument of power to enable men to exercise their authority without opposition. Marriage was an institution of social oppression under Victorian laws. He depicted a system of terror and power where women had limited options to curb the power of their masters:

> Every one of the subjects lives under the very eye, and almost, it may be said, in the hands, of one of the masters—in closer intimacy with him than with any of her fellow-subjects; with no means of combining against him, no power of even locally overmastering him, and, on the other hand, with the strongest motives for seeking his favour and avoiding giving him offence. (Rossi 1970: 136)

The patriarchal husbands became in Mill's description agents who could exercise power without restraint. Husbands were no longer the pillars of the moral superiority of Victorian social life; on the contrary, they became the primary agents of domination and inequality. They served a system of terror by benefiting from the advantages of their social position. Mill used performative interventions, such as depicting the opponents of equality as "barbarians" and portraying husbands as inflicting terror on their families. The aim of Mill's depiction of the terrors of marital life was to resignify the position of males in Victorian society. His intention for resignification was constructive. He wanted to transform marriage into "a school of moral cultivation." His use of the performative pointed toward a "model of equality of married people before the law" (Rossi 1970: 173).

Mill undertook a historical and sociological investigation to describe the formation of marriage as a social institution. Rather than utilizing the figure of the prostitute, which became a battleground for debates around women's sexuality and the Contagious Diseases Acts (CDA), he preferred to focus his rhetoric on women as slaves.[15] He argued that women were living in slavery because the current legal status of women was that of slaves.[16] By comparing an allegedly superior legal status of slaves in the US with the predicament of married women in England, he suggested that American slaves had more legal protection than English women (Rossi 1970: 160).[17]

Mill's silences about divorce and prostitution in *The Subjection of Women* have performative value, yet they do not function as interrupting *the police*. These silences do not disturb the social hierarchy of English society. During the period from 1865 to 1868, Mill was an MP in the British House of Commons. Instead of intervening as an activist, Mill's pamphlet was formulated from the position of a politician who makes a case for political enfranchisement.[18] The radicals claimed that divorce should be an important option for men and women, but Mill did not address divorce in *The Subjection of Women*. In her early letters, Harriet Taylor hoped that marriage would disappear in an egalitarian society and suggested that in a future educated society "no one would marry" (Rossi 1970: 85). More importantly, the radicals at the *Monthly Repository* claimed that marriage was prostitution and attacked Victorian assumptions about normative sexuality.[19]

Mill kept some of the rhetoric of the radicals, but he toned it down in important respects. Unlike the letters to Harriet Taylor in 1832–3, Mill's *The Subjection of Women*, which was published in 1869, did not raise the subject of prostitution in marriage.[20] Mill wanted to separate the argument about women's political rights from the debate about women's sexual rights, which was highly controversial because of the radical actions of Josephine Butler. Mill was worried that arguments that described married women as prostitutes would antagonize his audience. Rather than portraying male domination as repulsive, his aim was to convince his readers that men would gain from women's vote. He emphasized women's potential contributions to civic life because he believed that such arguments would convince his audience to accept the enfranchisement of women. The emphasis in his arguments changed from an early attack on the institution of marriage to the removal of the legal and social obstacles to women's empowerment. Because of the political consequences of the civil war in the United States and the abolition of slavery, he described women primarily as "slaves" and not prostitutes. Unlike Fox and Adams, he was not primarily interested in describing the social rituals of marriage, nor in providing religious arguments about the importance of divorce. The aim of *The Subjection of Women* was to convince its readers that women deserved political rights and that they deserved it because they needed to be equal to men.

I interpret Mill's silences as performative because his arguments were designed to advance women's cause according to what he judged as effective in a particular context. He did not want to associate claims about political goals such as women's vote to social practices such as divorce or prostitution. As with most of his progressive ideas, Mill was not facing a "particularly receptive audience" (Smith 2001: 192). ElisabethSmith argued that Mill's rhetoric about women's subordination adjusted to what he thought was politically feasible.[21] By refraining from deploying particular rhetorical tropes (such as "married women are prostitutes" and "divorce should be legalized"), his rhetoric appears less radical and powerful than the strategy of other radicals. Feminist scholars have noticed the contrast between his position and other radical arguments (see Rossi 1970: 22; Caine 1992: 36). Instead of understanding his rhetoric as weaker—and even defective by comparing it to the radicals' political arguments—Mill teaches us that particular forms of shaming have to be calibrated to a particular political context.[22]

But his reluctance to discuss divorce or to attack marriage as prostitution shows why this specific performative is not yet an interruption of conventional politics. Rather than taking into account *only* the content of political arguments, a performative understanding of shaming illuminates the context and the value of silences in a public argument. Yet his silences do not function as performative *and* unsettling, and I seek to illuminate the value of unsettling silences in the next section.

Mill's Disturbing Silence and the *Fox Affair*

> The path of emancipation rather appears as passing by way of the capacity to become different: not by becoming conscious, but by dizziness and loss of identity.
>
> Rancière (2011: 26)

In the context of the *Fox Affair*, Mill's refusal to talk about his sexuality in public undermines the assumptions that speech is *the* site of resistance to gender inequality. In this section I show that silence generated a space for Mill and Harriet Taylor to have "a livable life." Middle class respectability in Victorian England produced a certain distribution of roles that assigned men and women specific places in its heteronormative order. Marriage among middle class couples functioned like a factory, where reproduction and children were seen as the desired commodities which made life meaningful. But, as Rancière (2011: 181) noted, there are lines of escape from the factory of normative reproduction and a class "becomes dangerous" on the basis of "such lines of fracture." In this light, Mill's silence was disturbing when he sought to move away from middle class respectability. To stop being respectable is, like Rancière's worker's act of disruption, to stop being a worker. Not unlike Rancière's laborers, who acted in ways that that they were not supposed to, Mill and Harriet Taylor interrupted a mode of living that offered them given roles within a Victorian order of decency.[23]

Neither *constructive* nor *primitive*, Mill's silence led to a life that was organized against a dominant vision of intimacy and sexuality. Mill and Harriet Taylor's unconventional relationship was "a practice of freedom" that was made possible by their silence.[24] Butler argues that "modes of intimate association," when they produce sustaining web of relationships, "constitute a 'breakdown' of traditional kinship that displaces the presumption that biological and sexual relations structure kinship centrally" (2004a: 26). Within such relationships, a "durable tie can be situated outside of the conjugal frame." Intimate relationships open up the possibility of a critique of gender relations that is guided by "the question of what maximizes the possibilities for a livable life" and what "minimizes the possibility" of social and literal death (Butler 2004a: 8). But to enter into such a relationship and keep it functional one requires a certain mode of invisibility because, "while to be invisible within a local discourse may occasion the injuries of social liminality, such suffering may be mild compared to that of radical denunciation, hystericization, exclusion, or criminalization" (Brown 2005: 87). While they did not make a public case for the legitimacy of their relationship, Mill and Harriet Taylor's silence created a new mode of living.

Queer thinkers have reflected about how particular acts of shaming could be reappropriated and resignified. Butler argues that an insult could be performatively turned around and made into a "counter-hegemonic" gesture. The word "queer" can be mobilized from a term of insult into a political response that gives value to non-conventional sexualities and relationships. Butler suggests that a performative "counter-hegemonic" gesture responds effectively to hate speech:

> If hate speech constitutes the kind of act that seeks to silence the one to whom it is addressed, but which might revive within the vocabulary of the silenced as its unexpected rejoinder, then the response to hate speech constitutes 'the de-officialization' of the performative, its expropriation for non-ordinary means. Within the political sphere, performativity can work in precisely such counter-hegemonic ways. (1997b: 160)

Like Butler, Mill suggests a transformative strategy about political shame. First, in a letter to his radical Unitarian friend W. B. Adams, he argued that shame could be turned into power. Adams felt that he was shamed and despised because of his political convictions. Mill advised him to develop "an independent power" as a response to his critics—or the power to resist various attempts of shaming. Second, he advocated silence in a delicate affair involving Fox's potential adultery. His advocacy of silence is important because it speaks to how he presented his relationship with a married woman. In his *Autobiography*, Harriet and he decided to eliminate any indications of the couple's sexuality—or of what would have counted as an adulterous relationship in the eyes of the Victorians. They appealed to silence because they wanted to avoid conventional judgments about their sex life, as well as to protect themselves from being considered indecent.

Around 1832–3, Adams, Fox, and Mill were close friends and shared a similar frustration with the Victorian institution of marriage. In 1833, Adams was thirty-six years of age, Fox forty-seven, and Mill twenty-seven. They met regularly at Fox's house and constituted a British outlier of liberal intelligentsia "prominent throughout the Continent in the generation after Napoleon" (Smith 1973: 13). Fox was the most popular Unitarian preacher of the day, and unhappily married at the time of the articles about divorce. Adams was a brilliant engineer who invented a successful radial axle for railways in Britain.

Let us have a brief map of their personal connections at that time. Adams's future wife was Sarah Flower, the sister of Eliza Flower,

Fox's future wife. Fox was initially the mentor and friend of Sarah and Eliza because he was appointed the executor and the trustee of their wealth by their father. While Adams, Fox, and the Flower sisters had close personal ties, John Stuart Mill had a strong relationship with this group through Harriet Taylor, John Stuart Mill's intimate friend and future wife. Harriet Taylor was a Unitarian, went regularly to listen to Fox, and was Eliza Flower's best friend. Mill was introduced to the Taylors, John and Harriet, at Harriet's request to Fox. Harriet felt she wanted to improve her life and trusted that the Unitarian minister would recommend someone who would provide intellectual and spiritual excitement. By 1832–3, Mill and Harriet Taylor exchanged their views on marriage in private letters and their positions are often similar to those of Fox and Adams.

In 1832, William J. Fox was deeply involved in a relationship with Eliza Flower. In Fox's household, however, Mrs. Fox was not happy about her husband's relationship and wrote him a formal letter of complaint. Because divorce was impossible, considering Fox's position as a Unitarian minister, the only alternative was an arrangement between husband and wife. The arrangement, however, could not last more than two years. By its terms, they considered themselves separated, although they lived under the same roof (Mineka 1944: 193). Fox's congregation had a hard time accepting Fox's ambivalent relationship with the institution of marriage. A group within the Church wrote to Fox and demanded that he either set his house in order to Mrs. Fox's satisfaction or resign. Fox chose to resign, which he did in August 1834. He expressed his frustration at how various people shamed him about his private life. The interference of some Unitarians in his affairs was intolerable: selections were made from his private correspondence; his household accounts were analyzed; and Eliza Flower became a subject of public attacks (Mineka 1944: 194). Fox chose the strategy of meeting the charges head on. In his defense, he emphasized that it was the articles about divorce and women's oppression he published in the *Repository* that generated the public scandal. He advocated divorce as a solution to the subordination of English women, Fox explained, and the scandal was a result of his progressive views on marriage.[25]

Mill, Harriet Taylor, Fox, and Eliza Flower were close friends in 1832. Fox invited Mill to write regularly for the *Repository*, while Mill invited Fox to write for the *Westminster Review*.[26] By the summer of 1833, Fox became perhaps Mill's closest friend. Mill confessed to Fox that he could not go to Harriet's house every day, although he wanted to visit her "every evening" (*CW* XII: 134). He told Fox that he and Harriet "never could have been so near, so perfectly intimate" if they had not gone to Paris together (*CW* XII: 155). In the same letter, Mill articulated his conviction that "the experiment"—the arrangement that Mill, Harriet and John Taylor had—would succeed. In September, Fox was passing Mill's work to Harriet and served as an intimate friend to Mill. Mill suggested to Fox that the solution imagined by Harriet—the arrangement where she would have both John Taylor, her husband, and Mill in her life—was very hard for him. At the time, Fox was separated from his wife and in a relationship with Eliza Flower. Both couples were worried about respectability and public shaming. Mill, Fox, Eliza Flower and Harriet Taylor were exposed to public judgment because of their sexual transgressions.

The radicals articulated feminist and progressive opinions in various journals, but they were also exposed to the critique and ridicule of their political enemies. Mill was deeply engaged in a strategy about how to think and respond to public shaming. In his letters to Unitarian friends, Mill's advice about the threat of public shaming was specific to a particular context. He suggested that one would respond to shame by either rejecting one's intention to shame, as he advocated in his letter to Adams, or by refraining from explaining one's sexuality, as he recommended in his letter to Fox. To Adams, Mill wrote that shaming could be met by developing a power of one's own. In his letter, Mill proposed that shame can be turned into power if one does not accept the ridicule and humiliation of critics (*CW* XII: 109). Instead of accepting the charge that one is not good enough intellectually, Mill suggested that one could develop power independently of the diminishing evaluations of opponents.

Adams confessed to Mill that he loathed to be patronized. Mill responded by saying that he fully understood the humiliation of being diminished as a writer, yet he told Adams that he should not accept the shameful accusation. He explained to Adams that he should not see himself a "littérateur" who amuses people, but a thinker and writer who is a powerful independent force:

> In your loathing of the very idea of being patronized I can fully sympathize—but you are in no danger of that; because you are not a littérateur who administers to people's amusement, but a thinker & writer whose doings affect their substantial interests, & who therefore when you are not valued & esteemed, will be disliked & feared, but at least always treated *de puissance en puissance*. (*CW* XII: 109)

Mill does not subordinate this independent power to public adulation, because he knows that one could be disliked and feared for radical political views. While Adams was going to be shamed and treated disrespectfully, Mill suggested that he was going to be treated at least as a powerful force, or "*de puissance en puissance.*" Mill's advice to Adams was that public shaming could be rejected if one has independent power and does not allow oneself to be shamed.

Like Mill, Butler argued that when one takes particular uncomfortable political positions, one "braves the stigma." In her preface to *Precarious Life* she describes the shaming conditions around voicing dissent about the US war in Iraq: "To continue to voice one's views under those conditions is not easy, since one must not only discount the truth of the appellation, but brave the stigma that seizes up from the public domain" (2004b: xix). For Butler, "to brave the stigma" means to transform the humiliating component of a critique into positive action. It suggests that such strategy, although not easy, is possible. Mill's advocacy of being treated "*de puissance en puissance*" suggests a similar response to shaming.

Butler's fear in *Precarious Life* is that "shaming tactics" are not only silencing, but also produce a speaking subject who is seen as reasonable and civil. They also produce "reasonable opinion" within the public domain. Strategies of de-legitimizing one's ideas become regulative because they shape who counts as viable and what it is reasonable to articulate in public. Both Mill and Butler propose an affirmative project of using shame for radical feminist politics. Mill's "*de puissance en puissance*" and Butler's "brave the stigma" point toward a constructive approach to political shaming. They offer a strategy of transforming the pain and humiliation associated with unconventional ideas and political opinions.

However, Mill's response to shame is not only to become an independent power, which would be "disliked" and "feared." In a letter to Fox, Mill sketched a strategy of responding with silence to the public condemnation of intimate and sexual experiments. For Nussbaum, shame should be utilized to strengthen human vulnerability and common responsibility. Instead of thinking about shame *only* as a tactic to promote public values (vulnerability and responsibility), Mill shows us that shame can be deployed *to protect* from the value of public opinion and to mobilize experiments which might not be valuable according to dominant norms. Rather than expressing the *constructive* element of shame, Mill argued that Fox needed to defend himself by keeping his sexuality out of the public's curiosity. He suggested that Fox should deny sexual immoral relationships—and avoid engaging any arguments that would draw on his sexuality. Mill's advice about silence does not open up a space for making Fox's shame "available" to other people and closes off conversations about one's "common human vulnerability."

In 1834, when Fox had to address a crisis in his congregation about his affair, Mill believed that Fox should publicly deny having a sexual affair with Eliza Flower and urged Fox to use such fact as a political strategy in order to gain allies:

> We had a great deal more discussion after we left you, and we all (three) most decidedly think that since the crisis in the congregation appears to have been brought on principally by the belief that a fact, which would be of the greatest importance in their eyes, though of none at all in yours, is true—it would be very foolish that you should not have the full advantage of its not being true. Even supposing that your separation from the chapel were inevitable in every case, the effect on your future prospects will entirely depend upon that fact being denied or not—& whether you feel it consistent, or not, with your personal dignity to deny it, we are quite convinced that we, and all your friends, ought. While that fact is denied and deniable, all who are otherwise favorably disposed will not be afraid to stand by you. (CW XII: 188–9)

When thinking about the possibility of defending Fox, Mill claimed that it would be hard for his advocates (including himself) to defend an open sexual relationship with Flower. Such a relationship would be perceived as an "open profession and vindication of immorality." Interestingly, Mill did not say that he would see it as immoral, but that the danger was for Fox to be perceived as immoral.[27]

Instead of making public his sexual relationship with Flower, Mill's advice for Fox was to focus his strategy on defending his positions from the *Monthly Repository* about the immorality of marriage. Fox's defense in front of the congregation should not be made on rumors about his sexuality, but on principles that he advocated publicly. The refusal to speak was a strategy intended to reject the terms that the moralists deployed to frame Fox's alleged transgression. Mill was very careful to draft a strategy about how to engage with Fox's accusers. Fox should try to be silent on the question of sexual intimacy, and volunteer information only if he had to. If Fox were to be asked directly whether he had extra-conjugal sex, he should deny the accusation:

> We all think of great importance that every public mention of the charge should be accompanied by mention of your denying it—and also that the effect of this denial should not, unless it be absolutely necessary to your integrity, be inspired by the public profession of the extent to which your principles go in that one matter. (*CW* XII: 189)

Mill's advice was important because he was personally involved with the same question about how to respond to public accusations of adultery. The two feminists were very close to the indicted couple (Fox and Eliza Flower) and were facing the possibility of responding to the same charges of vice. For both Mill and Harriet Taylor, Fox should be silent about an eventual sexual contact with Eliza Flower. The minister should leave no room for interpretation about his relationships.[28]

In his letters to Adams and Fox, Mill was concerned with responding to public accusations. While to Adams he wrote that he needed to become an independent power, to Fox he recommended denying "altogether their [his critics] concern with it or right to enquire it." In both instances, Mill wanted his friends to gain power by not letting the accusers define their behavior. Writing to Fox, Mill expressed his worry that "the affair is left to its original promoters" (*CW* XII: 189). He wanted both Adams and Fox to react intelligently to defamations. They needed to change the terms in which the debate was taking place. Brown pointed out that "refusing to speak is a method of refusing colonization, of refusing complicity in injurious interpellations or in subjection through regulation" (2005: 97). Mill was concerned that allowing suspicions of immorality would damage Fox's reputation. While in his letter to Adams he advocated the transformation of shame, to Fox Mill proposed rejecting the accusation of immorality. Mill's refusal of a particular frame for non-normative sexuality does not represent a withdrawal from taking an active position in the affair. His rejection is performative and unsettles conventional norms about sexuality. It does allow the enforcers of police morality to define one's intimacy.

In Nussbaum's typology, *constructive shame* serves as a strategy to create a sense of vulnerability in other people. This is not the route, however, that Mill chose in his advice to Fox. He did not propose that

Fox should strip away his credentials—namely, his image of a moral person—and bring the readers to understand that they are not above people who are engaged in unconventional relationships. He did not tell Fox to use his sexuality to shame his readers because they live in privileged relationships. Mill did not want to reinforce the idea of "inclusion" in a greater community. On the contrary, he told Fox that he needed to protect his intimacy. While Mill's advice is not *constructive shame*, neither is it *primitive shame* because it does not represent a "threat to all possibility of morality and community, and indeed to a creative inner life" (Nussbaum 2001: 218). Mill's advice was an intervention to protect his friend from the power of public opinion. It shows that shame does not have to be always used to defend public values, but it could be aimed at protecting the value of an intimate relationship which was deemed immoral by the Victorian dominant public opinion.

To believe that one should always be open about one's sexuality—or to always theorize it, like Nussbaum suggests—is to ignore Eve Sedgwick's insights about the epistemology of the closet.[29] The assumption that one needs to think about sexuality by using the dichotomy between "closet" and "coming out" is problematic for a heterosexist culture at large, which utilizes such dichotomy to justify itself (Sedgwick 1990: 60–9). The meaning of this opposition is itself oppressive because it consolidates many other binaries such as heterosexual vs. homosexual, or silence vs. speech, which are generated by a heteronormative culture invested in producing strong dichotomies about people's identity and sexual behavior. Foucault showed us that "silence and secrecy are a shelter for power, anchoring its prohibitions," but also that "they also loosen its hold and provide for relatively obscure areas of tolerance" (quoted in Brown 2005: 86). Drawing on Foucault, Brown (2005: 86) insisted that silence about gay sex enabled silence to constitute both "a shelter for power" but also "a shelter from it." As such, there is an inherent risk when a silence is "broken" because one's otherness could be "violently" produced and one's identity becomes marked by "abjection, censure, or regulation" (Brown 2005: 86). In contrast with the philosophy that underlines Nussbaum theoretical model, Mill's advocacy of silence undermines the idea that exposing unconventional sexualities to public scrutiny is the *default* political action.

Mill's performative use of silence shows that hiding particular aspects of one's private life can protect people's intimacy. At the same time, Mill insisted that an important political act was to deny any wrongdoing. Denial became for Mill a strategy to oppose gossip and public defamation. Such denial has to be complemented by a public assertion of "principles" regarding the importance of transforming gender norms. Silence about one sex life is not silence about one's political values. Mill, Harriet Taylor and the radicals were committed feminists who displayed a powerful political activism. Mill's advice about Fox's sexuality does not represent what is problematic about silence, that is, the "habituation of being silent" and the gesture of "passive aggressiveness" (Brown 2005: 96). While silence about Fox's sexuality should protect him from the judgment of his congregation, the "profession" of his feminist convictions should complement such a strategic move. Neither routine nor aggression, Mill's advice to Fox's was intended as a gesture of friendship. It was an intervention to protect the life of a friend who was a sex dissenter.

Although Mill did not explicitly theorize silence as a "shelter" from the power of public opinion, he understood the costs of exposing one's sexuality to public scrutiny. Mill advocated silence not only in the case of the *Fox Affair*, but also when it came to his relationship with Harriet. In their letters written in the 1850s, after their marriage—during the drafting of the *Autobiography*—Mill asked Harriet "how much of the story it is advisable to tell, in order to make head against the representations of enemies" (Reeves 2008: 150–1). Harriet's response was that any sexual intimation should be left out of the picture and that the focus should be on their "strong affection" and "intimacy of friendship" (Reeves 2008: 151). Harriet, like Mill, conceived a strategy of defending the couple from sexual shaming. They saw this tactic as a lesson to people who necessarily associate friendship with sex and they wanted to keep the two apart: "It seems to me an edifying picture for those poor wretches who can not conceive friendship except in sex" (Reeves 2008: 151). They believed that it is better to remove any indication of sexuality from the story of their relationship. It seems that the *Fox Affair* made them realize the consequences and vulnerability that one has to face in a public sexual scandal.

Conclusion

As I argued in Chapter 1, Mill's relationship with Harriet Taylor was a performative intervention that expanded the meaning of "livable life." It was a "counter-hegemonic gesture" because Mill and Harriet Taylor were engaged in practices that undermined the assumption that intimacy should be regulated by a monogamous affective and sexual relationship (Butler 1997b: 160). While Harriet was formally married to John Taylor, she became an important source of strength and creativity in Mill's life. Mill argued that his work was a shared outcome of his and Harriet's mind. By keeping sexuality out of the public discussion, Mill secured to some extent his reputation against vicious attacks.[30] Mill and Harriet's relationship shows that not only spaces that *promote public values* are important, but also those that protect people *from* public scrutiny. It provided an "obscure area of tolerance" that helped them navigate the social world of the Victorians.[31] Such tolerance had not only a defensive quality, but also an affirmative dimension because, at least until John Taylor died, it allowed them to live their lives within an antinormative arrangement. This experiment both defied traditional gender expectations and avoided a confrontational attack on Victorian public sexuality. The experience of their friends provided them with a good appreciation of the dangers and costs of sexual shame, and their strategy was to deny any accusation that would involve sexual shame.

My investigation supports Sedgwick's case that "the epistemology of the closet"—or the dichotomy of thinking about sexuality in opposites such as hetero vs. homo, or closet vs. coming out—has been productive of modern Western culture and history at large. Such "epistemology" produces particular identities which are complicit in thinking about sexuality as being "out" versus being in "the closet." I focused on silence because it has the disturbing effect of producing the anxiety of *not* knowing what one *does* or *is*. As a result, the exact nature of Mill and Harriet Taylor's intimacy became a problem for many scholars, who could not fit such relationship into a pre-established schema of understanding. Mill and Harriet's silence is important because it draws an important contrast with models that emphasize the obligatory gesture of "coming out" of one's "closet." Although Mill, like Nussbaum, understood the importance of transforming shame into positive action, he also believed that his sexuality was an experiment in living. Mill's silence challenges Nussbaum's model that offers only a limited typology of democratic forms of employing shame. Mill neither advocated the value of his relationship as a public good, nor did he experience the destructive shame that Nussbaum believes paralyzes one's inner life. But his disturbing silence was a queer intervention and challenged a certain distribution of social positions. By taking on a type of relationship that was considered "immoral," Mill and Harriet Taylor troubled a hierarchy of available sexual roles.

I chose to emphasize the political nature of his relationship because it was important for Mill's positions on women's social life and rights. As *On Liberty* abundantly shows, Mill was very sensitive to the life and rights of those who did not conform with the values of the political majority. Mill's entry in his journal on March 26, 1854, reflects his commitment to sexual freedom. He notes that two things are required for improving human life:

> Firstly, that women should cease to be set apart for this function, and should be admitted to all other duties and occupations on a par with men; secondly, that what any persons may freely do with respect to sexual relations should be deemed to be an unimportant and purely private matter, which concerns no one but themselves. (Mill in Mazlish 1975: 328)

Mill felt that freedom about one's sexual choices is key for human improvement, but he, unfortunately, did not politicize the "deviant" character of his relationship with Harriet. His refusal to politicize it was followed by a strong tendency in Mill scholarship to ignore the political value of his intimacy with Harriet.

In Chapter 4, by drawing on John Stuart Mill and Josephine Butler's divergent strategies about advancing social and political rights in Victorian England, I theorize performative slurs as a queer strategy. The counter-figure of slurs is the second trope in my genealogical project that offers a different meaning to shame. I appeal to Rancière's "literarity" to argue that humiliating rhetoric was an element in the production of new political subjects in the Victorian public space. Unlike theorists of shame, who reject the use of political humiliation, I claim that slurs and the use of disgust in public arguments have political value and explore several tactics of Victorian feminists that displayed excessive language.

Notes

1. The trope of "speaking out" as opposed to remaining silent is key to a progressive narrative that emerged from the civil rights movements (see Turner 2010: 1–13).
2. See Foucault: "There is no binary division to be made between what one says and one does not say; we must try to determine the different

ways of not saying such things ... There is not one but many silences, and they are integral part of the strategies that underlie and permeate discourses" (1978: 27).

3. When Butler and Athanasiou discuss the value of the agency for contemporary feminist and queer movements, they draw on the example of *Women in Black* in former Yugoslavia who undertook "silent street actions" to disrupt political silence about the dead during the civil war (2013: 86–7). For Butler, such interventions were very effective because they were deployed against nationalism and because women did not only mourn "for those whom they know or those to whom they were related, but even for those they did not know, and never could have known" (2013: 87). Butler suggests that the practice of silence could become practice of resignification—or a moment of providing for "greater possibilities of life" (2004a: 223).

4. Silences—or even secrecy and anonymity—need to interrupt *the police* to count as disturbing a given political order. While Thomas (2016) shows the value of secrecy in certain political contexts, I highlight the performative *and* unsettling interventions that emerge from a refusal of publicity and visibility.

5. Nussbaum conceptualizes *constructive shaming* to distinguish it from shame that triggers bad feelings such as depression, rage, and inability to mourn (2004: 209). In contrast with *primitive shame*, constructive shame reinforces a sense of "common human vulnerability," a sense of "the inclusion of all human beings in the community," and shows people's interdependence and mutual responsibility (2004: 213).

6. Brown claims that silences offer ways of preserving certain practices and dimensions of life from "the scorching rays of public exposure" (2005: 85). Such conceit generates two misunderstandings. First, when silence is opposed to speech, everything that is embodied by the truth of speech is censored—or hidden—by silence. Second, if silence is the contrary of speech, then when an enforced silence is broken, what emerges from silence is authentic and true. See also Butler's (2013: 34–5) worry about discourses of sexual visibility and outness: "The prescription of certain cultural ideas about 'freedom' that involve hyper-visibility and discourses of 'outness' thus becomes a way of exporting and imposing certain first-world conceptions of freedom's contours." See Davis (2010: 50–1).

7. Although Mill refrained from tackling the question of divorce in *The Subjection of Women*, Adams argued that "marriage should be rendered a civil contract, capable of being dissolved like any other contract" (1833: 228).

8. Adams's arguments utilized an "orientalist" understanding of Turks (for Orientalism, see Said 1979). Edward Said calls "Orientalism" a system of political and cultural assumptions organized around the

idea that the East is inferior and alien to the West. While Fox, Adams, and Mill share a deep concern for conditions of inequality and call for gender equality, they articulate their positions by using an orientalist view of non-Western Eastern people. Adams argues that women's condition in England is similar to that of "inmates of a Turkish haram" (*On the Condition of Women in England*: 217). Fox designs a hierarchy of civilization, where the savage man "kicks and beats women," the semi-civilized "locks her up in a harem," and the three-quarters civilized "educates her for pleasure and dependency" (*A Victim*: 177). Mill argues that women in the harem of an Oriental do not complain about not having the freedoms of European women, and suggests that Oriental women are less civilized (Rossi 1970: 214). The strategy of shaming is double-edged in the feminists' writing. It calls for greater social equality, but it draws on distinctions such as the civilized West and the barbarian East for its deployment. For theories about colonization in 1830s England, in particular Mill's advocacy of systematic colonialism, see Bell (2010: 38–43).

9. Like Owen and Mill's resignification of the word "chastity," Adams's intervention against sexual purity aimed at unsettling a moral consensus about women's sexuality. Adams did not argue against fidelity toward one's partner, but against social norms that made women pay a higher price for sexual freedom. He made clear that he was not an advocate of "light love" because he believed that "constancy between the sexes is more productive of human happiness than any other condition" (Adams 1833: 229). Yet he believed that social norms unjustly discriminate against women. The male breach of a marriage agreement was "scarcely considered an offence," while in women it was "visited with remorseless and unsparing severity" (Adams 1833: 228). Because marriage was a contractual agreement, both parties should have the same rights in dissolving or changing it. However, the social norms strongly penalized women's transgressions, while it gently tolerated men's violations of the contract.

10. See Mill's commentary in his letter to Harriet: "Robert Owen's definitions of chastity and prostitution, are quite as simple and take as firm a hold of the mind as the vulgar ones which connect the ideas of virtue and vice with the performance and non-performance of an arbitrary ceremonial" (Rossi 1970: 83). By endorsing Owen's view, and also by communicating it to Harriet, Mill proposed a definition of sexuality that went against the norm. Mill criticizes some forms of traditional sexuality, while he justifies other problematic views on sexuality, such as that prostitution is demeaning (Zerilli 1994: 136).

11. In 1832, and for years afterwards, England gave limited protection to women. By marriage, a woman practically became the property of her

husband. A wife held no right even to dispose of her personal belongings; the husband was the legal owner of his wife's property and if she was able to make money, her earnings were legally his (Mineka 1944: 285). It was almost impossible for a wife to obtain divorce; the only ground was adultery, yet she could not appear as a defendant, plaintiff, or victim (Mineka 1944: 285). Divorce could be obtained by an Act of Parliament but the cost was prohibitive.

12. In *Antigone's Claim*, Butler (2000: 5) explains that the figure of Antigone is important for a politics of performativity because she "absorbs the very language of the state against which she rebels." Her politics becomes not "of oppositional purity but of the scandalous impure."
13. Although Fox's arguments have an important performative dimension that de-naturalizes traditional gender assumptions, they also contain assumptions that are problematic for feminists. For instance, the image of women as "fountains of honor," who purify the taste and reform social manners, puts women on a pedestal as angelic creatures who could civilize men (1832: 637). It is important to refuse Fox's idealization of women's nature. Yet, we also need to understand the political value of such idealization in the context of its utterance.
14. Because Mill believed that shame could represent a significant political weapon, he used particular terms by "expropriating" their conventional meaning. In Mill's rhetoric, "the barbarians" were people who refused to accept the relationship of equality between men and women. The opposition between civilization and barbarism was mobilized to show that the opponents of the suffrage should be ashamed of their political positions (Rossi 1970: 126).
15. I analyze Mill's involvement in the Contagious Diseases Acts debates in Chapter 4.
16. Although Mill strongly criticized the institution of marriage, he was also concerned to separate his challenge on legal norms from an indiscriminate attack on the sexual mores of his compatriots. He argued that some men were able to avoid the power and temptations that a legal regime gave to them (Rossi 1970: 161). Various checks on the absolute power of the husband, such as the ties between the husband and children, limit men's power (Rossi 1970: 161–2). Mill even argued that "men in general" did not inflict, nor use, the legal powers of tyranny that they had at their "disposal" (Rossi 1970: 162). He was careful not to sexually shame his readers by claiming that they were all rapists. Although he drew a clear distinction between the legal treatment and the actual treatment of wives, Mill emphasized that the actual treatment of women was not a sufficient argument to preserve women's legal slavery. The core of his argument was that "laws and institutions require to be adapted, not to good men, but to bad" (Rossi 1970: 163). Marriage laws were abusive, yet only "vile

malefactors" used such powers to oppress women. In his carefully crafted argument, Mill avoided indicting an entire population and suggested that social reform was possible because its audience understood the harm that particular people could inflict due to unjust laws.

17. For Mill, a female slave had the legal possibility—and it was considered a moral obligation—to "refuse to her master the last familiarity" (Rossi 1970: 160). Married women in England were worse off than slaves in the United States because they could be legally raped. Mill's provocative argument, while problematic because it overlooked the systematic rape of black women in slavery, rhetorically shamed the reader because it argued that English wives had fewer rights than American slaves.

18. In *The Dissenting Marriage Question*, Fox argued that the injustice within the institution of marriage led to prostitution, because "the streets of all large cities swarm with unhappy women, miserable agents of the temptation of which at first they were all the victims, alike suffering and corrupting" (1833b: 141). Such an image, emphasizing the direct relation between marriage and prostitution, would have been out of place in *The Subjection of Women*.

19. In the radicals' rhetoric, marriage was a social institution that was considered the main cause of men and women's suffering. Women were slaves, prostitutes, and victims of rape and murder. The radicals argued, among many other arguments, that the marriage contract was, unlike a religious ceremony, a civil transaction; that marriage was, in contrast with the beliefs of the Catholic Church, not a sacrament; that the imposition of a religious service was a violation of the liberty of conscience; that the religious service was a performance that ridiculed the love of God; that religious services required unfair taxes; that the time for the Dissenters to oppose oppressive religious practices had come (Fox 1833b: 137–8).

20. In a letter that he wrote for Harriet between 1832 and 1833, Mill compared married women to prostitutes. When there was a lack of affection in a family, and when women were dependent on a male's income for survival, they lived in a degraded condition, which "is the essence of all prostitution, the act of delivering up her person for bread" (Rossi 1970: 74). In the same letter, he argued that women needed to have political rights because women were dependent on fathers and husbands "for subsistence."

21. See Mill's comment in a letter to John Nicol, where he explained that he avoided the question of divorce in *The Subjection of Women* in part because of "the obvious inexpediency of establishing a connexion in people's minds between the equality and any particular opinions on the divorce question" (Smith 2001: 195).

22. I explain this claim in detail in Chapter 4. Elisabeth Smith suggested that Mill moderated his radical rhetoric because he had to appeal to a large political audience (2001: 193). Although he wrote a draft of *The Subjection of Women* by the beginning of the 1860s, Mill postponed publishing his pamphlet on women's rights until 1869 because he felt that he had a better political context for his ideas (Smith 2001: 196). He proposed a petition in the Parliament to give *unmarried women*—and not all women—the right to vote, left open some questions about the status of women enfranchised by his legal proposal, and advocated the employment of "feminine" attitudes for political gains (Smith 2001: 194–6).
23. Rancière's workers "composed and sang songs at the barrières which were as good as those to be heard in any bourgeois salon" or chose to consume their nights with writing (Davis 2010: 53–4).
24. Brown draws on Foucault to suggest that silence may function a practice of freedom—or "as a scene of practices that escape the regulatory functions of discourse." Brown is worried that "putatively emancipatory practices," such as the confession and the extraction of every detail into public discourse, while intended as practices of freedom, "instigate the further regulations of those lives" (2005: 85–8).
25. Fox was very much loved as a minister and was acquitted in September 1834 by a large majority. Although he was expelled from the association of Unitarian ministers of London, he remained the preacher of South Place Chapel until 1852. He gave his wife an allowance and moved to a suburb of London in 1835 with Eliza Flower and two of his children, while the third remained with the mother (Mineka 1944: 195).
26. In a letter to Carlyle, Mill described his new interest in the group of people organized around the Unitarian journal: "they are but Unitarians and liberals, unsectarianized, & with a larger & more tolerant spirit than common;" they "are decidedly *characters*, realizing an idea of their own & free from halfness of all sorts" (*CW* XII: 104).
27. Mill was well acquainted with the intimacy between Flower and Fox. He writes to Fox that although "our affairs have been gradually getting into a more & more unsatisfactory state," he was in "a higher state" with regard to his relationship to Harriet at the time of the Fox scandal (*CW* XII: 187). He knew that Fox might be conflicted about denying a clear sexual involvement with Flower, because that could affect his "personal dignity." Yet, Mill argued that Fox should deny it. In a subsequent letter on the question of "truth"—that is, on the question of whether Fox is intimately involved with Eliza Flower—he and Harriet believed that Fox should reject any involvement with Eliza Flower (*CW* XII: 178).

28. See Mill: "If they put that very question to you, no doubt you ought to say so—but I think not otherwise. It seems to me quite enough if you appeal to those articles in the Repository as containing your principles on the subject. You might say that you have acted no otherwise than in consistency with those principles; and if they ask you whether the particular fact is true, you might deny altogether their concern with it or right to enquire into it, but nevertheless profess your willingness voluntarily to give the information sought, by denying the assertion" (CW XII: 189).
29. Nussbaum (2010: 141): "In *On Liberty*, where reference to same-sex relationships would have been apropos, Mill certainly does not talk about sexual experimentation, or different forms of sexual life." Unlike Nussbaum, I believe that Mill's reference in *On Liberty* to "experiments in living" gestures toward what he calls an "experiment" in his relationship with Harriet.
30. Conservative critics did not fail to denounce the immorality of his relationship with Harriet. I explained that the conservative writer Abraham Hayward attacked Mill particularly because he had a relationship with a married woman. Hayward's condemnation was, however, an exception rather than the norm regarding the political rhetoric of his conservative opponents.
31. See Foucault's formulation, as quoted by Brown (2005: 86). Rossi, for instance, suggested that Mill and Harriet Taylor avoided a sexual relationship because of Victorian norms about respectability: "It may be that in the nineteenth-century Victorian England avoidance of the physical act of adultery and adherence to the formal obligations of the marital relationship were more significant than the existence of intellectual and personal intimacy between an unmarried man and a married woman" (1970: 10). As such, it seems that for Rossi they were both in a sexual closet.

Chapter 4
Performative Slurs: Political Rhetoric in Feminist Activism

> A girl who was committed to prison by the Bench at ———, said, "It did seem hard, ma'am, that the Magistrate on the bench who gave the casting vote for my imprisonment had paid me several shillings, a day to two before, in the street, to go with him." If the said Magistrate should chance to read *The Shield*, and would wish to hear a little more about this, I shall be happy to communicate with him.
> (Josephine Butler, quoted in Jordan and Sharp 2003b: 90)

On May 9, 1870, Josephine Butler was preoccupied with the campaign to repeal the Contagious Diseases (CD) Acts, which regulated prostitution in Victorian England. The CD Acts consisted of three laws passed by the British Parliament between 1864 and 1869, which affected the lives of many women and were opposed by many women's rights activists. Among feminists such as Florence Nightingale, James Stansfeld, James Stuart, Elisabeth Wolstenholme, and John Stuart Mill, Butler was the law's fiercest opponent. Because Butler argued that women needed to be protected from a piece of "vicious" and "evil" legislation, she became the most vocal defender of the prostitutes.

In a letter to the editor of *The Shield*, the magazine of the Anti-Contagious Diseases Acts Association, Butler made the case that the laws regulating prostitution had "demoralizing, brutalizing and oppressive" effects (Jordan and Sharp 2003b: 86). By channeling the voice of the prostitutes, she deployed shame rhetorically to show that upper class men were participating in the spread of prostitution. She strategically appealed to the threat of public humiliation. Butler used the confession of a woman to underscore the sexual involvement of an unnamed magistrate in prostitution. While Butler did not disclose the name of the magistrate, she gestured at the possibility that she might use such information to expose him as a hypocrite. Her implied threat was that *all* the magistrates in Kent might be in the same situation, and that they themselves could subsequently be exposed for their misdeeds, to the extent that they would have to endure public shame of their own.

The feminist activist utilized humiliation to open up the political space to experiences and ideas of those who were considered less than human. It performatively intervened in a public discourse organized to silence women engaged in sex work. Butler defended the prostitutes not only by showing that the magistrate was a hypocrite, but also by threatening public exposure of his sexuality. Since Butler was disgusted by the actions of judges, she often expressed her contempt toward their actions. Because the victims of prostitution were humiliated, Butler channeled women's voices to foment her own argument that upper class males should also themselves be ashamed of their own immoral behavior (Jordan and Sharp 2003b: 91). In Christina Tarnopolsky's typology of shame, Butler's rhetoric could be seen as an example of positive shaming.[1] By implying that the judges themselves hired prostitutes to do their bidding, Butler articulated what Tarnopolsky can argue is at the heart of "respectful shame," namely that "who you are cannot be captured by any particular norm or self-image you currently possess" (Tarnopolsky 2002: 20). Yet, Butler's intervention—her disclosure of magistrates that failed to embody the characteristics of a "just citizen"—is not primarily respectful, as Tarnopolsky defines it. It is deeply connected to humiliation and performs a rhetorical injury to the magistrate's social status.

The performative slur is the second counter-figure that I deploy to challenge a current understanding of shame. In this chapter, unlike political theorists who police humiliation as a strategic and moral tactic, I argue that slurs have value as a performative queer practice.[2] On the one hand, Butler's intervention is not an articulation of a *given* ideal, because it proposes a *resignification* of a norm that privileged some and excluded many. Instead of understanding public morality as reflecting the hierarchical opposition between moral judges and immoral sex workers, the Victorian feminist activist suggested that the reader should see such dichotomy as false. On the other hand, democratic equality means, in this context, the process of making visible the role of judges in producing prostitution; it seeks to identify them and challenge their position as the enactment of *police*. This new vocabulary of equality produces what Rancière calls "democracy," which is a struggle of those who do not count to interrupt a hierarchy of social roles.

Butler deployed the sex worker's bad reputation to turn the situation around and take control of it.[3] To speak the truth, the activist has to take the risk of "offending the other person, of irritating him, of making him angry and provoking him to conduct which may even be extremely violent" (Foucault 2010: 11). This act of disclosure is exposing the speaker to the risk of violence. Even while Butler maintains an overt demonstration of being "respectful" to the judge, at the same time, she also points to the humiliating possibility that the magistrate will be exposed as a client of prostitutes. Not only would such exposure be terrible for one's reputation, but it would show that magistrates are not neutral, impartial agents in a system that functions in an abusive manner. Yet Butler's vignette shows also how the sex worker interrupted an established order in which she did not have the right to speak, nor to exert herself as sovereign agent. In Rancière's terminology, this act was a "logical revolt" because those who are considered without a part—the *sans-part*—are just as capable of reasoning and fighting back as those who are powerful. By asserting her equal position, the sex worker, like Rancière's plebs, behaved as if she was an equal participant in the political process that condemned her for immorality.[4]

Nineteenth-century feminists' queer practices aimed at disturbing the norms about who counted as political subject and contested exclusionary social and political arrangements. By recovering strategies that seem disreputable, I argue that certain political gestures are important when they resignify conventions that limit "a livable life" (Butler 2004: 225). To offer an account about humiliation as a queer practice, I distinguish between two types of rhetoric.[5] A first type of political rhetoric is a queer practice if it seeks "collective political invention," "refigurative possibilities," and "transformative cultural practices" (Brown 1993: 406). In this political discourse, a new political subject is enacted, which is involved in the "agonistic theater" of politics and is interested primarily in forging an alternative future (Brown 1993: 407). In turn, a rhetoric of policing identities reiterates the intention of a regulatory and disciplinary society to mold its subjects. The subjects of *policed identities* become a vehicle of subordination through individualization and normalization, as every potentially subversive rejection of conventional norms has to be codified through law (Brown 1993: 399).

Queer practices, unlike a rhetoric about identities in liberal feminism, emphasize the value of becoming a political subject, rather than representing an identity in a political argument. Nussbaum tends to rely on a conception of identity that seems to be at the heart of mainstream feminist activism in United States, in which politics should represent the identities of hurt women.[6] In this liberal conception of feminism privileges hurt as the basis of political agency because women have been traditionally hurt by men. Unlike politics, which is seen as representing subjects, in a queer practice subjects manifest themselves as political subjects when they act. A theory of queer practice acknowledges that pain and injury is part of feminist rhetoric, but it claims that political feminist action has to be worried about the effects of *policed identities*.[7] In this respect, queer practices represent an important theoretical challenge to liberal feminism.[8] As such, it moves beyond types of political rhetoric such as *respectful* (Tarnopolsky 2010) and *constructive* (Nussbaum 2004).[9] In a queer practice one becomes a political subject when one struggles and asserts one's equality. By asserting a wrong, one creates a stage for politics and seeks to transform given identities. While a theory of queer practices does not reject the value of identities in politics, it emphasizes the value of dis-identifying from pre-established roles in a hierarchy.

Also, a queer conception of shame challenges the view that the humiliating rhetoric is always injurious in the way the speaker intends to be. Because there is a gap between speech and conduct, such a gap provides the possibility for political resistance, or what Judith Butler calls "the role of nonjuridical forms of opposition" and "ways of restaging and resignifying speech" (1997b: 23). Rather than starting from the premise that politics is a mirror for identities that are already given, a theory of queer practices begins with the idea that subjects become political in the process of asserting claims.[10]

This chapter makes two main contributions. First, I seek to de-police a rhetoric of humiliation by which the *sans-part* assert their position of equality. Josephine Butler and Mill deployed injurious rhetoric to argue that some men exercise power unjustly and used harsh language to stigmatize people who were in power. Although they did speak in the name of the victims of the upper class elite—which, as Rancière (2011: 9) told us, should worry us when it benefits its self-proclaimed representatives—the language they used had an "excessive" dimension. I interpret this feature of language, its "literarity", as an anarchic tendency to speak to anyone, and argue that the humiliating rhetoric of the Victorians was a populist tool that disrupted the social order. Their interventions sought to interrupt conventional norms about gender and produce new understandings about women's agency in politics.[11] Because they sought to challenge the Victorian political elite, they utilized pain and injury as performatives to resignify conventional understandings of gender.

Second, I contribute to the larger historical understanding of Victorian feminism by investigating Mill and Butler's distinct political strategies. Historians studying Victorian sexuality and the women's movement have thoroughly investigated the social and intellectual conditions surrounding the CD Acts.[12] Yet, this important historical literature has not compared Mill's and Josephine Butler's responses to the Acts. Both Mill and Butler were called to testify against the CD Acts in front of a Royal Commission, which was constituted with the intention of judging the value of the prostitution laws. Butler utilized humiliation as a catalyst to challenge narrow conceptions about women. Like Butler in her activism, Mill advocated for the "severity" of language when the circumstances were appropriate, but he did not employ it against the Royal Commission. Instead, Mill utilized humiliation to eliminate activists who sympathized with Butler's feminist goals. Rather than forming a coalition with Butler's sympathizers, Mill believed that each feminist group should have its politics (*CW* XXXII: 203).[13] He did not act by risking his position of power. Mill's humiliating rhetoric would have been effective if it had been aimed at forming coalitions with feminists he disagreed with.

In short, I make a case for humiliating rhetoric as a queer practice against a liberal feminist concept of shame. This perspective draws limits around respectful uses of shame and ignores the positive uses of its harsher articulations. My political history not only offers a deep contextual grasp of feminist figures, but also imagines alternative ways of using performative slurs in political activism.

The Contagious Diseases Acts and Josephine Butler's Rhetoric of Humiliation

Butler's political interventions were articulated at a moment when prostitution was severely condemned by the English political elite. Between 1864 and 1869, the British Parliament passed three laws regulating prostitution; these acts came to be known as the CD Acts. In 1864, the first law was passed in England as a temporary piece of legislation designed to contain the spread of sexual diseases in the armed forces. Two further acts were passed in 1866 and 1869, respectively: the act of 1869 extended the application of the original law to towns and naval ports in the south of England and in Ireland. According to this law, any woman suspected of being a prostitute could be arrested, required to sign a so-called voluntary submission form, and forced to undergo a medical examination. If she was found to be diseased, she could be confined to a locked hospital for nine months. If she resisted participation in the process at any stage, she "was liable to imprisonment." The legislation was enacted at the urging of officials in the War Office and the Admiralty who believed that the efficiency of the army was being impaired because of the spread of venereal diseases. The CD Acts protected all male clients from prostitutes, and powerful lobbies such as the Harveian Medical Society of London wanted to extend this legislation so that it would be applicable to the entire country (Jordan and Sharp 2003a: 3).

The CD Acts constituted part of a larger debate in Victorian England about women's rights and sexuality. The legal status of women was inextricably defined by social inequalities present during the first half of the nineteenth century. Married woman did not have a legal identity of their own in the eyes of the law. They could not own property, and they did not have legal rights to maintain the custody of their children (Griffin 2012: 5). A woman could not get divorced from an abusive or adulterous husband without an Act of Parliament, and only four women managed to obtain a divorce under these terms between 1670 and 1857. However, in the space of little more than thirty years (1870–1900), male legal and political privileges were "either swept away or substantially undermined" (Griffin 2012: 5). Women's political and legal rights were obtained partly because of the tenacious fight waged by a carefully organized women's movement. The second part of the century saw campaigns erupt which ultimately gave married women the right to own property, to improve their own employment and educational opportunities, gave mothers the same custody rights as fathers, repealed the CD Acts, and gave women the right to vote (Griffin 2012: 5). Married women were given the right to own property in two installments in 1870 and 1882, and the laws relating to child custody were changed to be in favor of women in 1873 and 1886. An English divorce court was created in 1857, and the Contagious Diseases Acts were suspended in 1883 and repealed in 1886. While the British Parliament was an exclusively male legislature until Nancy Astor took her seat in the House of Commons in 1919, women managed to gain representation in local government. In 1869, Jacob

Bright succeeded in restoring women's ability to vote in local elections; women also won the right to vote for school boards in 1870, and they were given the right to vote for the new county councils in 1888.

Although the campaign to repeal the CD Acts was part of a broader feminist movement, it represented a watershed because it brought into the public eye new ways of understanding male and female sexuality (Griffin 2012: 100–9). First, coupled with the rise of a series of "moral panics" about juvenile prostitution, venereal diseases and the murders executed by Jack the Ripper, the campaign underscored the possibility that male sexuality could pose a threat to the safety of women (Griffin 2012: 100). Campaigners who opposed the CD Acts presented the male elite as motivated by the desire to have unrestricted access to women's bodies. Josephine Butler, for instance, portrayed the supporters of regulation of prostitution as "sadistic aristocratic villains who conspired to control women through state sanction and monopoly" (Griffin 2012: 101). Second, the feminist movement was generally split between activists outside Westminster and parliamentarians who did not endorse the critique of elite sexuality (Griffin 2012: 101). In Parliament, both the advocates and the critics of the CD Acts "tended to speak as though the Acts affected only prostitutes and military personnel" (Griffin 2012: 101). In addition, the focus of pro-repeal speeches was "on improving the sexual morality of soldiers and sailors," and did not encompass the morality of the civilian population; it certainly did not call into question anything concerning the social elites (Griffin 2012: 102). Unlike the parliamentary critics of the CD Acts, the larger repeal campaign focused on the male monopoly of political power and on attacking the idea of the benign legislator and husband (Griffin 2012: 102).

Both Butler and Mill condemned women's subordination by resignifying traditional norms about womanhood. Rather than accepting women as an inferior term, Butler and Mill fiercely challenged political conceptions about the natural inferiority of women. They both underscored women's merits and qualifications to vote in elections. They wanted to show that English political institutions needed better conditions so as to cultivate women's social and political development.[14] However, they had different political targets and distinct ways of arguing against inequality and discrimination. While Mill focused his parliamentarian activity between 1865 and 1868 on advocating for women's right to vote, Butler was primarily interested in meeting her duties as an activist, writer, and public speaker and wanted to repeal the CD Acts. Although Mill testified as to the harmful role of the CD

Acts, he did not deliver any fiery speeches and was very cautious about using political arguments involving the CD Acts controversy (Reeves 2008: 431). Even more troubling, he was ashamed of some of the political actions of activists and called their rhetoric "vulgar."

Butler had a unique vision of feminist tactics and rhetoric. She is a rare figure within modern feminism, not only because of the sixteen years she spent relentlessly targeting the CD Acts, but also because she advocated many innovative feminist tactics such as militant acts, by-election campaigning, and extraparliamentary activity such as political rallies (Kent 1987: 8). Butler organized popular meetings about the CD Acts that were also a source of great popular entertainment (Walkowitz 1980: 104). Like other repealers, she challenged Liberal Party candidates at by-elections, and she actively campaigned against Liberals who supported the CD Acts (Walkowitz 1980: 106). Butler also used her sexuality, in addition to strong narratives about rape and corruption, to promote her cause. In Walkowitz's description,

> She was also sexually attractive to men. Meticulously coiffed, dressed in the height of fashion, she held popular audiences spellbound with tales of "instrumental" rape, police brutality, and aristocratic corruption. The voyeuristic character of these spectacles was undoubtedly enhanced by the physical charms of the "lady" speaker. (1980: 114–15)

Butler made women's sexuality a fundamental battleground for changing laws. Her repeal campaign was centered upon de-naturalizing ideas about sexuality. In particular, she opposed a vision of "a natural, uncontrollable male sex drive" (Kent 1987: 68). She resisted the belief that a slave class of "clean" women was required to serve male sexual appetites (Jordan and Sharp 2003a: 3). Although Butler primarily challenged sexual Victorian norms, property rights and political enfranchisement were also part of her larger campaign concerning feminist advocacy. Butler believed sexual autonomy and political rights could not remain separated. She argued that "we shall never have faith and courage enough in Parliament to attack this monster evil [of prostitution] in its sources until the conviction of women as well as of men are represented there" (Kent 1987: 13). In 1868, Butler and Wolstenholme formed the Married Woman's Property Committee in Manchester, which proposed a radical Bill that would have given married women the same property rights as men (Griffin 2012: 5). Because the radicalism of the Bill proved to be ultimately unacceptable, Parliament passed a substantially amended Bill that allowed women to have limited personal property, in addition to permitting them "to own their wages and earnings, certain investments, and property inherited as the next of kin of an intestate" (Griffin 2012: 5).

Performative slurs were part of Butler's performative interventions in the advocacy against the CD Acts. On the one hand, her strategy of moral progress was based on shaming upper class men for benefiting from the institution of prostitution. She asked Members of Parliament to behave like men, to "quit yourselves like men," and repeal "the wicked and abominable" CD Acts (Jordan and Sharp 2003b: 161). Shaming and humiliation targeted these men from their participation and role in a practice viewed as immoral: "make it a shame to see men bold in sin and profaneness, and God will bless you" (Jordan and Sharp 2003b: 160). In Butler's rhetoric, men were humiliated because they were faithless, lacked authentic masculinity, and drove women into entering prostitution. As a response to women's humiliating condition, Butler called for a war against those who engaged in practices that led women to prostitution (Jordan and Sharp 2003b: 129). She spoke vituperatively against the "hideous traffic" of women, against the "buying and selling of tender female children," against brothel-keeping, "patronized by the fashionable and the wealthy," against a "faithless, godless, despairing legislation" that made prostitution legal in England (Jordan and Sharp 2003b: 129).

On the other hand, like any performative strategy that operates under conditions of power, Butler utilized problematic religious language to challenge the laws regulating sexuality. Prostitution was morally reprehensible; it was a sin. She not only attacked the upper class elite, but also the practices of prostitution. She condemned not just those who were involved in it, but the act itself—and even the legalization that would have led to reducing the stigma associated with paid sex.[15] She frequently employed the terms "servants of shame" to refer to prostitutes, and called prostitution a "shame" (Jordan and Sharp 2003b: 165).

Butler's performative use of "prostitution" shows that her political rhetoric worked both with and against traditional notions of sexuality. She used religious language to unsettle received notions about women's sexuality, but she also accepted traditional notions about good sexuality in her activist work. For Butler, strong religious norms demarcated between moral and immoral sexual practices. Promiscuity was opposed to loving relationships. As Judith Butler pointed out, the use of the performative is double-edged, because it proposes new meanings to old conventions while instituting other norms. In Josephine Butler's rhetoric, the political elite was indicted as corrupted and hypocritical, but sexual practices such as paid sex or sex outside marriage were considered immoral and sinful.[16] Performative interventions are not only progressive politics; they generate changes in perception, while also strengthening particular oppressive norms.

In contrast to Mill's public opposition to the CD Acts, Butler utilized strong language to argue that MPs and magistrates had a direct stake in maintaining laws that rendered women sexually vulnerable. She showed contempt and disgust toward the hypocrisy of the upper class and called out the men who supported the abuse of women in Parliament (Kent 1987: 152). She frequently claimed that the persons who administered the Acts were "the same men who also bought their sexual services" (Butler quoted in Kent 1987: 153). She told the Royal Commission that she was troubled "at the sight of so many men with so base and low a moral character as you seem to have" (Kent 1987: 153). By calling men in the Royal Commission men of "base and low character," Butler not only shamed them for their actions, but also humiliated them. She was not afraid to sexually shame the all-male Royal Commission. While Mill suggested that the English public was directly involved in the issue of prostitution, and that men needed to pay for the costs associated with prostitution, Butler made the radical argument that the people who legislated were morally involved in prostitution. In her view, men in Parliament were directly responsible for "the miseries, the wrongs, the soul murders, and the destruction of young lives which have been going on for years past" (Kent 1987: 153). She utilized such language to shock, as well as to open up the possibility of fundamental changes within the political system.

Butler's performative rhetoric ran the risk of appealing to women's identity to use "recrimination" and "rancor" rather than to actualize a practice of freedom (Brown 1993: 390). Yet, her language was directed at generating a political movement that would repeal the CD Acts. The movement's goal was to transform social attitudes and influence opinion among the political elite (Walkowitz 1980: 90). The dissenters achieved their objectives. While, in 1869, the men and women who organized opposition to the prostitution laws were seen as "eccentric cranks" and religious zealots, by 1880 they had managed to impose their views on a significant portion of the general public and shape Liberal Party policy on the subject of regulation (Walkowitz 1980: 90). Butler's performative use of humiliation was part of a larger social movement to change public perceptions. The movement's strategy aimed at producing collective social transformation and legal changes by shifting a preconceived understanding of women's inferiority.

The social mobilization against the CD Acts drew on distinct vocabularies to express its opposition. Mill and Butler not only differed because Butler humiliated the male Victorian elite, but also because of the contrasting ways in which they deployed distinct performatives. While Mill articulated his opposition to the laws by employing secular language, Butler used powerful religious tropes to call for the repeal of the prostitution laws.[17] She frequently drew on Biblical passages and Christian metaphors to argue that the CD Acts were wrong (Jordan and Sharp 2003a: 283–9). In a speech in front of 400 women who supported the repeal, she described her involvement with the women's cause as a religious conversion (Jordan and Sharp 2003b: 126–7). Butler told her audience that she used to be very doubtful about the law. She "spoke and acted uncertainly and feebly," and waited "upon God and implored Him to put me beyond doubt" (Jordan and Sharp 2003b: 126). However, in her revelation, she felt "from a thousand channels, without or within, tides of evidence of the holiness of our work flowed in, and of the suitableness of women as God's agents in it" (Jordan and Sharp 2003b: 126–7). After the revelation, she did not doubt her mission anymore; that is, she saw herself as a person whose "mission" it was "to release the enslaved, loaded with chains of sin" (Jordan and Sharp 2003b: 128).

Both types of rhetoric were effective. Butler's speeches, which combined political principles with religious fervor, aroused "intense emotional loyalty" and "facilitated outreach among working men and women" (Walkowitz 1980: 101). Mill's secular rhetoric was appealing to the freethinking deists and Unitarians who dominated the National Association in London (Walkowitz 1980: 102). As Wendy Brown argues, liberal politics is organized around the formal legal autonomy of the subject and the formal secularism of the state (2008: 173). Yet, the movement against the prostitution laws undermines the assumption that religion is private experience, which needs to be "privately enjoyed" and "ideologically depoliticized" (Brown 2008: 169). A collective protest against the government's regulation of sexuality brought in not only working class secularists, but also working men and women who religiously objected to the laws (Walkowitz 1980: 102–3).

While the CD Acts opponents' rhetoric was effective, it was plagued by important flaws. Butler assumed that she was entitled to speak about the experiences of working class men and women because she understood their predicament. One of Butler's favorite strategies was to locate the damage that the CD Acts caused to women in her life. She criticized the law from the perspective of a mother who grew up in world where "vice was acknowledged as a necessity" (Jordan and Sharp 2003b: 99). She challenged the laws because she could relate to trauma suffered by women. She used vivid images to describe her pain. When she heard the news about the Acts being passed, she described herself as "filled with the deepest agony of the soul" (Jordan and Sharp 2003b: 98). She could not sleep for nights, because "her pillow was literally wet with tears" (Jordan and Sharp 2003b: 98). However, her critique of the prostitution laws came from the position that she lived the life of an oppressed woman. In her attack on the Victorian establishment as vicious and sinful, she was often willing to sidestep the differences between working class women and upper-middle class women like herself.

Butler's attitude toward working class women was not unique. The repealers' defense of so-called "prostitutes," as Walkowitz points out, was sometimes "ambivalent and contradictory" (103). A prominent trade unionist, Robert Applegarth, was the only member of the Royal Commission to suggest that not all but only registered prostitutes should be interviewed. He visited the districts with a high concentration of medical issues, interviewed women in the Royal Albert Hospital, and concluded that working women were bullied and abused under the Acts. Yet even Applegarth feared that the social underground of women who moved from "disorderly houses" to respectable houses would contaminate the respectable working class (Walkowitz 1980: 103). Because the language of the opponents of the law drew on Victorian ideas about political representation, it disregarded the voices of the women for whom such a political battle was deployed. Such marginalization shows not only the significance of the feminists' opposition to the CD Acts, but also their problematic role in articulating their dissent.

Victorian feminists reflected about how to respond to political denunciations and insults. Particular injurious words, such as shameless and immoral, intended to silence the supporters of the women's movement. As I showed in Chapter 2, Mill suggested to Adams that he needed a tactic with which he could turn painful feelings such as shame into a type of power. In Mill's view, one could transform a wrong by rejecting the shameful accusations of others. If a person is disliked and feared, then that individual can become powerful if she is treated by others *de puissance en puissance*, that is, as having "a power of their own." This tactic shows that the negative, dangerous side of shame can be re-worked for democratic purposes, when a wrong is reframed in an assertive political tactic.

Butler, like Mill, engaged in resignifying accusations and a rhetoric of inferiority. In a speech that Butler gave in front of the Ladies' National Association, she constructed a political scene in which she focused on the wrong that activists have to fight against (Jordan and Sharp 2003b: 175–6). She acknowledged that for a woman to be accused of being shameless or immodest was a very painful experience, because it "imparted a special sting associated with the pain which must be endured" (Jordan and Sharp 2003b: 175). In her view, the enemy had found the vulnerable point and pointed his arrows "with the words 'indecent, prurient, shameless' straight at the clefts of our armor" (Jordan and Sharp 2003b: 176). Yet, Butler told her fellow activists that "we are not going to die from these wounds" and that "their poison is converted into healing" (Jordan and Sharp 2003b: 176). More importantly, after turning shame into power, the repealers were going to "rise for the combat stronger than before" (Jordan and Sharp 2003b: 176). Like Mill, Butler suggested that it was possible to transform a past shameful accusation into a weapon, as well as to think about a strategy of empowerment. Both Butler and Mill were aware of the political potential of shame and reflected upon how to deploy it in their rhetoric.

When working as an activist, Butler was exposed to various verbal and physical attacks. She was heavily ridiculed by a Member of Parliament as being symbolic of, or tantamount to little more than, a "prostitute;" similarly, a journalist described her as "an indecent maenad, a shrieking sister, frenzied, unsexed, and utterly without shame" (Kent 1987: 10). Feminists' opponents did not use the language of sexuality by accident. As Kent observes, the anti-feminist language was political language: the anti-feminists were speaking in response to Butler's intention to undermine a sexual hierarchy that legitimized a particular form of male power (Kent 1987: 10). When it came to Butler's activism, shaming proved to be not only verbal, but also physical. In Manchester, Butler was attacked by a mob and "was covered with flour and excrement, her clothes had been torn off her body, her face was discolored and stiff with dry blood and she was so bruised that she could hardly move" (Kent 1987: 72). Butler understood exactly the intention of those anti-feminists who wanted to degrade her sexually. Describing her experience about an incident where a group of men threatened woman campaigners with bodily harm and the possibility of rape, Butler pointed out that women who ventured into the public arena were perceived as being equivalent to little more than prostitutes:

> We had no defence or means of escape . . . half of dozen fists were at my face at once, and the epithets applied were such as one only hears of in brothels. They filled their foul talk with allusions to the visits under the Contagious Diseases Acts. (Kent 1987: 72)

Butler rejected the term prostitute for her political activity, and she insisted rhetorically on the difference between speaking on behalf of prostitutes and speaking as a prostitute. The campaign against the CD Acts wanted to liberate prostitutes from "the darkest, cruelest slavery the world has seen" (Jordan and Sharp 2003b: 125). However, such a campaign needed to use sharp political weapons for fighting against "slavery." Butler understood very well the costs of her language and rhetoric. She thought that the repealers needed to learn from the gains of the progressive movement in the United States. In 1871, she defended her use of strong language by drawing on the words of William Lloyd Garrison and his tough abolitionist stance: "I should like to remind you of the words of Garrison, the liberator, he said, 'I am aware that many object to the severity of my language; but is there not cause for severity? I will be as harsh as truth and as uncompromising as justice'" (Butler as quoted in Frederickson 2008: 373). She also confessed that she had struggled with the experiences she had encountered as a result of being attacked by anti-feminists.

The resignification of shameful acts associated with feminism was incorporated in Butler's religious language. The strategy of converting "poison" into "healing" was an example of such resignification. She approached her role as a women's advocate by maintaining a deep allegiance to Christian discourses of redemption. Her work with prostitutes was shaped by a discourse of liberating prostitutes from shame. She explicitly embraced this type of discourse in the advice she gave to her colleagues: "you who are called the most difficult work . . . that of seeking to save the souls and bodies of the victims of the worst sin in the world. It requires a Christ-like, a God-like spirit . . . a consecration, a call to work" (Frederickson 2008: 384). Butler offered herself as an example of a person who could heal the wounds of women who had been shamed. She wrote about various spiritual experiences with women prostitutes. For instance, she visited a hospital where she met the chaplain who had "his hands pressed upon his ears, in order to shut out the sound of a torrent of blasphemy and coarse abuse hurled after him by one of the inmates" (Frederickson 2008: 384). She drew near to the woman, who was "hideous to look at, dying and raging." Yet "an unseen power" urged her to try to talk to her. Butler decided that she wanted to treat the woman with compassion and said a few words to her, which she did not remember, but they were spoken with love (Frederickson 2008: 384). The woman reacted very strongly to Butler's compassionate attitude:

> She gazed at me in astonishment . . . She took my hand and held it with a death grip. She became silent,—gentle. Tears welled from the eyes which had been gleaming with fury. The poor soul had been full to the brim of revenge and bitterness against man, against fate, against God. But she saw something new and strange. She heard that she was loved; she believed it and was transformed. (Frederickson 2008: 384)

The conversion of pain and shameful feelings into love was a major Christian theme in Butler's feminist work. It showed an alternative strategy of engaging with shame, which is different from Mill's idea of using shame as an independent power. While for Mill shameful feelings, particularly those regarding sexuality, had to be left out of public discourse, Butler believed that shameful sexualities *were* part of public discourse and needed to be articulated to protect sex workers. Mill focused on developing an individual strategy of responding to shaming, but Butler saw her task as being to highlight the plight of the prostitutes she defended. Because the male elite that benefited from a shaming discourse shaped the prostitutes' sense of sexuality and identities, this feminist counter-discourse had to make clear the power component inherent in sexual domination.

The strategy of resignification was intended as a political weapon to mobilize her fellow activists into continuing their work for social justice. In a public speech to the lady repealers, she outlined a strategy of tapping into mental resources to fight against the CD Acts. She pointed out the ways in which she understood that the subject of their work could prove embarrassing for her colleagues (Jordan and Sharp 2003b, 124–5). Activists for women's rights could get tired and lose faith. To help them deal with these ramifications of their work, she suggested that "the soul" had resources for overcoming pain and timidity:

> I well know that the mind cannot bear a long strain of one painful topic, and this subject is, of necessity, so sad and painful, that, in order to attain to faithful action, there must be another feeling and motive in the mind, powerful enough to overcome the fear of pain. (Jordan and Sharp 2003b: 125)

Butler acknowledged the pain and the sadness that the repealers experienced in their fight against the CD Acts, particularly when it involved difficult topics such as prostitution. Nevertheless, she believed that the pain was worth enduring because "a second feeling" proved these women with enough power to overcome the fear of pain.

Butler's strategy of shaming, including sexually shaming the political elite, was part of her broader tactic about how to use her emotions and harness their power to enact social justice. It called for the mobilization of negative emotions like shame and anger to be employed in a positive manner so as to challenge inequalities. Part of her strategy was the psychological transformation that activists experience. Psychological change helps them keep fighting against unjust laws. She was very aware that the repealers' work had to focus on a good use of emotional resources. She knew that "to escape pain" was less useful, because women needed to be "perseverant" in their work. Repealers needed to mobilize their anger, because they could be made capable of experiencing "a constant, sustained, and well-governed indignation." This type of "momentary flash of generous indignation against cruelty and wrong" would prove to be poor in its results "unless [it was] capable of expanding into the profound, patient and life-long hatred of injustice and oppression, which alone can work out social reform" (Jordan and Sharp 2003b: 125). In Butler's political rhetoric, sexual shame and contempt were included as strong, central elements. By showing the role that men played in the production of prostitution, she shifted the understanding of shame from "women [who] are [considered] sinful and disgusting" to being "men who use prostitutes [should be considered] sinful and disgusting." She used the voices of prostitutes to highlight her rejection of men's duplicity. Shame was for her a strategy with which she could speak the truth to the Victorian power elite and show the flaws in the democratic ideal that they held. Unlike Tarnopolsky's "respectful shame," her strategy was not purified of elements that had the potential to harm and humiliate.

Notably, Butler's rhetoric was inherently connected to what she called "the severity" of her language. She turned against men the shame, disgust, and contempt that prostitutes had to face. In May of 1870, Butler spoke at a conference with anti-CD Acts delegates. When speaking about "the moral reclaimability of the prostitutes," she knew that it is hard to persuade skeptics about the bad conditions that various women had to face. She initially considered the possibility of taking a skeptic into the "hiding places of shame," and showing to him that these women were "like ourselves, with heart and consciences, sorrows and joys, tender hopes and poignant regrets" (Jordan and Sharp 2003a: 122). She realized, however, that such an experience would be useless for many men. She doubted that even "the most powerful reasoning on this subject" would convince the skeptic, who claimed that women are beyond hope, as he called them "all kinds of ugly and ungracious names" (Jordan and Sharp 2003a: 122). Because it was impossible for some men to understand the condition of women who sell their bodies for sex, Butler argued that she could not to speak to them. However, partly tongue-in-cheek, she considered the question of whether she should speak about the "reclaimability of profligate men" to prostitutes (Jordan and Sharp 2003a: 123). So, she turned the tables against men who exploited women, and she explicitly reframed the initial accusation that prostitutes were shameful. Instead of shaming women, Butler shamed men for their role and participation in prostitution. She believed that women who sell their bodies had a better moral position than those men who benefitted from their services.

The *sans-part*, in the Rancièrian understanding of politics, enacted a rhetoric of equality through shaming their enemies. Like the sex workers, Butler shamed men because they were hypocrites and because they pretended to embody norms of religious and social respectability while at the same time seeking out paid sex. Prostitutes said to Butler: "we are awful sinners, but we are not hypocrites" (Jordan and Sharp 2003a: 123). They said: "we don't, after going about doing vile things under cover the darkness of the night, take our place smilingly in the day time among pure men and women, and go to church, maybe, on a Sunday" (Jordan and Sharp 2003a: 123). They expressed their disgust and contempt toward their clients: "it is shocking, disgusting, to see the crowds of married men, of middle-aged, of grey-haired fathers of families, who come to us" (Jordan and Sharp 2003a: 123). Butler drew a contrast between the class of women who were "sinful," but moral, and that class of men who hid their "sin" by pretending that they were morally superior.

Butler's rhetoric had the populist tendency to speak to anyone. Its character of wandering waywardly enacted what Rancière calls "literarity:" "It sets off anywhere at all, without knowing to whom it should and should not speak" (see Rancière in Davis 2010: 110). Although drawing on pain and injury, Butler resignified key aspects of women's agency in the Victorian political discourse. Her strategy gestured toward a positive future where sex workers are new political subjects. The risk in a policing rhetoric that deploys humiliation it to be dominated by a language of pain, suffering and fear, provided that the speaker does not put oneself at risk. Yet in Butler's language, women's agency—in particular, sex workers'—became a force to be taken seriously in the context of politics dominated by elite man. While she appealed to women's identities as "prostitutes," it signaled that political subjects could be actively involved in the "agonistic theater" of politics (Brown 1993: 408). If Rancière is right and democracy is not a form of representation, then democracy was enacted when Butler's speech did not make distinctions between forms of address. As a type of anarchist writing, her rhetoric rested on the capacity to wander freely and speak to all. Similarly, sex workers, even though they were deemed unworthy to speak, asserted their position of equality by refusing to accept the privilege of upper class men.

In the next section, I investigate Mill's opposition to CD Acts and compare it with Butler's tactical interventions in the prostitution debate. Although both Butler and Mill resignified traditional understandings about women's agency, Mill's refusal to build a coalition with anti-CD Acts activists is an example of policing activism.

Mill's Testimony against the Contagious Diseases Acts and the Policing of Feminist Activism

> No opportunity should be lost of getting rid of the different members whose votes are objectionable: and I cannot help thinking that if, in spite of all that can be done, the opposite party insist upon forming an independent Central Committee, and any of the members of the London Committee consent to join it in their private capacity, they should be requested to retire from the London Committee.
>
> (CW XVII: 270)

On September 20, 1871, Mill wrote to George Croom Robertson, a young philosopher whom Mill helped obtain a professorship at University College London. Because Robertson was also Mill's "man" in the London Committee for Women's Suffrage, Mill asked Robertson to get rid of Caroline Biggs, who intended to campaign for the repeal of CD Acts. Although Mill was in favor of the repeal of the CD Acts, he wanted Caroline Biggs to be excluded from the London Committee—or, to put it in his terms, "no opportunity should be lost of getting rid" of the "objectionable votes" of these women. Mill advised Robertson to eliminate Biggs and other members of the London branch of the women's movement from involvement with the Committee because they wanted to ally with Josephine Butler and other feminist activists who sought to repeal the CD Acts. Mill was worried that Josephine Butler's supporters intended to distance themselves from his political position and join the group of activists who were favoring non-traditional political interventions. For Mill, Biggs was "a quiet, steady opponent, who will betray you to the enemy, and take advantage from within of all your weak points" as long as "she remains in the Committee" (CW XVII: 270).

Mill had high hopes in 1870 about the success of the women's movement. Although he presented a petition in 1867 about the right to vote, which was defeated, a Bill giving women the right to vote was passed through the Commons in June of 1869; similarly, the Married Women's Property Act in 1870 gave women the right to hold property in their name after matrimony (Reeves 2008: 425). A Parliamentary Bill to remove the political restrictions on women was just prohibited from becoming law. Mill was thus very excited about the prospects of the progressive cause. He wrote to Charles Dilke, a radical politician: "I am in great spirits about our prospects, and think we are almost within as many years of victory as I formerly thought decades" (Reeves 2008: 429). Mill was also worried that the suffrage movement was linked to radical feminist causes such as the repeal of the CD Acts. As one of the founders of the London branch of the National Society for Women's Suffrage (NSWS), and as the author of *The Subjection of Women*, he was a powerful voice advocating in favor of the national feminist movement, but he considered that Josephine Butler's tactics were neither acceptable nor politically effective.

The appeal to harsh language was intended to persuade Robertson to take decisive measures against Butler's supporters. Because Robertson had to explain his decision to Caroline Biggs, Mill advised him to use "blunt language" and strong words such as "dismissal" (CW XVII: 275). More than that, he deployed severe words to describe his feelings toward Josephine Butler's sympathizers. The CD Acts activists were a "violent party," which lacked "consideration for the feelings of others," and who made "agitation for the suffrage vulgar and ridiculous" in the eyes of the majority of the English public (CW XVII: 269). Also, he believed that the general public would condemn the suffrage movement as being "indelicate and unfeminine" because of the repealers (CW XVII: 286).

By using harsh epithets such as "vulgar" and "ridiculous," Mill expressed his contempt toward feminist radicals, and his usage of these words became part of an effort to police political "enemies."

Radical feminists did not represent the feminist cause in a way Mill valued and appreciated. They discredited an important political movement—the women's suffrage movement—by exposing the unattractive side of the feminist campaign. In his letters, he made a clear separation between "us" and "them." "Us" were Mill and Robertson, who embodied "the advocates of moderation." The moderates were "farsighted" and "judicious" and realized the danger constituted by radicals. By contrast, "they," the supporters of abolishing the prostitution laws, utilized "common vulgar motives and tactics" to achieve their goal. "They" needed to be eliminated because of their behavior and tactics. Mill mobilized this binary, us vs. them, with political intentions. In his rhetoric, Caroline Biggs acquired a *policed identity* and became representative for the radical feminists. Biggs's identity in Mill's letters was shaped by her political allegiance, and her actions were interpreted through the narrow lens of her political sympathies. As an "enemy," Biggs risked indiscriminately pouring money into the CD Acts "agitation" (CW XVII: 259). Because Mill felt he had to defend his achievements and strategy, Biggs's role as an activist in the women's movement was relegated to a supporter of Butler's politics. Rather than imaging possibilities for coalition and grasping the force of radical tactics, Mill appealed to exclusion and humiliation to separate his politics from the threat of Butler's faction.

In my previous chapters, I showed that a liberal feminist model cannot capture Mill's employment of shame and humiliation. Shame—and shaming as it has been used as a strategy within this historical context—cannot be easily extricated from contempt and disgust. Because disgust and contempt need not to be excluded from political rhetoric, our task is to distinguish contextually between queer practices and modes of argumentation that police activism. The argument of this section is that the language of humiliation is counterproductive for feminism when it seeks to ban radical interventions and practices. I show here that, whereas Mill strategically avoided using harsh shaming in his public rhetoric against the CD Acts, he mobilized it against radical activists.

Like Butler, Mill viewed prostitution as being "evil." Contempt and disgust toward sex workers plagued some of his political interventions. Admittedly, this observation is not a new one within the broader context of Mill scholarship. Di Stefano (1991: 154–6) points out that Mill believed that disgust separates the lower from the higher classes of people. Zerilli shows that Mill's account of prostitutes is part of "a larger middle class cultural and psychological strategy" to "defend the bourgeois subjects against an abject social other" (1994: 136). Unlike Di Stefano and Zerilli, however, my interest is to illuminate the close association between different meanings of shame, which can hardly be thought of as reducible to strong binary dichotomies like the one represented by "respect" versus "humiliation." I focus on specific uses of performative slurs to achieve political goals and argue that Mill's use of shame and humiliation has relevance according to its particular context. His rhetorical strategy in the parliamentarian debates challenged previous norms about women's agency. He emphasized that rather than merely passive subjects of the state, women have the capacity to defend themselves and act against either controlling police officers or tyrannical husbands. His contributions to a feminist rhetoric in Victorian England were to resignify the notion of submissive women, underscore the larger social conditions of perceived social ills, and re-focus the debate on the male participation in the transmission of venereal diseases.

In 1870, Mill was asked to testify about the CD Acts. While it is not clear why the Royal Commission interviewed Mill, his opinion mattered. He was arguably the most prominent male feminist of his time, as he had voted against the extension of the law in 1866; in addition, his authority in the Victorian intelligentsia was "formidable" (Griffin 2012: 61). While his actual influence remains a topic of debate for historians, Mill was perceived as an important authority and source of legitimacy for the growing feminist movement. His arguments and public arguments influenced the way feminists articulated their political rhetoric and actions. While his impact was considerable, the extent of his power should not be overstated, as it still encountered boundaries. In Parliament, a group of radicals influenced by Mill and led by Henry Fawcett voted for women's rights. Despite this victory, Mill was not able to convince all the women's advocates of the validity of his view (Griffin 2012: 61). His position against the CD Acts was compatible with that of a moderate, parliamentarian feminist argument. Stronger arguments were made in the women's movement against the prostitution Bills. Unlike Butler, Mill did not argue that the male Victorian upper class should be ashamed of its participation in prostitution. More importantly, as Zerilli incisively points out, Mill did not defend the prostitutes because they were themselves at risk for infection (1994: 131). He did not argue that infected men not only transmitted diseases to their wives and children, but also passed such disease on to the prostitutes themselves. Unlike middle class women, the prostitutes did not constitute a subject of significant concern for some the women's rights advocates. Mill's caution and position as a politician shaped his rhetoric, and he consequently eschewed rhetorical tropes such as Butler's.

Butler and Mill's positions share common tropes but they also differ in some of their rhetorical accents. Like Butler, Mill argued that men—and not the prostitutes—should be held responsible for the costs of the CD Acts. He shifted the focus of the debate from an argument that blamed women for their immorality to denouncing men's participation in the transmission of sex diseases. Because men profited from prostitution, they should pay the costs that were associated with it. It was not the prostitutes that needed to be shamed and penalized, but the men who used them for sexual pleasure who should be held accountable. Like Butler, he also challenged the unfair treatment of women who were exposed to medical examinations and other types of surveillance by pointing out that men and women should be treated equally. If women are controlled and inspected regularly, then men need to be exposed to a similar treatment.

Unlike Butler, Mill's main strategy was to object to the Acts because they allowed for the abuse of power. He generally constructed his argument from the perspective of a civil libertarian who was worried about the extension of the state's power into the private lives of citizens. In addition to the standard arguments that Mill articulated in *On Liberty* about the right to have access to a private sphere and the limits of state's intervention, he claimed that the CD Acts were flawed based on utilitarian grounds. Mill's utilitarian claim was that the CD Acts multiplied the number of women involved in prostitution. For a utilitarian, it would be more efficient to repeal the Acts than to preserve them.

Whereas Mill's moderate position is different from Butler's radical stance, they share common concerns. First, Mill opposed the legislation because "it takes away" the security of women (*CW* XXI: 334). A woman could be taken before a magistrate and was liable to be imprisoned for refusing to sign a declaration. The main problem for Mill was that the police had significant authority to arrest women, and they could easily abuse this power. Mill's advice was that "we ought not to give powers liable to very great abuse, and easily abused, and then presume that those powers will not be abused" (*CW* XXI: 334). Mill was concerned that "modest women" could be arrested for prostitution and that the police would have loose criteria upon which to differentiate between a prostitute and a non-prostitute. Second, Mill objected to regular examinations of prostitutes because they did not allow women to defend themselves and to prove, for instance, that they were not prostitutes. Third, Mill's argument was that the Acts would lead to a greater amount of clandestine prostitution and that the Acts were not very efficient in realizing their goal. He explained his claim by noticing that, whereas some women could "withdraw from the profession," the vacancy they left would be filled by an additional number of women who would be brought into the profession (*CW* XXI: 345). If men felt more secure in utilizing the services of prostitutes because of the CD Acts, that fact and sense of security would "produce an increased demand for prostitutes" (*CW* XXI: 345). Fourth, Mill claimed that if a man infected his wife, then the wife was entitled to divorce him (*CW* XXI: 336). In the Victorian judicial practice, the right to divorce was not absolute, because the transmission of the disease did not have to lead to "complete dissolution of the matrimonial tie" (*CW* XXI: 344). Nevertheless, Mill advocated that the wife should have the right to divorce and to be entitled to financial compensations (*CW* XXI: 337).

These common concerns, however, point to why Mill felt he had to defend women, but that does not explain his opposition to radical suffragist tactics. Mill rejected the radicals' positions because he did not consider that they were *his* political responses. He made his evaluation clear by deploying various tropes that underscored his opposition to feminist radicalism. Unlike Butler's agitation, the London Committee was a "responsible and discreet body" (*CW* XVII: 259). The "unwise" feminists who sympathized with Butler, such as Caroline Biggs, were rejected because they caused "feverish bustle" or "feverish haste" (*CW* XVII: 259).

To preserve a given order in the women's movement, Mill policed the radicals and transformed them into enemies. This strategy appealed to a strong language to convince Robertson that specific exclusions were in order. It had the effect of both fragmenting an emerging movement and generating a split between moderates and radicals. His political strategizing was distinct from the defense of publicity in his previous work. As Zerilli shows, Mill's case against the secret ballot in the 1860s is based on the assumption that "the darker side of human character breeds in spaces of secrecy" (1994: 120). Mill felt that a certain degree of secrecy was in order to protect his London Committee. In his letters to Lord Robertson, he strove to distinguish his position from Butler's and others by requesting a "statement of reasons" so that he would show their "distinct differences of opinion" (*CW* XVII: 255). In the letter, he emphasized that his "statement" should be considered "private," because he wanted to avoid being exposed to the newspapers. He advised that Robertson should "vote simply against any new members of the London Committee" as they cannot be trusted, and "no reasons need be given." If Robertson needed a reason, he should argue about "the superior efficiency of a small Committee" (*CW* XVII: 255). The sharp dichotomies Mill uses, like the following binaries—responsible vs. haste, judicious vs. feverish, wise vs. unwise, good taste vs. vulgar—display his strong dis-identification from the radicals and their tactics.

What was Mill's relation with the actual institution of police? He worried about the nature of the police interventions and the lack of criteria to identify women. He was deeply concerned with the condition of working class women and sex workers. His concerns were justified. Mill's concerns with regard to the criteria of the police were based on the lack of clear analytical definitions of prostitution. While Mill deployed his usage of shame in a manner that proved different from Butler's shaming strategies, the CD Acts penalized any woman who was suspected of prostitution and required complex medical examinations. The boundaries between working class women, women living in non-marital relationships, single or married women with lovers, and prostitutes were not clear at all. Historians of sexuality describe an impressive amount of Victorian speculation about the exact nature of prostitution (Mason 1994a: 78–103). For instance, an impressive number of observations about working class girls (nursemaids, seamstresses, shop girls, and servants) show that they supplemented their income by occasional prostitution (Mason 1994a: 81). Many people lived in concubinage arrangements; in such non-normative relationships, "the woman's career has important affinities with prostitution or courtesanship" (Mason 1994a: 85). In addition, toward the end of the century, a new category of sexually transgressive women emerged, those "cultured women who lived on their own" but who took lovers (Mason 1994a: 86). When asked whether examining and licensing prostitutes were two distinct legal acts, Mill defended his objections to the CD Acts by saying that, for women, the distinction held some importance. When a person takes into account the feelings of women, then this consideration "makes a considerable difference" concerning whether women who are called to the police stations are called women or are labeled as licensed prostitutes (*CW* XXI: 339). Mill acknowledged that for the public the distinction was not very important; yet he argued that for the woman called to an examination, the point proved extremely important—as did the act of actually labeling them as prostitutes or not. While Mill articulated his position based on his sense of empathy with the "alleged" prostitutes, his rhetoric clearly differentiated between women who were legitimately at risk (prostitutes) and innocents who were mistakenly identified as prostitutes (middle class women).

Mill did not argue that the law is unjust because it violates the rights of prostitutes, but because it did not clearly separate between respectable and immoral women. By speaking for women, Mill emphasized the distinction between an identity ("prostitute") and a woman who had been called for medical examination. Like other activists and supporters in the women's movement, such as Josephine Butler, Mill took for granted a strong separation between respectable and depraved women, a distinction based on Victorian assumptions about class and gender that stigmatized working class women involved in sex work.

Because of his political activism on behalf of the women's movement, Mill's significance as a political thinker is hardly limited to that of being a paradigmatic representative of an "autonomous liberal individual." Arlene Saxonhouse argues that the rise of liberalism brought about a realm of privacy where "one practices individual freedom—a freedom from the intrusion and judgmental gaze of others" (2006: 79). Mill's *On Liberty* is, in Saxonhouse's view, an example of a liberal world that privileges privacy. By drawing clear boundaries around a private sphere, Mill articulates a space of "shamelessness," which "allows others to live free from those castigating glances of their neighbors" (2006: 79). Yet, Mill's liberalism proves more ambivalent and complex than Saxonhouse suggests.

Mill's opposition to the CD Acts demonstrates that, in addition to his concern about privacy, he was also willing to restrict and penalize the behavior of men and women. On the one hand, Mill drew on his defense of autonomy and privacy from *On Liberty* to argue his case in front of the Royal Commission. Two key arguments were deployed. First, women had a right to be protected from the intervention of the State, and they should not have been forced to act against their will. Second, even if the woman required help from the State, it is not the business of the State "to go out of its way" to provide facilities for the practice of prostitution. Women were entitled to a private sphere where the government should not impose its ideas on them. The government should not regulate activities that are only the concern of women. In front of the Royal Commission, Mill defended, as he did in *On Liberty*, the idea that the individual needs to be protected from the intervention of the government, and that women deserved to have the right to sexual autonomy.

On the other hand, he also claimed that penalties involving sexualities should not be placed on women, but, instead, on men. The focus of the CD Acts was to shame women and expose them to various invasive procedures that would limit the number of diseased people. Mill's strategy was to move the burden of proof from women to men, and also, to suggest ways in which the behavior of men could be restricted and penalized (CW XXI: 336).[18] By making this argument, Mill shifted the conversation about safety from women to men and showed that the object of the CD Acts—the prostitutes—should not be the target of social regulation. While in his previous interventions Mill's arguments were based on an individual's right to autonomy and to have access to a private sphere, his argument that men's sexuality needed to be regulated was based on the legitimacy of the government to be able to impose sexual control. Mill shifted the ground of his argumentation in his testimony against the CD Acts. Because the government had the (temporary) right to regulate people's sexuality, it should focus its attention on men.

Mill's argument was part of larger resignification tactic that challenged the condemnation of women's sexuality. Rather than accepting a narrow convention about women's role in prostitution, Mill refocused the blame on men. The CD Acts clearly involved invasive procedures that caused extensive mortification for numerous women. In a letter to Dr. J. J. Garth Wilkinson, Josephine Butler described in detail the pain and shame that women had to face when they were examined for sexual diseases (Jordan and Sharp 2003a: 21). For Butler, some of these interventions were similar to rape, because such interventions resulted women being "drenched in blood" and violated "with steel" (Jordan and Sharp 2003a: 21). Because of the shame, many women told Butler that, "I would rather go to prison than be examined" and "it is awful (both for the shame and the pain)" (Jordan and Sharp 2003a: 22). Mill understood the consequences of this type of interrogation. When one of the interviewers in the Royal Commission, Sir Walter James, asked Mill whether the personal examination was degrading and illegal, Mill recognized that the medical procedures could be very invasive and degrading for women, and more so for women than for men (CW XXI: 338). Mill argued that the very act of exposure was more shameful for women than for men, because "men are not lowered in their own eyes as much by exposure of their persons" (CW XXI: 338).

Notably, Mill's strategy of turning the object of shame from women to men was not just moderate; it also represented a complex political intervention that might have been different to execute in front of an all-male Royal Commission. While in his deposition Mill focused primarily on the sexuality of the prostitutes and the military personnel who were directly affected by the laws, he also gestured toward a broader critique of sexual practices in England. The activists outside Westminster argued that the Acts showed a powerful interest on the part of the male elite to have a "depraved access to women's bodies" (Griffin 2012: 101). Mill discussed the sexuality of people who were directly affected by the law, but he also used a variety of activist discourse tropes about the larger responsibility of the political elite regarding sexuality.[19]

The focus in Mill's strategy was to show that the Commission's attempts to blame prostitutes and brothel-houses for sexual illnesses was not justifiable. He wanted to move the argumentative thrust from being a message which suggested that "prostitutes are immoral and they need to pay for the damage" to consisting more of an attempt to understand the larger implication by and participation of the English public in the larger processes of the prostitution profession. In response to the question: "do you think prostitutes should pay for the Acts?" Mill stressed that, if the legislative measures were defended on the grounds of national health, then "it would be very fair that the English people should pay" (CW XXI: 338). When Mill was asked whether people should be taxed for the CD Acts, Mill responded that, if people want to be protected from sexual diseases, "the health of the community" was "within the province of Government" (CW XXI: 339). He stated the argument that by making the prostitutes pay for regulating their own sexuality, the government was avoiding its responsibility of charging the clients who benefited from prostitution.

Because he wanted to challenge the social and political convention that made men moral and women immoral, Mill's strategy of using shame was a queer practice. Like other supporters of the repeal in Westminster, such as James Stansfeld, he believed that men should pay for the costs of sexual diseases (Griffin 2012: 101). Stansfeld, a Liberal representing Halifax and a former Cabinet minister, was one of the leaders of the repeal and considered the Acts as legalizing prostitution. Both Stansfeld and Butler believed that men should pay for the costs of the related healthcare. Although Mill did not argue that the political elite was specifically to blame for diseases, he—like Josephine Butler—claimed that the general public was morally implicated in the proceedings of prostitution and that it should pay for health measures related to prostitution. For the defenders of the CD Acts, the prostitutes were the main cause of sexual diseases, and the government's job was to make the prostitutes bear the costs of the health problem.

Mill turned the tables on the CD Acts legislators and asked them to pay the costs that they identified as being the responsibility of the prostitutes. He also rejected the CD Acts because he thought that they represented the wrong intervention on account of their focus on prostitutes. He was asked whether prostitution was a moral evil. He responded that the sexual diseases were indeed "a great public evil" (CW XXI: 342). However, when pushed by the interviewer to agree with the necessity of the CD Acts, Mill refused to argue that these measures were justified; instead, he claimed that the State should accept the limits of its powers and that men should be penalized for getting sexual diseases:

> J. S. MILL: I think the State had better continue to suffer as much of that evil as it cannot prevent in other ways, by the application of military discipline and the correction of these practices among the soldiers.
> SIR J. S. PAKINGTON: Can you suggest any way other than that already adverted to, and which I have told you is already in exercise?
> J. S. MILL: You mentioned that the soldiers are liable to examination, but you have not mentioned, and I am not aware, to what degree, if the result of that examination proves them to be diseased, they are liable to penalties.
>
> (CW XXI: 342)

Why did Mill argue that people who engaged in illicit sexual acts should be "liable to penalties"? Mill's arguments about sexuality stemmed from a Victorian progressive view that male sexual needs were not fixed and that they could be improved by training. He shared the idea of the regulationists that sexual diseases produced highly negative consequences, and that the government should take measures to prevent the suffering caused by them. Nevertheless, though, his opposition to the CD Acts proved to be different from that of a conservative argument about the necessity of regulating people's sexuality. Conservative supporters of the law argued that the problem with sexual diseases was *not* a problem concerning male sexuality per se, but should only be focused on the sexuality of soldiers – or for "men drawn from 'among the lowest of population' and kept in an artificial state of celibacy" (Griffin 2012: 101).

Sexual moralism, which Mason describes as a mass movement with "tremendous ascendancy in respectable public discourse" based on anti-sensualism (1994a: 44), shaped Mill's ideas. While Victorian England was also a place for dissenting sexual cultures such as hedonistic cultures with numerous followers in London living by the creed "fucking is the great humanizer," Mill shared many assumptions of progressive anti-sensualists (Mason 1994a: 44). Anti-sensualism was "the creed of the forward-looking and optimistic: it had the aroma of modernity and change about it" (Mason 1994a: 284). The conventional explanation about Victorian sexuality was that anti-sensualism was a conservative, religious moralism with regard to sexuality. However, Mason challenged this view and argued that, for many progressives such as Mill, "an improved mankind is a less sensual mankind" (Mason 1994a: 285). Progressive anti-sensualists shared a "radical political programme" with regard to policies on sex that proved transgressive by conservative standards: divorce by consent, the acceptance of temporary unions outside marriage, encouragement of birth control (Mason 1994b: 118). Mill articulated most of the assumptions of progressive anti-sensualism, because he advocated for divorce under specific conditions, for the acceptance of non-traditional unions, and was a birth-control activist. While his progressive side led him to challenge conservative ideas about marriage and sexuality, he argued his position based on the logic that sexual restraint was superior to sexual drives (Mason 1994b: 10). His anti-sensualism becomes clearly articulated in a letter to Lord Acton, in which he writes that sexuality "will become with men . . . completely under the control of reason" (Mason 1994b: 9).

While Mill's opposition to the CD Acts stems from a progressive standpoint, his position cannot avoid including mortifying undertones. Zerilli shows that Mill accepted the view that prostitutes represented the "abject" and that the representation of prostitutes signaled the middle classes' fear and disgust:

It is not quite right to say, as Stallybrass and White do, that "the 'prostitute' . . . was *just* the privileged category in a metonymic chain of contagion which led back to the culture of the working classes." She was this and more—the abject: her condition, as the Royal Commission put it, was one of "absolute rottenness," her body "falling to pieces" (366). Sympathy for these "wretched women who haunted the camps" (368) slid repeatedly into middle class fear and disgust to produce the prostitute as the scapegoat for the haunting presence of the casual poor, and not least, for the disease that came back to haunt the bourgeoisie as the price for its ascendency to power (1994: 131–2).

Mill participated in the social articulation of prostitutes as the abject. He accepted the Royal Commission's view that prostitution was "evil" and that lower class prostitutes need to be represented as "degraded and demoralized, rather than as aggressive and sexualized" (Zerilli 1994: 133). Although his strategy was "an intelligent political strategy for combating sexual inequality," Mill sought to uphold a vision of Victorian femininity that marked prostitutes as despicable (Zerilli 1994: 130). In the process, contempt and disgust were part of how he differentiated between a "virtuous" and "vulgar" sexuality.

More importantly, not only Mill's political position was plagued by the harsh dichotomy between virtuous and vulgar sexuality, but he also employed insulting words for achieving political goals. As I showed in Chapter 2, Mill was primarily concerned with achieving the political right to vote for women, and felt that the "agitation" around the CD Acts did not help the passing of a voting bill (CW XVII: 278–9). He also did not agree with the type of politics that some repealers were promoting. The humiliating words that he used with regard to the repealers and their tactics, as well as the advice he gave to his protégé in the London Committee, shows that Mill utilized humiliation to eliminate those who opposed his ideas. Because he wanted to push Robertson to exclude the sympathizers of the CD Acts repeal, he expressed disgust and contempt toward them. Mill felt that the influence of the CD opponents was politically disastrous in the London Committee. In his view, the repealers were undermining his Committee because they cut its power with regard to other local Committees and made it "dependent on all the others" (CW XVII: 279). The other important political problem was that the many members of the Suffrage Society "disapprove[d] of the other agitation," and it was better for the London Committee to keep these political causes separate. Mill felt that he had to "stigmatize" a strategy which makes use "of one organization as a tool to bring money and influence for the other" (CW XVII: 279).

Because Mill was convinced that the two feminist causes should be kept separate, he wanted to convince Robertson of the necessity of "dismissing" Biggs. He believed that occasions like the one they faced asked for decisive actions. Because his "opponents" proved that they were not be trusted, Mill believed that the situation was "a battle," and that his adversaries did not deserve any generosity. Showing neither weakness nor kindness, political "enemies" should be eliminated from his organization by using "blunt language," if necessary:

> Nor, while I recommend the use of the mildest terms, such as "change" &c. in speaking of the dismissal, should I hesitate to use the word dismissal should it prove necessary: and it sometimes happens, more particularly

with the Manchester school, that blunt language is necessary for they can understand no other, and take the reticence of good breeding or kind feeling for signs of weakness of purpose. (CW XVII: 275)

Mill was not worried only about Caroline Biggs, but also about what he calls "common vulgar tactics" which have "been imported into the Woman's Suffrage Movement" (CW XVII: 276). He was worried that people in the Manchester Committee, which was a stronghold of the repealers, were advocating unpopular causes. He believed that actions such as Josephine Butler to make the Movement more appealing to the general public were corrupting the motivations of the activists. Although he argued that he did not want "to blame the various women who from motives of self-interest, of vanity or love of notoriety, employ such tactics," he felt that people "who condescend to no petty manoeuvres" should be stern and firm in their resolution (CW XVII: 276).

Both Mill's position toward prostitutes, and also, the strong language he used against radical feminists, showed what Foucault calls "a block of power relations" (1994: 283). For Foucault, a state of domination is when an individual or a social group manages to freeze power relations rather than reverse them. When those who are dominated cannot modify the asymmetry of power, freedom is harder to practice. Mill utilized harsh shame in his rejection of activists who employ "vulgar tactics," and felt that such an attitude was legitimate when his political ideal was threatened. Stigmatizing bad politics was necessary for achieving the goals of the London Committee, which, by "its calm and judicious conduct," offered "dignity and influence to the movement for Women's Suffrage" (CW XVII: 278). States of domination can be unblocked when one is willing to risk oneself, and as Foucault (2010: 12) argues in his description of parrhesia, even risk one's life. Coalition politics is not easy because it involves "trying to team up with someone who could possibly kill you because that's the only way you can figure you can stay alive" (Honig 1996: 267). Mill saw a coalition between the suffrage movement and anti-CD Acts activists as "suicidal" (CW, XVII: 286). This possibility of "death," which was also emphasized by Mill's worries about the ineffectiveness of the London Committee, made Mill resistant to any effort toward conciliation.[20] Mill privileged the idea of "dignity," as opposed to vulgarity, and refused to accept conflicts and harsh dilemmas within a space he wanted to control for political purposes. As a result, I argue that humiliation is not sufficient as a political goal, if we understand by humiliation only a deployment of insults and injurious language. It has to be attached to a queer practice of taking risks and to a strategy of creating political subjects.

Conclusion

I identified in this chapter two types of humiliation, one deployed as a queer practice and another as a tool of policing identities. On the one hand, performative slurs were articulated in the context of strategies to challenge narrow understandings about women's political agency in Victorian England. As Josephine Butler showed, humiliating people who were in power was a key strategy to confront traditional gender and sexuality dichotomies deployed by the upper class elite. Both Mill and Butler articulated risky political arguments that challenged and offended the political establishment. When activists put themselves in danger and their language aims at overcoming political hierarchies, humiliation becomes an act of speaking to all, rather than to a few. Because a queer practice is a political act that calls into question sexual and gender inequality, activists such as Butler and Mill utilized harsher shame to achieve their political goals.

Also, a queer practice is a process where those who have "no share" in the community struggle to be part of politics. August Blanqui named his profession as "proletarian" during his trial in 1832 because he wanted to make visible a class of people that was not seen, that is, the working class.[21] This tactic sought to demonstrate the equality of those who were not counted as part of the social order. In Rancière's interpretation, Blanqui became a political subject when he asserted the equality of the working class to other classes in nineteenth-century France. Mill and Butler resignified terms such as "men" and "women," which were deployed in a context of gender hierarchy, yet they felt reluctant to resignify slurs such as "prostitute." Unlike Blanqui, they did not become political subjects by making visible a class that was considered degraded.

On the other hand, humiliation was also utilized in the activists' rhetoric so that it strengthened hierarchies and diminished freedom. Mill sought to humiliate radical activists because he wanted the women's movement to separate itself from tactics that he did not agree with. He opposed "us," a moderate party, and "them," a party that made use of non-conventional tactics. Unfortunately, Mill's strategy of divorcing the two feminist causes undermined what could have been a process of building an alliance and reinforced a political conflict within the women's movement. Mill's single-mindedness about the political vote did not allow him to see that a coalition between the repealers and himself, although costly, could have been possible in the London Committee. A politics of agonism, which takes seriously the use of harsh and injurious language, has to be mindful about the context when humiliating language is used. Mill was clearly involved in conflictual politics and wanted radical feminists eliminated, but he was not prepared to think about the Committee as a space for political conflict. In this sense, he did not put into practice what Honig finds critical for coalition politics, namely that "when you feel like you might 'keel over at any minute and die,' when 'you feel threatened to the core,' then you're really doing 'coalition work'" (1996: 267). He seemed to have ignored that politics is an assertion of a wrong which itself creates parties in a political dispute.

In Chapter 5, I continue my analysis of feminist activists and thinkers but I focus on tactics to resignify abjected identities. The third counter-figure of my genealogy is shame as a line of escape. To show that shame introduces the capacity to dream about escaping disciplinary norms, I focus on Victoria Woodhull, a controversial nineteenth-century American feminist. She performed and theorized a political term, "free lover," which was used with shaming intentions. Woodhull utilized strong affective responses in her political life, and responded harshly to being shamed and humiliated because of her alternative sexual practices. She believed that a political strategy of exposing people's unconventional relationships would lead to sexual revolution. Although her strategy of outing had important drawbacks, it constitutes an important starting point to imagine the deployment of queer practices in politics.

Notes

1. For Tarnopolsky (2002: 20), Socrates serves as an example of a critical voice who possesses the power to destabilize established notions about the democratic city. Butler, like Socrates, wanted to disrupt the ideal image of the "just citizen" by showing that the magistrates participated in those very "vices" that they were called to punish.
2. Political theorists such as Tarnopolsky and Nussbaum view humiliation and stigmatization as politically illegitimate. Tarnopolsky argues that, unlike humiliation, *respectful shaming* offers a model of respect—or attaches dignity to shame—in a manner that incorporates "openness to discomfort and perplexity" that serves as a crucial part of democratic engagement (Tarnopolsky 2010: 166). *Respectful shaming* is modeled on Socrates' shaming interpellations that encourage Athenians to live more justly (2002: 109–13). Shaming opens up a space of discomfort that counteracts the politics inherent in "flattering shame," which is focused only "on the pleasures of mutual recognition" (Tarnopolsky

2010: 166). For Tarnopolsky, shame fulfills a positive function, because it destabilizes an image of omnipotence and normality that stifles any possibility of contestation of conventional notions about democracy. As such, a democratic conversation involves the painful shaming of one's fellow citizens as "part of an on-going project of collective deliberation and reflection" (2002: 185). Humiliation is illegitimate because "this kind of judgment is likely to be self-shattering and to involve a global assessment of the self as completely unworthy" (Tarnopolsky 2010: 156). It is also illegitimate because humiliation is associated with "subordination" and "associated harms" in pornography that threaten core elements of a liberal society (Nussbaum 2004: 139). For another liberal argument about the illegitimacy of using humiliation in public discourse, see also Margalit (1996).

3. For this strategy, see Foucault's description of Diogenes' actions (2010: 261).
4. See Davis (2010: 81–4) for a description of Rancière's reading of the roles of plebs in the Aventine Secession of 494 BCE.
5. I draw here on Wendy Brown (1993: 399); discourses that aim at constructing *politicized identities* and discourses that seek *transformative political interventions*. Drawing on Nietzsche, Brown notes that politicized identities are an effect of *ressentiment*, that is, "the moralized revenge of the powerless, 'the triumph of the weak as weak'" (1993: 400). The *ressentiment* toward the politically powerful produces multiple effects. It generates an affect (rage, righteousness) that "overwhelms the hurt," a person responsible for the damage, and "a site of revenge to displace the hurt" (1993: 401). *Politicized identity* is "premised on exclusion," is "fueled by the humiliation and suffering" imposed by its historical impotence, and is more likely to punish and reproach than to find "venues of self-affirming action" (1993: 403).
6. For Janet Halley, US feminism represents "a subordination theory set by default to seek the social welfare of women, femininity, and/or female or feminine gender by undoing some part or all of their subordination to men, masculinity, and /or male or masculine gender" (2006: 4). As a result, feminism is primarily a theory based on the subordination of women by men. Nussbaum articulates this vision of feminism when, for instance, she reads Mill as a strong ally of Andrea Dworkin. In Nussbaum's argument, had Mill acquired a more sophisticated psychology of emotions and desires, he would have agreed with Dworkin, for whom "fantasies of domination and subordination" led to the abuse of women by men (2010: 137). In this reconstruction of Mill's political psychology, Dworkin's cultural feminism that emphasizes the pain and injury of women is an improved alternative to Mill's feminism. See also Anne Phillips's (2001: 256–61) critique of Nussbaum's liberalism. For her, Nussbaum seems to sometimes endorse the view that gender is

a "detachable category," that she simply opposes "choice" to a world where one's life is dictated by others, and that she keeps in place a hierarchy where reason trumps emotions.

7. I work with the term *policed identities* rather than *politicized identities* because it better captures what Brown finds problematic in the notion of identities. The term *police* offers a stronger account of how identities are "effects of domination" that impose suffering through the production of guilt, through establishing suffering as the measure of social virtue, and through casting "privilege" as self-recriminating (Brown 1993: 403).

8. A queer feminist conception of agency focuses not on the type of subversive acts, but rather on its effects in a specific context: "the question here is not whether denaturalizing political strategies subvert the subjugating force of our naturalized identity formation, but what kind of politicalization, produced out of and inserted into what kind of political context, might perform such subversion" (Brown 1995: 55). Brown worries that a feminist discourse emphasizing women's victimization intensifies the regulation of gender and sexuality and assists rather than "contests" hegemonic forms of gender identity (2005: 91). Both Butler and Brown turn our attention to the political risk of a subversive politics. "Affirmative resignification" runs "the risk of re-installing the abject" as a site of opposition (Butler 1993: 185).

9. While in their strong versions, both Brown's and Rancière's theories seem to elide the potential of identities to create political interventions, critics showed that terms such as "women," "feminist," "gay," "queer," or "trans" can enact powerful politics. For a critique of Brown, see Bickford (1997). Also, see Davis's (2010: 88–90) discussion of the relationship between queer theory and Rancière's political subjectivation.

10. Like Catharine MacKinnon, Tarnopolsky and Nussbaum seem to share the view that language injures and that words constitute "a certain kind of conduct" (Butler 1997b: 17). As such, humiliation leads to harmful consequences such as self-shattering and subordination.

11. The sex workers' agency is, however, limited by the fact that Josephine Butler speaks for them, rather than allows them to speak for themselves. This gesture of appropriation is part of Butler's colonialist mindset that privileges the white middle class subject (see Burton 1992, for this argument).

12. See Walkowitz (1980); Kent (1987); Mason (1994a, b); Griffin (2012).

13. Mill was skeptical about interfering in the politics of other groups because he did not want the CD Acts repealers to have power in the London Committee for Women's Suffrage. Because he felt that political groups advocating for women should organize themselves, he advised Josephine Butler not to "waste energy" in "guiding the hand of others" (*CW* XXXII: 203).

14. Butler (1997b: 89) identifies performative interventions such as the use of language by subjects who have been excluded from enfranchisement. These interventions represent a "performative contradiction," because only by "seizing the universal language of enfranchisement" the conventions are exposed as narrow and contradictory. Performative contradiction is not a "self-defeating enterprise;" on the contrary, it represents "the continuing revision and elaboration of historical standards of universality proper to the futural movement of democracy itself" (1997b: 89).
15. See her comment on a prostitute's remark about the benefits of legalizing her work: "What a terrible thing, by legalising sin, to drown souls in perdition like this" (Jordan and Sharp 2003b: 78).
16. Like the language of "sin," the liberal language of "land ownership" could be either a weapon for challenging oppression or for supporting it, or it can be both simultaneously. In her conversations with Athena Athanasiou, Judith Butler (2013: 22–3) explores whether the language of "possession" works as a performative practice in the context of the Israel–Palestine conflict. She asks herself whether "possession" could be the name for a counter-movement for Palestinians, provided that such language naturalizes the subject as "one who possesses itself and its objective world." She suggests that political mobilization which appeals to the language of land property works "with and against traditional norms of sovereignty" (23).
17. For Mill's secularism, see his opposition to claims that are rooted in God and nature (Rossi 1970: 128).
18. See Mill (CW XXI: 336): "A woman can only communicate it [the disease] through a man; it must be the man who communicates it to innocent women and children afterwards. It seems to me, therefore, if the object is to protect those who are not unchaste, the way to do that is to bring motives to bear on the man and not on the woman, who cannot have anything to do directly with the communication of it to persons entirely innocent, whereas the man can and does."
19. However, Mill's argumentative turn, from shaming women for their sexuality to shaming men, is not unusual within the broader context of feminism's responses to discrimination. See the current laws that were passed in France (2016), Norway (2008), and the UK (2009) that punish customers who buy prostitutes, as opposed to punishing sex workers. Radical feminists achieved the repeal of the law before Mill's objective was accomplished. The CD Acts were repealed in 1886, after a hard-fought battle.
20. It was not until 1918 that English women over the age of thirty obtained the right to vote, provided that they met minimum property qualifications.
21. For a description of Rancière's understanding of Blanqui as a historical figure, see Davis (2010: 83).

Chapter 5
Shame as a Line of Escape: Victoria Woodhull, Dispossession, and Free Love

> It can now be asked: What is the legitimate sequence of Social Freedom? To which I unhesitatingly reply: Free Love, or freedom of the affections. "And are you a Free Lover?" is the almost incredulous query. I repeat a frequent reply: "I am"; and I can honestly, in the fullness of my soul, raise my voice to my Maker, and thank Him that I am, and [that] I have had the strength and the devotion to truth to stand before this traducing and vilifying community in a manner representative of that which shall come with healing on its wings for the bruised hearts and crushed affections of humanity.
>
> (Woodhull quoted in Carpenter 2010: 51)

In a speech given on November 20, 1871, in what was "the first free love lecture presented to Northeast audiences ranging from 2,500 to 4,000," Victoria Woodhull embraced the label of "free lover" which had been conferred on her, so she could resignify its meaning in a positive light (Frisken 2004: 126). Woodhull was the most prominent advocate of free love in the United States during the nineteenth century. In her speech, she asserted that she had "an inalienable, constitutional, and natural right to love whom [she] may" and "to change that love every day if [she] please[d]" (Woodhull in Carpenter 2010: 52). Her defense of free love appealed to the right to privacy, which she borrowed from John Stuart Mill's famous defense of individual rights in *On Liberty*.[1]

However, in addition to defending her position by drawing on her constitutional right to free speech, she then executed an unexpected move by reversing the accepted meaning of an injurious term—*free lover*—and transforming it into a term with positive connotations. Because the term *free lover* was used with the intention to harm, Woodhull's intention was to change a slur into a performative assertion of power. Although Woodhull pointed out that *free lover* operated as a shaming interpellation, she claimed that her enemies were unaware that the word was "handed over to us already coined" by associating the two most beautiful words "in the English language," free and love (Woodhull in Carpenter 2010: 53). *Free lover* became for Woodhull a powerful weapon to denounce abuse in marriages, the social and legal subordination of women, and organized sexual hypocrisy.

Woodhull's strategy of turning an insult into a term that she could use to wield power is similar in many respects to Judith Butler's celebrated articulation of individuals who are "critically queer." Like Woodhull, Butler investigates the critical potential of an insult to be resignified into an assertion of power (1993: 172). Because of its use as a "paralyzing slur" and based on its condemnation of "pathologized sexuality," the term *queer* becomes a tool of empowerment and "affirmative resignification" (1993: 169). While Butler is skeptical that resignifying the term—and articulating an affirmative meaning of queerness—eliminates its history of repudiation, *queer* is important because it becomes an instrument of "collective contestation, the point of departure for a set of historical reflections and futural imaginings" (1993: 170–3).[2] Although Butler is interested in queer both as a mark for "the *limits* of agency" and "its *enabling conditions*," the emphasis in her work is on turning away from past degradations toward a hypothetically positive future.[3] This positivity emerges from the affects' capacity to generate a different subjectivity, which is open to transformation and "being undone" by others (2004a: 20).

Queer theory offers a strong reflection about affects but Rancière gives us an important apparatus to illuminate antagonistic political tactics. In this book I argue that shame is what interrupts *the police*, and I do so also because Rancière's political vocabulary does not offer a direct conceptualization of affect.[4] While Rancière's use of the contrast between politics and *the police* seems to be "unduly rationalistic" (Davis 2010: 97), I appeal to queer theory to draw on the political potential of affects. Instead of appealing to a logic where individuals are seen as deliberate and in control, Butler urges us to think about the self as "driven by passions it can not fully consciously ground or know" (2013: 4). Shame—along with other terms that are associated with stigma such as guilt and melancholia—is productive because of the role it plays within the context of a democratic project.[5]

I interpret Woodhull's strategy of deploying shame as a line of escape and draw on scholarship that illuminated her role in nineteenth-century US political history (Frisken 2004; Carpenter 2010). In a genealogical project to unmoor shame from liberal theory, my third counter-figure is unconventional relationships. In living her life as a free lover, Woodhull produced a "line of escape" by making visible a different partition of what was sexually acceptable. In Rancière's thought, lines of escape are strategies deployed by non-normative people to refuse a hierarchical identity and create a stage for conflict. In his analysis of workers' history, he claims that "lines of escape" emerge for "those minorities who can no longer tolerate the labour of workshop, nor yet its manners and talk—in other words, can no longer tolerate *being a worker*" (Rancière 2011: 181). I demonstrate that Woodhull's role in exposing the Beecher sexual affair was part of her tactic to refuse the role of a "decent" woman. By disclosing the adultery of Henry Ward Beecher, who was a famous pastor and antislavery advocate, Woodhull set in motion the "most controversial sex scandal in the nineteenth century," known as the Beecher-Tilton scandal (Frisken 2004: 86).[6] Against a progressive activism that policed "promiscuity", she "proliferated strategies" by which sex radicals moved "in the space of the bourgeois and let their dreams wander there."[7]

Further, I contribute to queer feminist scholarship by identifying commonalities and differences between the rhetoric used by Woodhull and English Victorian feminists such as Josephine Butler and John Stuart Mill. Rather than accepting the negative consequences of living an unconventional life, Woodhull turned shame into a tool of political conflict. Woodhull's response to shaming became a unique tactic in the effort of nineteenth-century feminists and sex radicals to counteract the effects of stigmatization. Her innovative tactics offer an example of interventions that seek to challenge sexual norms, which exclude and silence sex dissenters.

In the first section, I analyze the role of shame in Woodhull's life as well as her conception of free love. Specifically, I focus on her public arguments and relationships that contested the ideal of monogamous heterosexuality. In the second section, I investigate Woodhull's strategy of sexual exposures and argue that it sought to interrupt a narrow conception of sexuality. I also show in the third section that her actions were met with strong negative responses from *the police*. Woodhull was jailed and banned from lecturing in some cities. Claiming that Woodhull's sexual exposures were dangerous, conservative activists passed a new federal statute against obscenity, known as the Comstock Law. Despite the interventions of moralists and advocates of proper sexual behavior, I conclude that Woodhull's strategy is a line of escape because it offered the possibility of imaging new types of sexual relationships.

Woodhull's Shaming and Sexual Transgressions

Woodhull was a radical figure in the history of the US women's movement. She deployed various political actions to criticize traditional assumptions about the presence of women in public life. Her actions unsettled accepted notions about women's sexuality. She advocated free love, the elimination of marriage as social institution, and the value of participation in democratic politics. In this section, I show that Victoria Woodhull was attacked and shamed for her advocacy of free love. I interpret her sexual transgressions as interventions seeking to offer legitimacy to new forms of intimacy.

Although Woodhull championed women's rights and the importance of love for human sexuality, her political ideas were plagued by ambiguities. Like English feminists who intervened performatively in political debates about women's gender and sexuality, Woodhull both drew on the assumptions of her time and contested them. Ambiguities and even contradictions represent, from this perspective, an inevitable feature of radical dissent. As Butler (1997a: 15) argues, disruptive interventions in normal politics are made possible by norms that one does not choose. Radical dissenters changed gender and sexual representations by articulating them in a new vocabulary and their interventions drew on representations that made them possible. While problematic, Woodhull's contradictions are inherent to progressive strategies of contesting conventional social norms about gender and sexuality.[8] Notwithstanding her progressive political goals, Woodhull believed that black men should be forced to wait for women to achieve the universal right to vote (Carpenter 2010: xix). She also excluded black women from the universal category of women (Carpenter 2010: xix). While she strongly advocated in favor of what we today call sex education, she condemned the practice of masturbation (Woodhull in Carpenter 2010: xiii). Victoria's journal, *Woodhull & Claflin's Weekly*, condemned abortion but favored birth control (Marberry 1967: 16). Woodhull's contradictions are important because they illuminate the ambiguous relationship that dissenters have with traditional conventions. Their politics does not only change traditional political norms, but also incorporates elements that are part of an exclusionary vocabulary that draws on the relation between gender, sexuality, class, and race.

Further, Woodhull's usage of the term *free love* expressed a dynamic imprecision. When she spoke about *free love*, she often implied that sexual non-monogamous relationships have great value. Yet, she also understood *free love* not as sexual but as spiritual love. *Free love* was opposed to crude and vulgar sexuality. The term *free love* had a contested meaning in the public discourse of nineteenth-century American politics. Joanne Passet emphasized the various usages of the term and pointed out that it could have referenced monogamy, chastity in monogamy, multiple partners in heterosexual relationships, or the denunciation of marriage.[9] As queer is used today with distinct intentions, the term *free love* was deployed according to the goals of various speakers. Many utilized the term as a shaming word to condemn various sexual and gender behaviors that were considered immoral. A free lover was adulterous or morally corrupted. By contrast, sex radicals mobilized the word to challenge traditional social institutions such as marriage and family. A free lover was an individual who chose to live freely against conventional sexual and gender norms.

Sex radicals resignified the word to undercut the shame associated with it. Some, like Woodhull, used the term in association with a strong connotation of spiritual love. Love was used as opposed to the satisfaction of primary instincts. Woodhull called for free love and freedom within sexual relations and condemned "free lust" (Carpenter 2010: xxii). In her writing, lust represents the "animal" instinct, which she views as the antithesis of noble, spiritual love (Woodhull in Carpenter 2010: 63). Many sex radicals argued—"to the displeasure of monogamists"—for the legitimacy of having multiple lovers (Carpenter 2010: xxi). Woodhull explicitly utilized the polysemy of free love to signify a higher, spiritual love, as well as non-monogamous relationships. She utilized this ambiguity to argue against her political opponents that free love has a higher value than traditional relationships.

The sexual politics of Woodhull led to vicious attacks concerning her feminism. Her political opponents shamed her. For instance, strong condemnations—similar to the caricatures that exposed Mill as a cross-dresser—were aimed at her sexuality. Illustrated sporting newspapers such as the *Days' Doings,* which sought to shock and entertain people, contributed to Victoria Woodhull's fame and that of her sister (Frisken 2004: 2). They presented the sisters primarily as sexually promiscuous, using a number of visual codes to suggest their weak morality. In Figure 5.1, a cover image of Woodhull and Claflin,

156   Counter-Figures

Figure 5.1:   The Woodhull sisters (*The Days' Doing*, February 26, 1870) (photo courtesy of Indiana University libraries)

her sister, shows them receiving clients for their broker firm. They are in their office and are surrounded by four men. The caption under the image is a combination of neutral and gender inflected language. The sisters are identified as "financiers," yet they are also labeled as "lovely" to clearly indicate their gender. The *Day's Doing*'s writers marked the sisters' establishment as "gorgeous" and intimated toward the similarities between their office and a brothel. The visual codes, however, tell a much stronger narrative about their sexuality. Claflin leans over the table in a very seductive position. The position of the man's hand next to her is very ambiguous. The reader does not know whether the man is merely gesturing with his hand or whether he is actually touching Claflin's thigh (Frisken 2004: 3). The sisters are depicted as being visually close to their clients; this portrayal opens up possibilities for intimate physical contact. The intention of the caricatures was not to present Woodhull and Claflin as professional individuals, but as seductive women whose morality was flawed. The caricatures sought to impute the sisters' politics on their alleged immoral behavior and prostitution.

Woodhull suffered greatly because she was depicted as a dangerous and promiscuous figure. She emphasized that she became a target for conservative advocates of sexuality, because of her outspokenness and fame. Her business as a stockbroker was severely damaged. Although she published materials about adultery in *Woodhull & Claflin's Weekly* that were published in other journals, she was imprisoned for a month on charges of obscenity. She lived "in comatose state" for many hours, because of society's judgment on her actions (Carpenter 2010: 196). She presented her life as shaped by "intense mental anxiety" and describes her condition in 1873 in *The Elixir of Life* as "pitilessly lambasted and caricatured in lewd and impossible positions by execrable artists, in the public press" (Woodhull in Carpenter 2010: 196).

While Woodhull was shamed by the conservative press, progressives who did not agree with her politics also attacked her. A renowned abolitionist, Harriet Beecher Stowe, in her serial "My Wife and I" in the *Christian Union,* introduced a character named Audacia Dangyereyes, whom most readers identified as Victoria Woodhull (Gabriel 1998: 105). For many Americans living after the Civil War, Harriet Beecher Stowe's writings embodied everything that was "good, womanly and sincere" (Gabriel 1998: 106). Her book *Uncle Tom's Cabin* had made her a literary luminary and a moral compass in the nineteenth century. However, Stowe depicted Woodhull in "My wife and I" as a "lusty, badly spoken political candidate and editoress of a newspaper called the *Emancipated Woman*" who coerced men to subscribe to her journal (Gabriel 1998: 105). Audacia's paper attacked "Christianity, marriage, the family, state, and all human laws and standing order, whatsoever" (Stowe quoted in Gabriel 1998: 105). Stowe rejected the sexual politics that undergirded Woodhull's writings and public speeches. She labeled Woodhull's politics as vulgar and violating decent sexual norms. For her, Woodhull was a mortal enemy to civilization and she believed that Woodhull's revolutionary politics would bring about violence and bloodshed. The writing in the *Emancipated Woman* was "coarse in expression, narrow in education, and wholly devoid of common decency in [its] manner of putting things" (Stowe in Gabriel 1998: 105). Like Stowe, Henry Ward Beecher denounced Woodhull and Claflin from his Plymouth Church pulpit as horrible examples of vice, and referred to them as "the two prostitutes" (Marberry 1967: 27).

Considering that the campaign against her and her sister portrayed them as vulgar and dangerous prostitutes, Woodhull understood the motivations of the critics. Her politics challenged both a conservative vision about the role of women in the public sphere and a progressive vision that endorsed monogamous sexuality as its ideal. She knew that moralists on both sides wanted to defend the sacredness of marriage. They mobilized gossip, whispers, and innuendoes to penalize her for transgressions (Gabriel 1998: 112). By arguing that men and women needed to be treated fairly, Woodhull was denouncing a sexual code that imposed a different standard upon women. In her public interventions, she lambasted the fact that men were allowed to have sexual affairs without penalty, while women were severely punished and humiliated for their sexual freedom. In her view, women should be treated according to the same standards as men when it came to choosing a profession or expressing their sexuality (Gabriel 1998: 112). Free love was a political term that called for a critique of marriage as the social institution with a privileged role in organizing sexuality.

Woodhull's presentation of her womanhood created a new subject of politics, which opposed not only the image of women as household workers, but also the assumption that women's sexuality should be policed by political figures such as Stowe and Beecher. She acted like a migrant that moved between classes, when she criticized both groups of moralizers. Like Rancière's (2011: 181) workers, she became dangerous because she introduced disorder where there should have been a class separation. The worker who, without having learned to spell, tried to make poems and dream about a different life, initiates what Rancière (2011: 181) calls "a line of fracture" into the class of producers. On such lines of fracture, a class—or a group of people—become dangerous, when they cannot tolerate being defined as "workers"—or in Woodhull's case, as "women." Because these new subjects of politics talk and behave in a different manner, they are not unifying a group but dividing it. This division, as Rancière (2011: 181) argues, "produces minorities." This process of creating a disagreement emerged when Woodhull articulated a "wrong" in the public space. And this wrong, which will be exemplified by Woodhull's exposure of Beecher, became a line of escape from factions that wanted to police her sexuality.

While Woodhull was attacked by both factions, she pondered about how to react to the various tactics designed to shame her. Her responses to a scandal in her family show that she was aware of the damaging effects on public shaming. In 1871, Victoria's mother brought Victoria's husband in front of the judge. She accused him of threatening to kill her. Victoria's husband, Colonel Blood, testified that Victoria's ex-husband, Dr. Woodhull, lived in the same household with them. Victoria was asked to explain the unusual arrangement in her life. This type of subject was a favorite topic for arbiters of public opinion, particularly because a famous advocate of free love lived with a husband and an ex-husband in an unclear arrangement. The attacks on Woodhull's morality were brutal and Victoria hoped for a long time that her ideas would speak for themselves. She wished that her reputation would not be tarnished (Gabriel 1998: 110). On May 22, 1871, she wrote a letter to the *New York Times* in which she explained her position:

> Because I am a woman, and because I conscientiously hold opinions somewhat different from the self-elected orthodoxy which men find their profit in supporting; and because I think it is my bounden duty and my absolute right to put forward my opinions and advocate them with my whole strength, self-elected orthodoxy assails me, vilifies me, and endeavors to cover my life with ridicule and dishonor. (Woodhull in Gabriel 1998: 110)

Woodhull realized that her ideas and life were going to be the subject of public humiliation. While she accepted the position of being a subject of public scrutiny, she explained that her former husband lived with her because he "was sick, ailing, and incapable of self-support" (Woodhull in Gabriel 1998: 110). She claimed that she felt that it was her duty to care for him, and that her husband, Colonel Blood, cooperated in this gesture of charity. Although she considered her act "one of the most virtuous acts of her life," various papers "have stigmatized her as a living example of immorality and unchastity" (Woodhull in Gabriel 1998: 110). Woodhull understood that she had to challenge the public perception, which typecast her as the sexual villain. Rather than accepting being humiliated by her opponents, she decided to fight with arguments in public interventions.

Woodhull's arrangement with Dr. Woodhull and Colonel Blood represents an example of a practice that proves oppositional to the existing conception of normative sexuality. Like Mill's arrangement with Harriet Taylor and John Taylor, which I described in Chapter 1, Woodhull's queer relationship challenged a restrictive conception of sexuality, and it did so by articulating the possibility of a queer temporality. The imagination of new sexual roles was disorderly, and it created a break into conventional expectations about intimacy. This arrangement was dangerous because it offered a large audience the possibility to dream, and this dream was useless "for the improvement of their material life" (Rancière 2011: 182). If straight time is a naturalized temporality, then queer time opens a different temporality, which is threatening because it contests entrenched notions of property.[10] This dream creates the impulse to queer "normal" time (Muñoz 2009: 25). Woodhull's arrangement contested the idea that a woman was the sexual and emotional property of one man; it opposed the assumption that a woman should not live in the same household with two former or present sexual partners; and it confused the boundaries between sexuality and marriage, and undermined the assumption that monogamous marriage was the only legitimate institution for intimacy. Like Mill's relationship with a married woman, Woodhull's relationship with two men was "a line of escape" from traditional ideas about sexual property.

While Woodhull was shamed and attacked for her domestic situation, she refused to play the role of a victim and scapegoat. Woodhull displayed courage, which Butler (2013: 67) argues represents a virtue in the practices of "crafting oneself." She claims that as some people struggle "against the categories of gender that secure contemporary ideas of personhood," they are involved in a mode of self-making or self-poiesis that risks "intelligibility" (2013:67). Woodhull lived in critical relation with norms that defined what was sexually intelligible. Yet, by advocating the legitimacy of free love, she argued for a particular recognition of her sexual freedom. Because she repudiated a hypocritical view of sexuality, Woodhull justified a living arrangement that unsettled public morality. As such, she did not want only to be disruptive but advocated free love to enlarge a restrictive monogamous heterosexual ideal.

Woodhull's example is particularly relevant in light of contemporary debates about kinship and legitimate sexual relationship. Many European and US citizens reject the conception of family that allows the adoption of children by same sex couples. Butler points out that families "who do not approximate the norm" are seen as unreal or less important than heterosexual monogamy (2000: 78–9). Her theoretical proposal is that relationships that fall outside such a model open up new ways of thinking about humanity and kinship. Butler's Antigone offers an example of a heroine who performs kinship as "a public scandal" (2000: 58).[11] The figure of Antigone unsettles the assumption that the violation of the incest taboo, which is associated with various sexual and gender transgressions such as gay relationships, should produce *only* horror and moral revulsion. Like Butler's Antigone, Woodhull's actions do not represent "an assimilation to an existing norm;" they "upset the vocabulary of kinship that is a precondition of the human, implicitly raising the question for us of what those preconditions really must be" (2000: 82).

Unlike Mill and Harriet Taylor, Woodhull made sexual politics the center of her defense. She admitted that she advocated "free love in the highest, purest sense, as the only cure for immorality" (Woodhull in Gabriel 1998: 110). In Chapter 2, I demonstrated that Fox, the Unitarian married minister at the *Monthly Repository*, was caught in a public scandal concerning his relationship with Eliza Flower. Mill and Harriet Taylor decided that they needed to defend their relationship without exposing it to the public. They also encouraged Fox and his lover to keep the relationship private. However, unlike Fox, Woodhull was not in the position to defend herself by denying the allegations. The details of her household arrangement were already public knowledge. Woodhull had to respond to the specifics about her intimate life, which had been made public by her mother. Silence was not an option for her. Woodhull wanted to tackle the sexual norms directly and acknowledged that she lived in a house with her husband and ex-husband. Unlike Mill, Woodhull was neither silent nor cautious in her use of sexual shaming. Unlike Mill and Josephine Butler, Woodhull disclosed the sexual practices of people who hypocritically attacked free love in public while they condoned it in private conversations.

When Butler discusses Antigone's performative intervention, she focuses primarily on mourning as a political gesture. For Butler, mourning functions as an act of recognition. Relationships that are denied legitimacy, or those who call for new terms of sexual organization, are prohibited from being publicly acknowledged and valued. Such relationships "involve persons who are restricted in the very act of grieving, who are denied the power to confer legitimacy on loss" (2000: 79). Butler theorizes mourning as a political act that defies prohibitions, which lead to "a socially instituted melancholia" (2000: 80). As I will show in the next section, and in contrast to Butler's emphasis on mourning, I find that Woodhull deployed shame to criticize a rigid organization of sexual roles. Her defense consisted of an aggressive strategy by which she could expose her critics as hypocrites and as closeted free lovers. The performative act for Woodhull was not to publicly mourn a sibling, as Antigone did, but to challenge the meaning of what counts as sexually legitimate in the public space. Shame constituted for Woodhull a mode of political action that compelled her to act in ways that she did not imagine prior to this event.

Shame as Dispossession

Woodhull's relationship with shame takes the form of what Butler and Athanasiou call a mode of dispossession (2013: 1–9). The concept of dispossession is constituted by a paradox. On the one hand, to be dispossessed means to be subjected to "processes and ideologies by which persons are disowned by normative and normalizing power" (2013: 2). These powers define what is intelligible and legitimate while they "regulate the distribution of vulnerability." It implies "injuries, painful interpellations, occlusions and foreclosures," which are modes of subjugation that "call to be addressed and redressed" (2013: 2). As I previously argued, Woodhull was exposed to shaming and various public injuries. She was depicted and attacked as a prostitute, exposed to public ridicule, and vilified as the embodiment of immoral behavior. Her critics defended a normative regime that was organized to uphold heterosexual monogamy, and controlled who counted as a legitimate public voice. But this normative regime evaluating Woodhull's transgressions was less an internalization of an ideological formation regarding normal sexuality than the fear about losing one's place in a given order. These attacks represented the response of those who saw a woman behaving in ways that did not fit with normative "womanhood" and sought to police what

Rancière calls "the flight that carried minorities of the working class to the other side of the cultural barrier" (2011: 205).

On the other hand, unlike the first side of dispossession, which is "forcible" and "privative," dispossession generates various performative actions by moving one outside oneself. Because one is not only a rational autonomous individual, one is moved by others in ways that "disconcert, displace and dispossess" (Butler 2103: 3). Once the self is conceptualized as driven by passions one cannot fully consciously "ground or know," shame generates important interventions in the public life. When an affective wrong is articulated publicly, then a stage is constructed for a disagreement to be articulated. By exposing the sexual practices of the political elite, Woodhull's goal was to challenge the idea that monogamous sexuality is a viable ideal. Woodhull considered "sexual exposures" to be a crucial weapon for achieving a fundamental transformation of North American society. The intent of political exposures was to interrupt conventional notions about human sexuality, which seek to repress new sexual and political experiences. Because it is a mode of dispossession, shame is therefore not only coercive and privative. It also generates new political interventions, which aim at undermining a narrow conception of sexuality.

In this section, I focus on Woodhull's disclosures of Henry Ward Beecher's sexuality. I identify the conditions and the historical circumstances underlying her political strategy, and also I compare her strategy with that of Mill's, Josephine Butler's and the *Monthly Repository*'s feminist tactics. My contention is that, because of the constant shaming that she had to face in public, she lived in a state of being dispossessed. Such a state was not only an impediment to her life, but also generated a sophisticated political intervention, which was the exposure of Henry Ward Beecher. Woodhull utilized outing as a political strategy to respond to her critics who denounced her practice of free love. In her view, shaming was not just an accidental by-product tangentially associated with political change; instead, it was part of a necessary change which must be enacted in order for justice to be achieved.

The strategy of resignifying the shame associated with immoral sexual practices is constituted by an ambivalent rhetoric. While Woodhull sometimes utilized the word prostitute in a negative manner, she also deployed it positively to challenge the view that married women were superior to prostitutes. Like W. J. Fox and the radicals at the *Monthly Repository*, Woodhull focused her attacks on marriage by describing it as an institution promoting loveless sexuality.

For her, marriage laws were prostitution laws: "The marriage law is the most damnable Social Evil bill—the most consummate outrage on woman—that was ever conceived" (Woodhull in Carpenter 2010: 218). She saw no "moral" difference between a married woman who lives with a man who can provide for her, and a prostitute, who becomes paid at the same price (Woodhull in Carpenter 2010: 61). She pointed out that the only difference between a married woman and a prostitute was "a licensed ceremony, and a slip of printed paper costing twenty-five cents and upward" (Woodhull in Carpenter, 2010: 60). She also defined prostitution as an activity that implied *more* than paid sexual intercourse. For her, prostitution meant "all sexual commerce that has not a proper basis in love and desire" (Woodhull in Carpenter 2010: 232). She claimed that many wives are prostitutes in their relationships with their husbands, because men wanted "sexual gratification without regard for the effect it had upon their victims" (Woodhull in Carpenter 2010: 232). Also, she did not use the word prostitution only as an indictment, but also as a positive term. Like W. B. Adams, the British radical from the *Monthly Repository*, she attacked traditional sexual norms. For Woodhull, a man who visited prostitutes was "accepted into society." If he was rich, he was "eagerly sought" by mothers and daughters for marriage. A prostitute, however, was considered too vile for beings "worthy for Christian burial" and was looked upon as a degraded human being. Woodhull wanted to sympathetically describe the condition of prostitutes. Because she drew frequent comparisons between married women and prostitutes, she claimed that many prostitutes were freer than married women. Her political and sexual ideal was free love, which meant a type of freedom that sidestepped the distinction between marriage and prostitution.

The focus of Woodhull's critique of marriage was sexual and social coercion, which represented a strong theme for sex radicals in the US. Her opposition to marriage was not only derived from the importance of individual consent in sexuality, but also from a critique of gender and sexual discrimination. In contrast with the English radicals, her rhetoric denounced particular groups of people (political elite, lawyers, priests) who benefited from discrimination and argued that an entire class participated and financially gained from prostitution laws (Woodhull in Carpenter 2010: 235). While the English radicals did not directly attack the priests collectively as a caste, Woodhull condemned their role in performing religious ceremonies. She suggested that even polygamy—or relationships with multiple sexual partners—would be a better situation than marriage. In her view, marriage existed because a group of interested people wanted to make money out of people's desires and passions. Priests made money "for forging the chains" of marriage, and lawyers "got bigger" fees for "breaking the fetters" (Woodhull in Carpenter 2010: 225). Coercive arrangements represented the foundation of monogamy. Because sexuality was a healthy practice when people were not coerced into participating in it, and because marriage was an institution founded on coercion, "promiscuous intercourse" was better than "monogamic intercourse" (Woodhull in Carpenter 2010: 247). While legal marriages presupposed oppression, free relationships undergirded by the ideal of free love were better than any type of coercion.

To achieve her objectives, Woodhull mobilized various feelings so that her readers would participate in the condemnation of inequality. Like Josephine Butler, she deliberately used a strategy of summoning emotions such as shame and anger. She sexually shamed the male political elite for their involvement in prostitution. Because politicians and lobbyists had money and time to spend on sexual favors, she argued that people who condemn prostitutes should channel their anger toward the "best men of the country" (Woodhull in Carpenter 2010: 235). She claimed that the bills regulating prostitution were wrong. For health reasons, it would be better to "deny admission" to men who visited the prostitutes. She argued that the prostitutes were not the agent of venereal diseases, but rather, that that role fell to the men who visited them. Men, not women, should be examined first in medical inspection: "Now if they really wish[ed] to stop these diseases and make the business safe, why [do they] not register and examine every man who visits these houses before he is admitted?" (Woodhull in Carpenter 2010: 235). Like Mill, she tried to channel people's anger on men rather than on women. The shaming of prostitutes was, for Woodhull, a political strategy that subordinated women to the interests of powerful men. Her response was to shame men for their involvement in what they publicly attack as immoral.

Like the English feminists, Woodhull wanted to disturb a narrow view of women's sexuality. She offered a positive meaning to shameful words such free lover and prostitute, which were utilized to silence and exclude. Yet, none of the feminists that I investigated in previous chapters used political outing as a response to shaming. Her performative tactic is a unique feminist intervention. In the words of a contemporary, the Beecher scandal "struck everybody, who was not familiar with the cool audacity of the author of it, with astonishment (Doyle 1874: 44).

Woodhull's disclosure of Beecher was part of a larger campaign to prove that social revolution was inevitable. In addition to revealing the adultery of a popular minister such as Beecher, Woodhull uncovered the sexual debauchery of a Wall Street broker, Luther Challis. Woodhull also accused the conservative editor of a Spiritualist journal, the *Religio-Philosophical Journal*, S. S. Jones, of supporting a mistress.

The exposure of Beecher, Challis, and Jones was part of a larger political tactic that her allies, sex radicals, used in a campaign to establish "what they call[ed] a single standard for all" (Frisken 2004: 86). The sex radicals were "an uncompromising network" of people, who "saw the sexual liberation of women as key to all other reform" (Frisken 2004: 14). They demanded "plain speech" about the subject of human sexuality and continued to struggle to make information about human sexuality available in the public sphere (Frisken 2004: 15). Like the sex radicals, Woodhull was neither interested in criticizing adultery, nor in seeking revenge against the accusations directed toward her of being shameless. Disclosures were primarily an act of justice that challenged a widespread culture of sexual secrecy. Like other sex radicals such Henry T. Child, she believed that "the bubble reputations which we are seeking are too often a cloak for hypocrisy and conceit" (Child quoted in Frisken 2004: 86).

Exposing and troubling the conventional norms about sexuality was an act that required a stage. This new stage was needed because political spaces were organized so that they did not make visible the reality of sexual practices that were *not* monogamous and respectable. Woodhull's exposure is, in this sense, a theatrical act. A marginal on the political scene and a free lover, she pretended that she was already equal with her political targets, and as such, an equal participant to a political process from which, in fact, she was excluded. As Rancière emphasizes, the *sans-part* have to be actors because they need to pretend that "[they] are something [they] are not in order to become it" (Davis 2010: 86). The *sans-part* need to construct a common space that was not there before, and in this process they become political subjects. This new political scene allowed the sex radicals to show that people's imagination can wander in those spaces where conventional sexuality demarcated between proper and immoral.[12]

When she talked about the details of Beecher's affair, Woodhull's intention was to show that marriage, like slavery, was an institution that supported a system of organized injustice. Like slave owners, people who benefitted from marriage needed to be publicly denounced. Shaming Beecher became a key tactic for those who had been excluded from living a livable life. Beecher himself was not unfamiliar with resignification tactics that produced a political stage. Like many progressives and abolitionists, he directed theatrical performances that offered portrayals of the slave auction, which at the time were known as "mock auctions." He used this mock auction technique several times to raise money and appeal to the good conscience of the North.[13] By exposing Beecher as a "hypocrite," Woodhull appealed to the same tradition of moral perfectionism that undergirded Beecher's mock auctions (Frisken 2004: 87). Sex radicals like Woodhull shared with Beecher the conviction that exposing people's immorality would help "cleanse the social order" (Frisken 2004: 87). In her statement, Woodhull argued that the act of exposure is comparable in its "criminality" to the act of liberating a slave (Woodhull in Doyle 1874: 32). As such, Woodhull considered her action of exposing Beecher to be as subversive as liberating slaves.

Various rumors about Beecher's sexual infidelity circulated not only in Brooklyn—where Beecher's church, Plymouth Church, was situated—but also within different groups of the women's movement (Doyle 1874: 13). Woodhull claimed that she had discovered the details of the sexual affair from two renowned women's rights advocates, Pauline Wright Davis and Elisabeth Cady Stanton (Carpenter 2010: 110–11). At the beginning of the scandal, she knew "of one man, a public teacher of eminence, who lived in concubinage with the wife of another public teacher of almost equal eminence" (Woodhull in Gabriel 1998: 111). Later, she hinted in some of her public interventions that a famous pastor who was privately supporting free love had had an affair with the wife of a famous journalist, Theodore Tilton. However, the charges were not made explicit and detailed until November 2, 1872, when Woodhull chose to present a full condemnation of Beecher in an article published in *Woodhull & Claflin*. Woodhull began her piece by arguing that her article would "burst like a bomb-shell into the ranks of the moralistic social camp," because it was "a series of aggressive moral warfare on the social question" (Woodhull in Doyle 1874: 14). It was a revolutionary act targeting the institution of marriage, which "as a *bond* or *promise* to love another to the end of life, and forego all other loves or passional gratifications, ha[d] outlived its day of usefulness" (Woodhull in Doyle 1874: 14).

Her case against marriage was based on the idea that people already lived by the ideal of free love. Marriage was a relict of the past that "most intelligent and really virtuous [...] citizens ha[d] outgrown," and as such, they despised it as representing another form of slavery

(Woodhull in Doyle 1874: 14). People only submitted to the appearance of fidelity because they feared the shame of public opinion, which "no longer represent[ed] the convictions of anybody" (Woodhull in Doyle 1874: 14). Woodhull's rhetorical strategy was powerful because she appealed to the antislavery rhetoric of Beecher. People needed to see the institution of marriage as similar to slavery; like slavery, she argued, marriage was going to be replaced by other forms of social arrangements. She justified her disclosure for the role it played as part of a larger social revolution that would lead to the elimination of both slavery and marriage. Until the social revolution would be completely realized, people would live in immoral arrangements (Doyle 1874: 15). They "tremble[ed] on the brink of the revolution and hesitate[ed] to avow their convictions," and they acted upon free love while "'professing obedience' to old institutions" (Woodhull in Doyle 1874: 15). An "organized hypocrisy" took over modern societies. Woodhull framed the exposure of Beecher as an act of justice and saw herself a person who would lead the movement in announcement of the "higher order of life" (Woodhull in Doyle 1874: 15).

Woodhull took an act that was generally seen as immoral, adultery, and resignified it as positive. As Butler argued in her work, performativity holds an important political promise, which is that a speech act takes a "non-ordinary meaning" and functions in contexts where "it has not belonged" (1997b: 61). Woodhull's disclosure exposed the invisibility of people whose sexuality was condemned. While conversations about adultery were supposed to be kept private in the United States in the nineteenth-century, Woodhull made the subject a political topic. Also, she made people dream that the demarcation between proper and improper sex could be interrogated and disturbed in a public conversation.

Woodhull spoke for the first time about Henry Ward Beecher's affair at the National Association of Spiritualists, in September 1872 at Boston. The movement for free love was in bad shape: "the press refused all notice of the new reformatory movement;" the sisters were in a desperate struggle for "mere existence;" Woodhull's candidacy for presidency was unnoticed; and "a new batch of slanders and injurious innuendos permeated the community in respect to my condition and character" (Woodhull in Doyle 1874: 22). The anxiety about her career and the free love movement were high. She felt she was "distrusted and unpopular," with "no consolation but the consciousness of having striven to do right" (Doyle 1874: 22). For Woodhull, the decision to expose Beecher's affair came as an act of inspiration: she described her state as being "taken out" of herself (Doyle 1874: 22). The exposure was not her conscious decision because it came from a place that was unknown to her. In a rhapsody of "indignant eloquence," she divulged the details of the Tilton and Beecher story. This moment shows that shame does not only injure but also generates performative action—or what Butler calls "insurrectionary speech" (1997b: 144). Insurrectionary speech is speech that is unpredictable. It demonstrates that agency is not only the agency of the rational subject. It breaks with the presumption of the sovereign subject because it unsettles the assumption that autonomous agents cause their actions.

While she described herself as "inspired" when she decided to act, Woodhull began to reflect more deeply about the tactic which she chose to promote. Because she took outing seriously as a political strategy, she had to study the history of reformers to see whether the use of this strategy had been justified in the past. Like Josephine Butler, she understood that William Lloyd Garrison, a prominent abolitionist, offered an important lesson to progressives by not attacking slavery in the abstract, but by making it particular to "great and influential men, North and South, in the community" (Woodhull in Doyle 1874: 16). People's reputations had to be tarnished during a social revolution. Because Garrison "pointed out and depicted the individual instances of cruelty," he "dragged to light and scathed and stigmatized the individual offenders" (Woodhull in Doyle 1874: 16). Sexual exposures, from a gesture of indignation, became a strategy of political "warfare." She learned from Garrison how to utilize actual and vivid pictures of cruelty and how to mobilize public opinion against atrocities (Woodhull in Doyle 1874: 16). In short, she realized that political shaming was a justified tactic to advance her cause. Her insurrectionary speech sought to expose the hypocrisy of marriage and broaden a narrow view about human sexuality.

Woodhull's actions, which were deployed in a moment of political passion, were imagined as a contribution to a larger social movement. She believed that the Beecher scandal would have powerful effect on the Socialist cause in the US. In her view, the institution of marriage would be superseded because of the viability of "new socialistic arrangements" (Doyle 1874: 15). While she believed in the aims of the radical Socialism, she recognized that it was a risky strategy. Challenging conventional norms about sexuality by mobilizing affects could generate a strong backlash. By drawing on William Garrison's experience with social reform, she explained that she learned from his experience as a radical fighter against slavery. People shamed Garrison and refused to listen to his ideas.[14] Similarly, people could see Beecher and others as victims; in fact, they denounced her as "a malignant and cruel wretch for not covering up scenes too dreadful to be thought upon" (Woodhull in Doyle 1874: 17). Although people would be shocked and feelings would be hurt, Woodhull believed in social reform and drew comfort from the work of the "brave old cyclops," who "hammered away at their anvils," "forging thunderbolts of the gods" (Woodhull in Doyle 1874: 17). Because Woodhull assumed that her actions were justified as part of a larger revolution, she argued that "every revolution ha[d] its terrific cost, if not in blood and treasure, but then still in the less tangible but alike real sentimental injury of thousands of sufferers" (Woodhull in Doyle 1874: 16). The sex scandal was a sign of an age that was "pregnant with great events" and could become "the crack of doom to our old and worn out, and false and hypocritical social institutions" (Woodhull in Doyle 1874: 40). As a "messenger of a new world," Woodhull deployed political outing to unleash new political energies.

Woodhull justified outing as an act of denouncing hypocrisy and condemnation of political cowardice. Shaming was a critical tool in the toolkit of an "agitator" and "social revolutionist" to fight against marriage, which pushed everybody into living a false life. Her actions were at the heart of a movement aiming at reforming social and gender relations. In her story about Beecher, she did not condemn men because of their sexual practices, but because of their hypocrisy. Henry Beecher "had done the very best which he could do under the circumstances—with his demanding physical nature, and with the terrible restrictions upon a clergyman's life, imposed by that ignorant public opinion about physiological laws" (Doyle 1874: 24). She admired "the immense physical potency of Mr. Beecher," his urgency for intimacy, and "the embraces of the noble and cultured women" (Doyle 1874: 40). Woodhull did not condemn Beecher because of his adulterous relationships with another woman. Beecher's capacity for love "[was] one of the noblest and grandest of the endowments of this truly great and representative man" (Doyle 1874: 40). Because he, like Woodhull, believed in free love, she denounced him because

> he ha[d] permitted himself to be over-awed by public opinion, [and he had] profess[ed] to believe otherwise than as he [did] believe, [and he had also] helped to maintain for these many years that very social slavery under which he was chafing, and against which he was secretly revolting both in thought and practice. (Doyle 1874: 40)

She criticized him for being a "poltroon, a coward and a sneak," not for anything he had done, but for failing "to stand shoulder to shoulder with [her] and others who [were] endeavoring to hasten a social regeneration which he believe[d] in (Doyle 1874: 40).

Although Woodhull argued that she was the "champion" of the "very right to privacy and of individual sovereignty," she used "means" that were legitimate during war (Woodhull in Doyle 1874: 38). Because she saw a war existing between conformism and social revolutionaries, she perceived Beecher either as her "auxiliary in a great war for freedom" or as "a violent enemy and a powerful hindrance to all that I am bent on accomplishing" (Woodhull in Doyle 1874: 38). She apologized to Beecher for interfering in his life. In her view, Mr. Beecher's congregation did not have the right to know the details of a private affair. Nevertheless, like Josephine Butler who portrayed herself as a female Christ, she needed to bring "not peace but sword." While she was convinced that Beecher had the right to privacy, she also "[had] to invade the most secret and sacred affairs of his life, and drag them to the light and expose him to the opprobrium and vilification of the public." Because the social cause trumped privacy, Woodhull had ideological legitimacy and authority to perform such political evisceration.

By outing Beecher, Woodhull exposed the norms of intelligibility that constructed a particular kind of sexuality as central to human life. She made visible that heterosexual monogamy was a powerful, albeit changeable, political norm. It showed that people live in various relationships that are not included within traditional institutions such as marriage. In addition, her actions indicated that conventional norms could be opposed and resignified. By using the term free love, she intended to transform an insult into a positive interpellation. She believed that shame could become a positive weapon in a struggle against a narrow conception about sexuality and gender. Rather than perceiving shame as an impediment to imagination, Woodhull shows that shame has a productive and performative capacity. As such, shame is not only the fear of producing "the new," of changing what is taken for granted as an established convention. Like the term identity in Butler's work, shame is neither a "natural" nor a "fixed" concept (1999: 201). Woodhull showed that shaming could generate alternatives to nineteenth-century conventional politics. Her tactic of shaming "hypocrites" was designed to disrupt and radically alter established notions about sexuality.

The Police and How to Close the Lines of Escape

In the previous section I showed that shame had two major effects on Victoria Woodhull. On the one hand, public shaming led to injuries and suffering in her life. On the other hand, shame generated political interventions that interrupted a conventional normative view about sexuality. Like Butler's theoretical account of "queer," Woodhull's conception of a "free lover" was mobilized to create new political alternatives. Her public actions undermined a puritanical vision about women's sexuality. Woodhull's outing was a powerful act of political subversion, because she wanted to expose the sexual hypocrisy of the upper class social elite. While she intended to advance the cause of sexual dissenters, she did not anticipate the magnitude of the conservative opposition to her ideas. Her opponents put her in jail and passed a law, the Comstock Act, which made it illegal to send obscene materials through the mail.

Along similar lines, the strategy of transforming the word "queer" into a positive term involves risks. Butler was aware of the risk of utilizing an "impure" material for such conversion:

> Performativity describes the relation of being implicated in that which one opposes, this turning of power against itself to produce alternative modalities of power, to establish a kind of political contestation that is not "pure" opposition, a "transcendence" of contemporary relations of power, but a difficult labor of forging a future from resources that are inevitably impure. (Butler 1993: 184)

Although Butler understands that recuperating the word queer for its use in future actions is not a "pure" strategy, she emphasizes that these interventions oppose rigid gender norms. While creative tactics such as political exposures have their undesirable consequences, they are important because they seek to create a larger space for alternative sexual and gender behaviors.

While women often felt sexual disgust because marriage was a coercive institution, Woodhull believed that their feeling of disgust can lead to new possibilities for intimacy. Married women had to live with sense of disgust and powerlessness. Marriage was the only institution "among pretendedly enlightened nations" that gave men the right to rape. It submitted women's' bodies to unwanted fluids:

> Compelled to submit their bodies to disgusting pollution! Oh, Shame! where hast thou fled, that the fair face of womanhood is not suffused with thy protesting blushes, stinging her, at least into self-respect, if not into freedom itself! Am I too severe? No, I am only just. (Carpenter 2010: 219)

Disgust and shame not only produced powerlessness, but also served as a resource to women's empowerment. In Woodhull's public speeches, her rhetorical move was to transition from women's disgust to women's realization that shame leads to political freedom. "Pollution" was a word that marked the reprehensive quality of sexual intercourse. It exposed its disgusting nature when one was coerced into it. Woodhull's exclamation, "Oh, Shame!" revealed the strong relationship between disgust and shame. It suggested that a "pure" body was touched by the corrupted influence of male force. The act of obligatory intercourse was associated with pollution and disgust, and proved shameful. At the same time that she recognized this negative dimension of shame, Woodhull also invoked shame as a possible resource for change. Shame triggered "protesting blushes," which had the effect of "stinging," or calling for particular forms of response and action. For Woodhull, shame led to "self-respect" and "freedom." Women could gain sexual autonomy if they could understand that men use women's bodies to leave them "degraded, debauched and diseased" (Woodhull in Carpenter 2010: 219).

In a short vignette, Woodhull offered an example of how shame acquires this ambivalent nature. She described a casual conversation with a married woman about sexuality and promiscuity. Both she and her interlocutor were traveling. Because the married woman had heard about Woodhull's life and political beliefs, she asked her whether she was promiscuous. Woodhull told her that, in order to answer the question, she needed to know whether she had sexually known other people than her husband (Woodhull in Carpenter 2010: 230). The woman answered affirmatively, and said that she lived at the moment with her fourth husband. Woodhull replied with "affected disdain," "Madame, you are altogether too promiscuous for me" (Woodhull in Carpenter 2010: 230). Woodhull utilized this conversation in one of her most famous speeches about free love to show that shame can be transformed in an expression of power. Rather than accepting the terms of the question, namely that she, unlike the respectable woman, was promiscuous, she turned the table against this conception of sexuality. She demonstrated that most people live a sexual life that they are willing to condemn in others. She did not allow herself to be sexually shamed, and criticized "hypocrites" who imposed a false morality by revealing their own immorality.

While she strongly asserted her political convictions in public settings, a strategy of political outing had important risks. The exposure of Beecher led to an important conservative backlash against free speech about women's sexuality. Woodhull and her friends anticipated that "some kind of legal action would follow the exposure" (Frisken 2004: 87). She even knew that her piece in *Woodhull & Claflin's Weekly* about Beecher would leave her vulnerable to prosecution for libel. Yet, she expected neither the intervention of the federal government, nor her prosecution under an obscenity statute (Frisken 2004: 87). Her strongest adversary was Anthony Comstock, a New York dry-goods salesman. Comstock, acting in the interest of public morality and backed up by the Young Men's Christian Association (YMCA), wanted to punish Woodhull and her sister for the exposure. Although Comstock failed to convince the state attorney to proceed against the sisters, he obtained a federal warrant for their arrest, had federal marshals take them into custody, and imprisoned them in Manhattan's jail (Frisken 2004: 95). At the hearing in a federal court, Assistant US District Attorney Noah Davis commented that "the defendants had not only circulated obscene literature, but they had attacked in a most abominable manner the character of one of the best and purest citizens of the United States, and that it was well worthwhile for the Government of the Unites States to vindicate him" (Davis quoted in Frisken 2004: 96). Woodhull and her sister were not the only sex radicals who were indicted by Comstock. Freethinkers such as George Francis Train were arrested for publishing controversial material and thrown into jail (Frisken 2004: 103). Woodhull and Claflin's imprisonment shows both the high personal costs of individuals who challenged traditional notions of sexuality and the damaging consequences of sexual shaming.

In addition to being jailed, Woodhull was prohibited to lecture in Boston by Massachusetts governor, William Claflin. Beecher's sister, Harriet Beecher Stowe, probably influenced the decision (Frisken 2004: 104). In their indictment of Woodhull, the federal attorney, Noah Davis, argued that they had a moral obligation to stop sex radicals such as Woodhull. Similarly, the governor of Massachusetts emphasized that Woodhull represented a public danger for Boston:

> We have enough bad women in Boston now, without permitting this one to come here to further demoralize us. Why, she might even repeat the vile stories about Mr. Beecher, or even attack some of us in Boston. No, sir! This can not be permitted. (Davis in Frisken 2004: 104)

Because of her outspoken sexual opinions, and because of her use of sexual shaming, Woodhull became an enemy to people like William Claflin who wanted to protect public morality. In his justification of the ban, the governor emphasized that Woodhull was not only dangerous for her opinions, but also because she could attack "us." In his view, sexual shaming was a strategy that could become a powerful enemy, and only the act of banning Woodhull could prevent her from condemning him, as well as other public figures. The Beecher affair resulted not only in Woodhull being banned from lecturing in some cities, but also in the passing of a new federal statute against obscenity, known as the Comstock Law (Frisken 2004: 122). The law against obscenity included newspapers, and Comstock assumed unprecedented federal censorship powers. Conservative politicians used Woodhull's example to propose new federal regulations of obscenity.

The police are not only the expected usual suspects, but also presumed allies. Woodhull was attacked not only by the conservative establishment, but also by other sex radicals. After the exposure of Beecher, Joseph Treat, a veteran of Ohio's free love community, contested Woodhull's credentials and accused her of prostitution. He claimed that Woodhull and her sisters prostituted themselves in times of financial hardship (Frisken 2004: 112). By using Woodhull's argument that free speech should be a protected value, he claimed that "any attempt to prevent [my exposure], will be already more than Free Speech—will be *Confession*" (Treat in Frisken 2004: 112). Of Victoria, Treat wrote that she sold herself for money:

> Last March, on your Chicago trip, Colonel not being with you, you rode in a sleeping-car with a prominent business man of Boston, well known also in this city . . . He said the conversation mutually recognized the fact that you were one thing on the platform, and another off it. "And what do you charge a night when you are not on the platform?" said he. "Two hundred and fifty dollars." He paid it and then and there mingled the rushing tide of his life with yours. ("Elect to End Party Politics")

In his exposure of Woodhull, Treat used the same justifications that Woodhull utilized against Beecher. He accused Woodhull of being a hypocrite; that is, he claimed that her discourse and her actions were in conflict. He argued that the exposure was done "in good faith," and that he was compassionate toward the people he indicted (Frisken 2004: 112). However, Treat wanted to discredit Woodhull as an advocate of free love.[15] Woodhull was in the difficult position of defending her reputation while asserting her support for the principles of sexual honesty. Treat's attack on her—and his accusation that she was a prostitute—shows the danger of using humiliation in a public discourse. While Treat claimed that he wanted to emancipate

Woodhull, political outing became a strategy of discrediting people's reputation and contesting their moral authority.

Yet, the conservative uses of sexual exposures—and its reappropriation by people who wanted to harm Woodhull—does not represent a convincing argument against employing exposures to challenge traditional norms about women's sexuality. Butler (2004a: 223) showed that resignification can be either mobilized to generate radical democratic actions or uphold restrictive political norms. The justification of resignification depends on the context and the political goals of a particular act. Whereas Woodhull exposed Beecher's sexuality to broaden a monogamous political mindset, Treat sought to depict Woodhull as a prostitute. Woodhull mobilized exposures to enlarge narrow sexual norms, while Treat wanted to enforce binary distinctions such as prostitute vs. free lover. The tactic of sexual exposures should be also evaluated by investigating the historical consequences of its impact. Woodhull was taken by surprise when she understood the strength of the opposition against her actions. She neither anticipated she would spend time in jail, nor the costs she had to pay for her actions. She was neither responsible for the Comstock laws against "obscenity," nor for Joseph Treat's attacks.

While the exposures of Victoria Woodhull were novel tactics in American politics, they were rapidly turned into a material for sustaining the same hierarchies of power that Woodhull criticized. Woodhull's actions were spectacular, and they offered a reconfiguration of the perceptible by creating a scandal. Like the crowds that stormed the Bastille, Woodhull's politics show that any deployment of divisive politics produces a stage and a spectacle (Hallward 2006: 111). Woodhull's show was an improvised and unauthorized emergence of a democratic voice. It brought visibility to sex radicalism, and as such, enacted what Rancière sees at the heart of political emancipation, namely "the claim to visibility" (Hallward 2006: 117). If Woodhull's politics was a theatrical performance, the counter-political action of *the police* is to eliminate the spectacle of the disorder. What William Claflin, Anthony Comstock, and Joseph Treat wanted was to re-establish the smooth circulation of traffic, which was interrupted by a demonstration of protest. In saying "There is nothing to see" they wanted to block the lines of escape Woodhull's intervention created and eliminate the possibility that other types of sexual intimacy are possible.

Conclusion

The aim of this chapter was to show that Woodhull's interventions in the politics of sexuality of the US in the nineteenth-century offered a "line of escape" from conventional monogamous sexuality. Her deployment of shame was a political act that produced a stage for articulating a conflict. Woodhull's disruptive intervention was theatrical because it gestured toward the location of "a place for the out-of-place" (Hallward 2006: 118). This space was a territory of impurity, which allowed for the imagination of crossing boundaries, not unlike the Rancièrian space where tailors might pose as "dandies from the world of fashion" and respectable married men fall under the spell of actresses and prostitutes (Hallward 2006: 119). In other words, Woodhull staged equality by showing that there is an uncertain line between proper sexuality and immoral practices.

Shame's capacity to be a line of escape cannot be captured without understanding that it functions as dispossession. One is dispossessed when one is judged as being less valuable than the person who embodies monogamous heterosexuality. One is dispossessed when one has to pay a substantial price for deviating from the norm. The idea of dispossession articulates the privative and painful effects of political shaming. But shame has an important capacity to generate novel political actions. When one is dispossessed, one is exposed, made vulnerable and moved toward others. Dispossession unsettles the idea of the autonomous individual and shows that particular political practices are not a result of strict rational choice. Shame generates political acts such as Woodhull's exposures, which trouble a sexual regime that is derived from heterosexual monogamy.

Woodhull's actions show not only a demand for visibility of those whose lives are made invisible, but also a disruption of what counts as intelligible according to traditional sexual and kinship norms. The counter-figure of unconventional relationships is important to contest contemporary politics which imagines sexual subversion according to established conventions such as marriages. Same sex marriages model themselves upon heterosexual marriages in legal terminologies. The risk is to lose a creative dimension by replicating an existing model of intimacy. While same sex marriages challenge in many ways the heteronormativity of US politics, alternative interventions that deeply unsettle existing institutional arrangements point to new ways of life. These new modes of living can be produced outside restrictive understandings of sexuality. Rather than accepting marriage as the fundamental structure of human intimacy, Woodhull spoke about the significance of sexual relationships that transgress accepted conventional norms. Her living arrangements with her husband and her ex-husband represented an illustration of this new life. Her outspokenness about the importance of free love is a strong argument about the necessity of imagining new ways of living, which move away from a standard model about one's intimacy.

In this chapter, I was inspired by the queer theoretical move to transform a shameful slur into an empowering concept. These interventions that seek to modify the injurious content of slurs are not only strategic acts, but also ways of losing the proper boundaries of oneself. While she was in an unconscious state during the speech where she exposed Beecher for the first time, Woodhull was told that she used "naughty words" upon that occasion. When she reflected on her actions, she believed that she did not swear profanely, but "divinely" (Doyle 1874: 15). While shame is seen as a block to political imagination, I focused on Woodhull's example to offer an account of actions that unsettle conventional ideas about women and sexuality. Such political experimentation needs to take into account the risks involved in sexual exposures. Notwithstanding Woodhull's intentions, her sexual disclosures were deployed to promote a conservative backlash against the freedom of speech. The politics of contesting gender hierarchies has to be aware of the kind of interventions it mobilizes in particular historical contexts. Political interventions call for both innovative tactics and the anticipation of a backlash against such actions.

Notes

1. In a speech she gave in 1873, Woodhull explicitly drew on the authority of Mill, when she said that "all reformers have learned to love." She quoted a passage from the *Principles of Political Economy* in which Mill advocated for the right to free speech (Woodhull in Carpenter 2010: 172).
2. Butler's piece on the concept of "critically queer" in *Bodies that Matter* (1993) inaugurated a strong interest that queer studies cultivates in relation to its history of injuries and stigmatization. This concept opens up a powerful interrogation about the term *queer* in its capacity to be used as a tool in support of anti-homophobic politics, and more importantly, which helps bring about social justice. While *queer* for Butler is primarily a word associated with gay and lesbian politics, the term itself became a rallying point with which to challenge the mechanisms of state power

that imposes particular identities on sexual subjects (Eng et al. 2005: 1). The political promise of the term *queer* resides in its "broad critique of multiple social antagonisms, including race, gender, class, nationality, and religion, in addition to sexuality" (Eng et al. 2005: 1). Butler mobilizes queer to resignify the shame associated with sex and gender transgressions, because the term remains "never fully owned, but always and only redeployed, twisted, queered from a prior usage and in the direction of urgent and expanding political purposes" (1993: 173).

3. Butler's theorizing of queer, which set the terms for "the turn to stigma in queer studies," is predicated on an affirmative and positive story (Love 2007: 18). Love makes this point poignantly: "stigma is crucial, but its acceptance is conditional on its ability to be 'turned' to good use in an antihomophobic political project" (2007: 18). While resignifying shame is a productive political project, Butler claims that shame is neither redeemable nor completely transformed in this process (2003: 472). Butler notes that an affirmative project of transforming negative emotions, be that melancholia, shame, or loss, could not purge injury and loss from people's subjectivity. Mourning will not replace feelings associated with melancholia. Both mourning and melancholia constitute each other. The distinction between the two might not hold, because "they are, inevitably, experienced in a certain configuration of simultaneity and succession" (2003: 472).

4. For Davis, Rancière "does not appear to be interested in the powerful affective dimension which is usually involved in the experience of non-recognition" (2010: 97).

5. "To be undone" means that one not only *does* one's sexuality, or one's gender, or one's emotions, but also that one's "individual personhood" is dependent on norms that one does not choose (Butler 2004a: 1).

6. The impact of this scandal was hard to quantify, yet we know that it "brought low one of the last powerful symbols of the Republican party and abolition" (Frisken 2004: 84).

7. See Rancière (2011: 178) for how workers, by participating in *goguettes*, challenged the distribution of their roles as working people. *Goguettes* were singing societies that also served as places for drinking and socializing.

8. The Equal Rights Party chose her in 1872 to run as their candidate for the Presidency on the same ticket as Frederick Douglass. The strategy of this progressive party was to open up a larger conversation about the exclusion of women and black people from voting.

9. See Passet (2003: 2): "Mainstream newspaper editors and clergy, free love's most vocal critics, called anyone who deviated from the customary ideals of proper behavior a 'free lover.' Nineteenth-century sex radicals further confused matters because they could not agree on the term's application in daily life: for some it meant a lifelong and monogamous

commitment to a member of the opposite sex, others envisioned it as serial monogamy, a few advocated chaste heterosexual relationships except when children were mutually desired, and a smaller number defined it as variety (multiple partners, simultaneously) in sexual relationships." Despite the fact that the term free love had many meanings, Passet also observed that sex radicals were united against the idea of coercion in sex and wanted to advocate the right of women to determine the uses of her body (2003: 2).

10. See Rancière's (2011: 175–200) description of how French workers were policed through ideas of work and private property. The most important thing in the act of policing was the elimination of an alternative to current working conditions: "The morality of the goal was certainly less important than the abolition of any outlet toward other worlds or other conditions" (184).
11. Because Antigone expresses her love for her dead brother by mourning him, she repeats kinship as "an aberrant repetition of the norm." This action raises the possibility of a new articulation of the standard convention about love between siblings (Butler 2000: 58).
12. See also Rancière (2011: 178).
13. The tactic was intended to shame slavery's defenders by highlighting its immoral underpinnings. In 1848, Paul Edmondson was a free black man who had two daughters held captive in jail, waiting to be sold on the slave market (Dorrien 2001: 195). In response to Edmondson's request for help, Beecher, who was well-known as an antislavery advocate, organized a mock auction. He directed a play in which slave owners were buying Edmondson's daughters. This production demonstrated how badly the sisters were treated. The play endorsed an anti-abolitionist sentiment, so the people who supported slavery were exposed as cruel and selfish. Beecher raised the funds to buy the girls' freedom. The case gained national attention, and Beecher was placed at the forefront of the antislavery movement (Dorrien 2001: 195).
14. See Woodhull's (Doyle 1874: 17) statement: "The world cried shame! and said it was scandalous, and stopped their ears and blinded their eyes, that their own sensibilities might not be hurt by these horrid revelations."
15. Treat's allegations contributed to the degradation in the public perception of Woodhull's persona. The commercial press described her as a woman who advocated harlotry; her critics became more vocal in denouncing her (Frisken 2004: 112–13).

PART III
QUEERING SHAME

Chapter 6
Does Queer Political Theory Have a Future?

> Let us begin with an empirical given: police intervention in public spaces does not consist primarily in the interpellation of demonstrators, but in the breaking up of demonstrations. The police is not that law interpellating individuals (as in Althusser's "Hey, you there!") unless one confuses it with religious subjectification. It is, first of all, a reminder of the obviousness of what there is, or rather, of what there isn't: "Move along! There is nothing to see here!"
>
> (Rancière 2001, Thesis 8)

I started this book with the observation that shame is a widespread feeling in our neoliberal academia. While this feeling often produces a deep sense of anxiety and inferiority, I sought in this book to sketch the possibility of a queer political theory that may constitute an alternative to (only) feeling powerless. Reimagining queer political theory can start from understanding and illuminating how many of us are already talking back to police officers. My effort in this study was to show that shame disturbs the soul, or the already known architecture of the prison. But talking back to *the police* occurs—and occurred historically—in modalities that are still unknown. These situations are made unknown by a deep investment in forgetting how shame and its capacity to provoke activism have a history. Currently, shame is constructed in a presentist mode—*this is what shame is*—because capitalism blocks any account of unstable histories that led to our conception of affects and sexuality. Yet queer genealogy refuses this idea of a "thick" present which seduces us into thinking that shame does not have a history. The idea that shame feels only in particular ways is a consequence of the neoliberal investment in the value of the present.[1]

To contest a current view of shame, this book deployed three counter-figures to enact the disruptive potential of this affect. They emerged from feeling "irritably attached" while reading queer and feminist political theory (Davis 2009: 2).[2] Because the terms of my experience are historical and collective, I became curious about the ways in which this affect had been policed and controlled. To engage in this investigation, I had to analyze the terms of what counted as shame in contemporary queer feminism. I felt that the scholarship I read was too invested in mapping good and bad forms of democratic shame. I felt the need to argue that, rather than saying "Move along! There is nothing to see here!," political theorists needed to become curious and perhaps willing to be surprised by feminist history. I wanted to find instances in which nineteenth-century feminists felt the need to say "But officer . . ." and then observe what could emerge from this interruption.

Feeling irritated but also surprised were key affective moves in writing this book. I thought it was wrong, on the one hand, to think about some of these Victorians either as not queer enough or as old school liberals. But I also find it wrong for queer accounts to ignore the narrative about the origins of Anglo-American feminism. This narrative is deeply entrenched in how feminism is taught and made visible in nineteenth-century scholarship. I was annoyed by both of these moves, and I sought to create new Victorian actors that are simultaneously not queer and not feminist enough. I centered this new political stage on my subjects' experiences of being disoriented and of having to invent a new map for themselves. My frustration with queer and feminist theory led me to interrogate the terms that demarcated this experience of irritation and surprise.

Also, writing a genealogical investigation of shame made me conscious about a potential alliance between the history of political thought and queer studies. Therefore, the question became for me: does queer political theory have a future? In answering this question, my first move was to shift from a Foucauldian perception of *the police* to a practice of interruption such as "But officer . . .". Differently put, instead of understanding *the police* as an ideological apparatus that produces our soul, I re-thought *the police* as an apparatus that fears the spectacle of its disruption. *The police* seek to shame us so that we will stop demonstrating and contesting its mechanisms and power. At the beginning of *Discipline and Punish*, Foucault wrote in an enigmatic and troubling way about a sense of shame "constantly growing" over the last 200 years (1995: 8). Yet shame is not only a disciplinary affect that creates a prison through its repetition, nor is it merely an affect that interpellates one into feeling bad, for example, in obeying the demand of the police officer. Shame is also a tool that can be reversed against the growth of disciplinary power. Rethinking *the police* helps us rethink the role of shame in exercising power. Shame can surprise us if we do not let ourselves get caught in anticipating and reproducing its effects. That is why I wanted to think about queer political theory as unexpected, when it seeks to turn around received understandings of politics.

But an aversion to surprise is, as Sedgwick (2003: 130–1) indicated, deeply ingrained in the queer relationship to time and affect. It is located in a certain vigilance about being deemed inferior, so that "no time could be too early for one's having-already-known, for its having-already-been-inevitable, that something bad would happen" (Sedgwick 2003: 131). This aversion to surprise can be traced to the formation of the soul in Foucault's theory. This soul, saturated by shame, is an "effect and instrument of political anatomy" and "the prison of the body" (Foucault 1995: 30). Reductions in penal severity have historically contributed to a reorientation of punishment from tortured bodies to a bodiless reality. This shame-filled soul has created an industry of psychologists and moralists, whose task is to heal the wounds of feeling inferior and bad (Foucault 1995: 10). Also, the soul produces paranoid responses that, as Eve Sedgwick claimed, tend to reproduce disciplinary power. She observed (2003: 131), when commenting on D. A. Miller's book *The Novel and the Police*, that one could always say: "*Anything you can do (to me) I can do worse*, and *Anything you can do (to me) I can do first*." Fearing surprise means that the soul is already a prison that one can hardly escape. This aversion to surprise is not an enemy of *the police*; on the contrary, it functions as a modality to re-enact the same reactions that generated fear and discipline in the first place.

Feeling irritated but also surprised helps queer political theory to become more curious about what counts as "feminist" or "democratic."[3] In a queer conception, the adjective "democratic-feminist" would not precede a particular act, as if we already know what democracy and feminism are. These terms are not givens; they become subjects of production and contestation. Instead of reflecting a fixed identity, the content of these terms becomes a space for polemic. Performative acts are part of struggles to propose new meanings to contested concepts. Because they have a destabilizing component, performative interventions are subject to being labeled offensive, disgusting, or inappropriate. When what is not counted as proper, that is, the vulgar, becomes a territory for contesting normal politics, then this space could generate a new understanding of what counts as feminism. Rather than assuming that feminists know from the beginning what constitutes a democratic or feminist practice, queer practices capture the fluidity and novelty of political interventions.

My second move in answering the question about the future of queer political theory was to performatively intervene in the field. Queer genealogy illuminates the *sans-part* in a particular field of inquiry and exposes the process by which these actors are made invisible. The types of political action that I focused upon—disturbing silence, performative slurs, and unconventional relationships—have the status of the *sans-part* because they do not count as politics for many political theorists. To make them political, I sought to disturb entrenched positions in queer feminist theory. I understood shame as a process of "dislocating positions" through its enunciation and conceptualized it along the lines of what Benjamin Arditi and Jeremy Valentine (1999: xii) call "polemicization." I asked queer theorists to look at figures such as J. S. Mill, Josephine Butler, and Victoria Woodhull, who do not figure in the theorists' analyses because they are either forgotten or deemed liberal, and I asked feminists to reconsider the grounds for seeing something as feminist. In this vein, shame is both an enunciation of a wrong—"I feel bad when you consider me inferior"—and a catalyst for the emergence of a political subject. My cross-pollination of Rancière and queer theory sought to identify actions that could change the conventional view about shame as a "bad" emotion for democratic practices.

The payoff in illuminating the *sans-part* is to make queer practices visible, rather than to engage with what political theorists already demarcate as democratic.[4] The term allowed me to describe interventions that do not count in a liberal feminist framework. I focused on the "origins" of Anglo-American feminism—or what became canonical as "first wave feminism"—to show that we can perceive "new" practices by using a different vocabulary. I located the kind of shame that interrupts *the police* at the level of visceral experiences that have the affective structure of antinormativity. This affective structure was felt as excessive or disorderly in certain "situations" (Berlant 2011: 5) and was articulated through silence, insults, and illicit relationships. The term "situation" captures here a state of disorientation, as embodied in actions that could help us challenge current conceptions of shame. And as in "situations," my account of queer practices focuses on how "a relation of persons and worlds is sensed to be changing" while the rules that structure it are in chaos (Berlant 2011: 6). Instead of insisting on known democratic actions, queer political theory offers an alternative view of agency that takes into account experiences that are not yet theorized and formulated. With a new sense of curiosity, political theorists may notice that shame is not only obstructive and traumatic but also potentially productive of a new understanding of equality. The attention to practices allows one to capture theatrical performances which produce a new space for politics.[5] Mill's silence in Westminster, Butler's theatrical interventions, and Woodhull's loud proclamation that she is a free lover constitute acts that enact a different organization of given roles. Rather than reproduce politics-as-usual, these interventions produce a different, theatrical politics.

The third observation that I make about queer political theory is that it needs to address the dichotomy between traumatic and affirmative politics. In some theoretical accounts, political action is either traumatic, by which is meant bad and oppressive, or political, by which it is understood as affirmative, positive, and constructive.[6] In contesting this dichotomy, my study has shown that nineteenth-century feminists reflected on and understood the capacity of shame to fight against *the police*. Mill suggested that to respond strongly to public shaming is to demonstrate that one is an independent thinker who has "a power of his own." Josephine Butler claimed that feminists could transform the "poison" of shame into "healing" through political action. Woodhull argued that disgust and shame did not merely produce powerlessness, but also served as a resource for women's empowerment. But as nineteenth-century feminists engaged with the question of transforming the negative effects of shame, they were also too eager to see its effects as redemptive and beneficial. As Leo Bersani (2009: 24–5) reminded us, we need to break the direct relationship between shame and its presumed redemptive *telos*—be that autonomy, healing, or empowerment. Shame's transformative capacity can be seen—in a Rancièrian sense—not primarily in its result but in its potential to articulate a wrong and to incite one to dis-identify with a given identity in a hierarchical order.

Rather than understanding trauma as the opposite of a creative life, Butler suggests that possibilities for freedom emerge from "undoing" various attachments that humans have to pain and humiliation (1997a: 61). Similarly, Berlant (2011: 81) sees trauma as *not* making the experience of "the historical present impossible but possible." Trauma opens up a future that is queer because it does not have a given script. As such, trauma "transforms the work of survival without much of a normative plot or guarantee" (Berlant 2011: 81). The consequence of this approach is that experiences that are seen as fundamentally negative need to be rethought in feminism. If shame, humiliation, masochism, and sadism represent critical experiences for human subjectivity, they need to be reflected upon and, as Butler suggests, "occupied" (1997a: 104). If they do not represent the opposite of positive feminist agency but rather constitute it, then only a thorough analysis of their role can help to build a stronger feminist theory. Butler shows us that an investigation of the traumatic and productive iterability of power leads to performative gestures. Instead of ignoring the dark side of human subjectivity, queer political theorists can learn how to better mobilize it for their political interventions.

An orientation to what Oliver Davis (2009: 1–2) calls an "allergic awareness," or sensitivity to hierarchy and authority, is central to doing theoretical work in new ways. Laurent Berlant's (2011: 139) psychosocial analysis of the word smart indicates that "smartness is what hurts . . . it's sharp, it stings, and it's ruthless." If feminists are invested in smartness, and if smartness is a defense that aims to ward off traumatic surprise, Berlant seeks to imagine a distinct agency according to an embodied "impersonality," where subjects could embrace their own bodies "at the pinnacle of their greatest humiliations" (2011: 143). Similarly, Judith Butler's tactic of resignification can be instrumental in developing awareness about feminists' relationship to shame. A strong suggestion implicit in Butler's argument is that one does not choose merely to shame others, but rather shaming is constitutive to political agency.[7] Because in my study I have shown why these responses to shame are critical for understanding nineteenth-century feminism, to *not* focus on such tactics would mean ignoring significant dynamics that have shaped feminist history.

Now, what are the larger implications for queer and feminist political theory if we know that shame interrupts *the police*? My first claim is that the future of queer political theory is wrapped up in understanding its potential to make visible and name what is considered illegible. If equality in terms of new gender and sexual relationships has a future, then that future calls for a new vocabulary and practice that grasps what is excessive and considered not yet respectable. To further this project, I have shown that rather than taking for granted the value of monogamous heterosexuality, queer theorists can imagine novel forms of intimacy. Also, I have shown that injurious language has real value because it introduces an order of equality in a language that is policed by notions such as civility and dignity. Humiliating and injurious words need not be excluded from the attention of queer feminists but can be incorporated into theoretical reflections that draw on and sharpen activist tactics. I have argued that silence about one's practices preserves a space for experimentation and creativity that falls outside the scrutiny of established public norms. Silence, as with any other type of non-speech act, can disrupt entrenched assumptions about what counts as legitimate political language.

Sexuality is a privileged location to grasp how to trouble *the police*. If desiring sex is a process that requires a disruption of the self, then any feminist activist and theorist should think twice before separating sexual shame from activism. Rancière's lesson for queer feminist theory is that sexuality can be socially dysfunctional (Bersani 2009: 30), not only when coming (*jouissance*) is selfish but also when it destroys the self to create new sexual migrants. Mill, Harriet Taylor, and John Taylor were nineteenth-century sexual migrants when they chose to live in a relationship that was *not* monogamous. As Bersani (2009: 24–5) argues, shame is disruptive when it shatters the boundaries of the self with the aim of discarding a previous, rigid psychic structure. Similarly, Rancière asks us to see that politics, not unlike sex, interrupts a rigid order of the known as new subjects emerge from contesting *the police*. If the sex *police* is an internalized structure, it can be dismantled through practices that do not require redemptive politics. Yet, unlike Bersani, I believe that the practice of destroying a sexual hierarchy does not have to be primarily anti-egalitarian. Sex has an egalitarian intention when subjects disturb the accepted divisions within sexual hierarchies. As migrants who move at the borders between sexual classes, these subjects refuse the policing of their sex and enact an egalitarian politics.

To make visible what is considered illegible is a project in realizing queer utopia. I find the project of queer utopia very appealing when it insists that queerness is already here, located in the ongoing practices of migrants that interrupt a given definition of what can be felt and seen. With the work of José Esteban Muñoz (2009), queer utopia has been understood as the province of hope, in contrast to the anti-relational thread in queer theory that underscores the value of negativity. For Muñoz, the anti-relational move in queer theory focused too heavily on sexual transgressions and scenes of *jouissance* as opposed to those moments in the present, such as the encounter between a young white lesbian and an older gay white man, that point to possibilities that are not yet articulated, a queerness that is not yet conscious (2009: 3).

The utopian possibilities in my book are filled with hope but also with moments of irritability and of feeling wronged that generate a new affective orientation. Not only is drinking Coke in a quotidian act of queer relationality utopian and hopeful, but so are those acts that put one in danger in a given hierarchy. I wanted to show that risk and feeling bad are deeply utopian in their potentiality, not much different from what Muñoz argued when he noted that the disappointment needs to be risked if certain impasses are to be resisted (2009: 9). These feelings invoke, in addition to hope, a wrong and a political scene that emerges from feeling inferior. And this moment of enunciating the wrong acts against *the police's* demand to show your papers.

This queer utopia is not, however, open only to people who, when asked to show their papers, do have some sort of papers. The *sans-part* do not struggle to assert their equality only by talking back, having non-normative relationships, or being silent when they should not be. Some *sans-part*, for instance, do not have papers at all. In their position, it is hard to see exploitation and monogamy as the enemy. Some *sans-part* feel lucky to be exploited, or to be part of "the proletarian economy in [a] crummy service-sector [job]" (Berlant 2011: 171). There are key differences among those who struggle to be counted, but there are also similarities. As Berlant reminds us, "citizens without capital and migrants with fake papers are in proximate, interdependent boats structurally and affectively" (2011: 172). In some accounts of queer theory a strong emphasis is placed on refusing to look down on those who do not want to be part of a queer utopia. Many of the *sans-part* live in what Berlant describes as a structure of "cruel optimism," or a desire "to stay proximate, no matter what, to the potential openings marked out by fantasies of the good life, self-continuity, or unconflictedness" (Berlant 2011: 185–6). But some of these accounts have a tendency to exaggerate the separation between the desire for the normative good life and a queer utopia. For instance, Berlant writes about the subjects of her analyses as if they are not sometimes queer in their desires, as they are not challenging *the police* by refusing to accept what their families and authorities tell them to do. There is a loss in abandoning the sharp focus on antagonism as a function of politics and in forgetting that *the police* always say "Move on!"

This is why, rather than saying with Berlant (2011:261) that politics is a "commitment to the present activity of senses," I obsessively argued that shame—the feeling that you have been wronged, the disidentification with a previous given identity, and the articulation of conflict—interrupts *the police*. If a queer utopia is to be welcomed by those who have never heard about it, then the first move is to understand how they are already creating it. While a commitment to sensorial experiences can reproduce an already drafted map of feelings, perhaps a commitment to refusing the imposition of norms illuminates where and how queer utopia lives in the present moment.

My second claim is that political theorists can embrace their mistakes and lose some of their investments in successfully resisting within political science. As both Kaufman-Osborn (2010) and Brown (2010) notice, theorists are under an increased pressure to justify their work in the language of the ideology of the market. As in other disciplines, the work of teaching and research becomes a measurable tool in the need to advance the value of students as human capital. What is to be done? The feeling of powerless leads to imagining scenarios where political theorists become "unabashed mongrels" and learn from other new fields of inquiry (Kaufman-Osborn 2010: 669) or "hit the streets" and recover the value of public life (Brown 2010: 684). Both capture what I think is crucial in the work that political theorists do, that is the effort to "assist in giving form to emergent realities that otherwise remain beyond our ken" (Kaufman-Osborn 2010: 669). Yet both are also alternatives to feeling disempowered and capture the pull to have a map or a direction that we can share with others and feel safer.

An effort to illuminate and produce new types of politics, however, does not need to appeal to a narrative of success. Rather than producing a new map, we can start from what queer political theory already does. Brilliant scholars show how to oppose frames of normalization in our field. They suggest a queer political theory that lives with interpretative contradictions or one that shifts prevailing narratives about consent and harm (Schotten 2009; Fischel 2016).[8] Others create new alliances between Laclau's conception of the political and queer theory (Castro et al. 2016). New theoretical work may not need strong calls to action, not even new names attached to what it does. Although Brown (2010: 683) believes we suffer from "impoverished classificatory schemes," labels such as "allergic political theory" or "the political theory of feeling bad" may generate novel categories in the field.[9] Yet to forcefully break away from the *police*, theorists need to do much more of what they do badly. They need to make crucial mistakes such as break away from political science departments or start sections in the American Political Science Association that do not make sense (in this sense, "allergic political theory" is a wonderful candidate). "Excessive practices" can open up lines of escape, which come with risks and disciplinary shaming. Such acts can dislocate the soul—and perhaps surprise may be courted again. Rancière's lesson about writing is that it is powerful when it steals away "to wander aimlessly without knowing who to speak to or who not to speak to" (2004: 8). Perhaps this is one route to be taken. We need to expect that we will be met with ridicule and urged to behave like adults and move on. Yet only a serious commitment to be wrong and to fail can make us say and do things we have never imagined.

Notes

1. Harry Harootunian alluded to this process when he argued that "the present was both severed from its historical past and indefinitely deprived of a future from which it once derived expectation" (2007: 472). Both the past and the future can be accounted in new ways, provided that one is able to "conjure the past into its existence" (Doan 2013: xii).
2. Rancière points to the potential of shame to offer a litigation of what is perceived and create a different circulation and division of roles and places (Davis 2009: 1–2, 14).
3. Locke favors an approach that asks feminists to pay attention to traditional feminist-democratic practices of "inclusion" (2007: 148).
4. Like Nussbaum, Locke centers on shame's destructive potential as an obstacle to a creative life and progressive politics, and she primarily conceptualizes shame as being at odds with democratic agency. Rather than seeing that shame could be a litigious practice that transforms politics-as-usual, Jill Locke (2007: 47) argues that "shame and shaming per se" ought not occupy "a central position in feminist-democratic politics" (2007: 47).
5. Both queer theorists and Rancière insist on shame's disturbing capacity. Sedgwick (2003: 36) insisted on the potential of shame to be the "disruptive moment" in a circuit of identity-constituting communication. Like Rancière, Sedgwick (2003: 38) understands that politics is a moment of creating a spectacle so that the feminist activist is also an actor or a performance artist.
6. At the heart of Locke's (2007) concerns about shame is her assumption that shame's traumatic content negates any positive self-affirming experiences. Her claim is that we do not have evidence to show that shame has any positive transformative potential.
7. Butler's conception of power demonstrates what is weak about Locke's argument that feminists should not focus "on shaming those who shame us" (2007: 159). Locke ignores that shaming is intrinsic to many feminist responses to their opponents.

8. A Nietzschean queer theory can be affirmative in "one's profound no-saying to present existence" and stake its future "on the eradication of the past, not on its preservation" (Schotten 2009: 198, 206). Queer political theory also shows that requirements of consent and age, when they are legislated in the arena of sex, "carry unexpected and unjust consequences" (Fischel 2016: 6).
9. Brown (2010: 683) argues that the institutional categories that political theorists use such as "historical" or "normative" do not appear to address power while this separation intensifies their "seeming irrelevance."

References and Further Reading

Primary sources:
John Stuart Mill's writings:
John Stuart Mill (1963–91) [referred to as: CW], *The Collected Works of John Stuart Mill*, general editor F. E. L. Priestley and subsequently John M. Robson, University of Toronto Press: Toronto and London, 33 vols. Vol. I: *Autobiography and Literary Essays* (1981); II, III: *Principles of Political Economy* (1965); X: *Essays on Ethics, Religion and Society* (1969); XII, XIII: *Earlier Letters, 1812–1848* (1962); XIV, XV, XVI, XVII: *Later Letters, 1848–1873* (1972); XVIII, XIX: *Essays on Politics and Society* (1977); XXI: *Essays on Equality, Law and Education* (1984); XXII, XXIII, XXIV, XXV: *Newspaper Writings* (1986); XXVIII, XXIX: *Public and Parliamentary Speeches* (1988); XXXII: *Additional Letters of John Stuart Mill* (1991). Accessed from *The Online Library of Liberty* at <http://oll.libertyfund.org/index.php?option=com_staticxt&staticfile=show.php&title=165>

Rossi, Alice (ed.) (1970), *Essays on Sex Equality*, Chicago: University of Chicago Press.

Pyle, Andrew (ed.) (1995), *Liberty: Contemporary Responses to John Stuart Mill*, Bristol: Thoemmes.

John Stuart Mill in the nineteenth-century caricatures:
'Mill, John Stuart', *Punch,* 1873a, May 24, p. 216.
'Mill and Miller', *Punch,* 1873b, November 29, p. 222.
'Miss Mill joins the Ladies', *Judy,* November 2, 1868, pp. 46–7.
'Parliamentary', *Judy,* July 24, 1867, p. 156.

The writings of feminist Unitarians:
Adams, W. B. (1833), 'On the condition of women in England', *Monthly Repository*, 7: 73, pp. 217–31.
Fox, William J. (1832), 'A political and social anomaly', *Monthly Repository*, 6: 69, p. 637.
Fox, William. J. (1833a), 'A victim', *Monthly Repository*, 7: 73, pp. 164–77.
Fox, William. J. (1833b), 'The dissenting marriage question', *Monthly Repository*, 7: 73, pp. 136–42.

Harriet Taylor's writings:
Jacobs, Jane E. (ed.) (1998), *The Complete Works of Harriet Taylor Mill*, Bloomington, Indiana: Indiana University Press.

Josephine Butler's writings:
Jordan, Jane and Ingrid Sharp (eds) (2003a), *Josephine Butler and the Prostitution Campaigns: Diseased of the Body Politics* (vol. 1), London: Routledge.
Jordan, Jane and Ingrid Sharp (eds) (2003b), *Josephine Butler and the Prostitution Campaigns: Diseased of the Body Politics* (vol. 2), London: Routledge.

Victoria Woodhull's writings:
Carpenter, Cari M. (ed.) (2010), *Selected Writings of Victoria Woodhull: Suffrage, Free Love, and Eugenics*, Lincoln, NE: University of Nebraska Press.

Books and articles:
Abbey, Ruth (2011), *The Return of Feminist Liberalism*, Montreal: McGill-Queen's University Press.
Ahmed, Sara (2004), *The Cultural Politics of Emotion*, New York: Routledge.
Annas, Julia (1977), 'Mill and the subjection of women', *Philosophy*, 52: 200, pp. 179–94.
Arditi, Benjamin (2007), *Politics on the Edges of Liberalism: Difference, Populism, Revolution, Agitation*, Edinburgh: Edinburgh University Press.
Arditi, Benjamin and David Valentine (1999), *Polemicization: The Contingency of the Common Place*, Edinburgh: Edinburgh University Press.
Barry, Kathleen (1979), *Female Sexual Slavery*, New York: NYU Press.
Bell, Duncan (2010), 'John Stuart Mill on colonies', *Political Theory*, 38: 1, pp. 36–64.
Berlant, Lauren (2011), *Cruel Optimism*, Durham: Duke University Press.
Berlin, Isaiah (2002), *Liberty: Incorporating Four Essays on Liberty*, ed. Henry Hardy, Oxford: Oxford University Press.
Bersani, Leo (2009), *Is the Rectum a Grave? and Other Essays*, Chicago, London: University of Chicago Press.
Bickford, Susan (1997), 'Anti-anti-anti identity politics: feminism, democracy, and the complexities of citizenship', *Hypatia*, 12: 4, pp. 111–31.
Brennan, Teresa (2004), *The Transmission of Affect*, Ithaca: Cornell University Press.
British Magazine (1833), *British Magazine and Monthly Register of Religious and Ecclesiastical Information, Parochial History, and Documents Respecting the State of the Poor, Progress of Education*, vols I–IV, 1832–1833.
Brown, Wendy (1993), 'Wounded attachments', *Political Theory*, 21, pp. 390–410.
Brown, Wendy (1995), *States of Injury: Power and Freedom in Late Modernity*, Princeton, NJ: Princeton University Press.

Brown, Wendy (1997), 'The impossibility of women's studies', *differences*, 9: 3, pp. 79–101.
Brown, Wendy (2005), *Edgework: Critical Essays on Knowledge and Politics*, Princeton, NJ: Princeton University Press.
Brown, Wendy (2008), *Regulating Aversion: Tolerance in the Age of Identity*, Princeton, NJ: Princeton University Press.
Brown, Wendy (2010), 'Political theory is not a luxury: a response to Timothy Kaufman-Osborn's "Political theory as a profession"', *Political Research Quarterly*, 63: 3, pp. 680–5.
Brown, Wendy and Janet Halley (2002), 'Introduction', in W. Brown and J. Halley (eds), *Left Legalism/Left Critique*, Durham, London: Duke University Press, pp. 1–37.
Burton, Antoinette (1992), 'The white woman's burden, British Feminists and "The Indian woman", 1865–1915,' in N. Chaudhuri and M. Strobel (eds), *Western Women and Imperialism*, Bloomington, IN: Indiana University Press, pp. 137–57.
Burton, Antoinette (1998), 'States of injury: Josephine Butler on slavery, citizenship, and the Boer War', *Social Politics*, 5: 3, pp. 338–61.
Butler, Judith (1993), *Bodies That Matter: On the Discursive Limits of Sex*, New York, London: Routledge.
Butler, Judith (1997a), *The Psychic Life of Power: Theories in Subjection*, California: Stanford University Press.
Butler, Judith (1997b), *Excitable Speech: A Politics of the Performative*, London, New York: Routledge.
Butler, Judith (1999), *Gender Trouble: Feminism and the Subversion of Identity*, New York, London: Routledge.
Butler, Judith (2000), *Antigone's Claim: Kinship between Life and Death*, New York: Columbia University Press.
Butler, Judith (2003), 'Afterward: after loss, what then?', in David L. Eng and David Kazanjian (eds), *Loss: The Politics of Mourning*, Berkeley, London: University of California Press, pp. 467–75.
Butler, Judith (2004a), *Undoing Gender*, New York, London: Routledge.
Butler, Judith (2004b), *Precarious Life: The Powers of Mourning and Violence*, London, New York: Verso.
Butler, Judith (2007), *Who Sings the Nation-State? Language, Politics, Belonging* (with Gaytari Spivak), Calcutta, New York, Oxford: Seagull Books.
Butler, Judith (2009), 'Performativity, precarity and sexual politics', *Revista de Antropologia Iberoamericana*, Madrid, 4: 3, pp. i–xiii.
Butler, Judith (2013), *Dispossession: The Performative in the Political* (with Athena Athanasiou), Cambridge, US: Polity Press.
Caine, Barbara (1992), *Victorian Feminists*, New York: Oxford University Press.
Caine, Barbara (1997), *English Feminism, 1780–1980*, New York: Oxford University Press.

Carver, Terence and Samuel Chambers (2008), *Judith Butler's Precarious Politics: Critical Encounters*, London: Routledge, pp. 109–27.
Castro Varela, Maria do Mar, Nikita Dhawan and Antke Engel (eds) (2016), *Hegemony and Heteronormativity: Revisiting 'The Political' in Queer Politics*, Burlington, VT: Ashgate.
Chambers, Samuel (2013), *The Lessons of Rancière*, Oxford, New York: Oxford University Press.
Chambers, Samuel (2014), *Bearing Society in Mind*, Lanham, MD: Rowman and Littlefield International.
Cocks, Harry G. (2010), *Nameless Offences: Homosexual Desire in the 19th Century*, London, New York: I. B. Tauris.
Cohen, Cathy (1997), 'Punks, bulldaggers, and welfare queens: the radical potential of queer politics?', *GLQ*, 3, pp. 437–65.
Cvetkovich, Ann (2003), *An Archive of Feelings: Trauma, Sexuality and Lesbian Public Cultures*, Durham, NC: Duke University Press.
Davis, Oliver (2009), 'Rancière and queer theory: on irritable attachment', *Borderlands*, 8: 2, pp. 1–19.
Davis, Oliver (2010), *Jacques Rancière*, Cambridge, UK: Polity Press.
Dean, Jodi (2008), 'Change of address: Butler's ethics of sovereignty deadlock', in Terrell Carver and Samuel Allen Chambers (eds), *Judith Butler's Precarious Politics: Critical Encounters*, Abingdon, New York: Routledge.
Dean, Tim (2009), *Unlimited Intimacy: Reflection on the Subculture of Barebacking*, Chicago: University of Chicago Press.
Doan, Laura (2013), *History, Sexuality, and Women's Experience of Modern War*, Chicago: University of Chicago Press.
Disch, Lisa (1999), 'Judith Butler and the politics of the performative', *Political Theory*, 27: 4, pp. 545–59.
Di Stefano, Christine (1989), 'Rereading J. S. Mill: interpolations from the (m)otherworld', in Marleen S. Barr and Richard Feldstein (eds), *Discontented Discourses: Feminism/Textual Interventions/Psychoanalysis*, Urbana: University of Illinois Press, pp. 160–72.
Di Stefano, Christine (1991), *Configurations of Masculinity: A Feminist Perspective on Modern Political Theory*, Ithaca, NY: Cornell University Press.
Donner, Wendy (1992), 'John Stuart Mill's liberal feminism', *Philosophical Studies*, 69: 2/3, pp. 155–66.
Dorrien, Gary (2001), *The Making of American Liberal Theology: Imagining Progressive Religion, 1805–1900*, Westminster: John Knox Press.
Doyle, E. P. (1874), *The Romance of Plymouth Church, its Pastor, and his Accusers*, Hartford, CT: Park Publishing Company.
Drabinski, John E. (2012), 'Affect and revolution: on Baldwin and Fanon', *PhaenEX* 7: 2, pp. 124–58.
Duggan, Lisa (2003), *The Twilight of Equality?: Neoliberalism, Cultural Politics, and the Attack On Democracy*, Boston, MA: Beacon Press.
Eisenstein, Zilah (1981), *The Radical Future of Liberal Feminism*, New York and London: Longman.

Elden, Stuart (2016), *Foucault's Last Decade*, London: Polity.
Elster, Jon (1998), *Deliberative Democracy*, Cambridge: Cambridge University Press.
Eng, David L., José Esteban Muñoz and Judith Halberstam (eds) (2005), *What's Queer about Queer Studies Now?* Durham, NC: Duke University Press.
Fiol-Matta, Licia (2002), *A Queer Mother for the Nation: The State and Gabriela Mistral*, Minneapolis: University of Minnesota Press.
Fischel, Joseph J. (2016), *Sex and Harm in the Age of Consent*, Minneapolis: University of Minnesota Press.
Foucault, Michel (1978), *The History of Sexuality: Volume 1*, New York: Pantheon Books.
Foucault, Michel (1994), *Ethics, Subjectivity, and Truth*, ed. Paul Rabinow, New York: New Press.
Foucault, Michel (1995), *Discipline and Punish. The Birth of Prisons*, New York: Vintage Books.
Foucault, Michel (2003), *Society Must Be Defended: Lectures at the Collège de France, 1975–1976*, trans. David Macey, New York: Picador.
Foucault, Michel (2005), *The Hermeneutics of the Subject: Lectures at the Collège de France, 1981–1982*, New York: Picador.
Foucault, Michel (2008), *The Birth of Politics: Lectures at the Collège de France*, London: Palgrave MacMillan.
Foucault, Michel (2010), *The Birth of Biopolitics: Lectures at the Collège de France, 1978–1979*, trans. Graham Burchell, New York: Picador, Palgrave Macmillan.
Foucault Studies (2013), 'Foucault Studies Special Issue: Foucault and Feminism', *Foucault Studies*, September issue.
Fraser, Nancy (1998), 'Heterosexism, misrecognition and capitalism: a response to Judith Butler', *New Left Review*, 228: March–April, pp. 140–50.
Frederickson, Kristine W. (2008), 'Josephine E. Butler and Christianity in the British Victorian Movement', unpublished Ph.D. dissertation, Department of History, University of Utah, UMI Number: 3337531.
Frisken, Amanda (2004), *Victoria Woodhull's Sexual Revolution: Political Theater and the Popular Press in Nineteenth Century America*, Philadelphia: University of Pennsylvania Press.
Gabriel, Mary (1998), *Notorious Victoria: The Life of Victoria Woodhull, Uncensored*, Chapel Hill, NC: Algonquin Books.
Gibson, Ian (1978), *The English Vice: Beatings, Sex and Shame in Victorian England and After*, London: Duckworth.
Gleadle, Katherine (1998), *The Early Feminists: Radical Unitarians and the Emergence of the Women's Rights Movement, 1831–51*, London: Palgrave Macmillan.
Goffman, Erving (1963), *Stigma: Notes on the Management of Spoiled Identity*, New York: Simon and Schuster.

Gordon, Kristyn (2007), 'Theorizing emotion and affect: feminist engagements', *Feminist Theory*, 8: 3, pp. 333–58.
Green, Jonathan (1998), *The Cassell Dictionary of Slang*, London: Cassell.
Griffin, Ben (2012), *The Politics of Gender in Victorian England*, Cambridge: Cambridge University Press.
Gutmann, Amy and Dennis F. Thompson (1996), *Democracy and Disagreement*, Cambridge, MA: Harvard University Press.
Habermas, Jürgen (1999), 'A short reply', *Ratio Juris*, 12: 4, pp. 445–53.
Halley, Janet (2006), *Split Decisions: How and Why to Take a Break from Feminism*, Princeton, NJ: Princeton University Press.
Halperin, David M. (1995), *Saint Foucault: Towards a Gay Hagiography*, Oxford: Oxford University Press.
Halperin, David M. (2002), *How to Do the History of Homosexuality*, Chicago: University of Chicago Press.
Hallward, Peter (2006), 'Staging equality: on Rancière's theatrocracy', *New Left Review*, 37: 109–29.
Harootunian, Harry (2007), 'Remembering the historical present', *Critical Inquiry*, 33: 471–94.
Hemmings, Clare (2005), 'Invoking affect', *Cultural Studies*, 19:5, pp. 548–67.
Honig, Bonnie (1993), *Political Theory and the Displacement of Politics*, Ithaca, NY: Cornell University Press.
Honig, Bonnie (1996), 'Democracy, dilemmas and the politics of home,' in S. Benhabib (ed.), *Democracy and Difference: Contesting the Boundaries of the Political*, Princeton, NJ: Princeton University Press, pp. 257–77.
Honig, Bonnie (2013), *Antigone, Interrupted*, Cambridge: Cambridge University Press.
Jeffreys, Sheila (1997), *The Idea of Prostitution*, Melbourne: Spinifex Press Pty Ltd.
Joannou, Maroula and June Purvis (1998), *The Women's Suffrage Movement: New Feminist Perspectives*, Manchester: Manchester University Press.
Jones, Gareth S. (2014), *Outcast London: A Study in the Relationship between Classes in Victorian Society*, London: Verso.
Kamm, Josephine (1977), *John Stuart Mill in Love*, London: Gordon and Cremonesi.
Kaufman, Gershen (2004), *The Psychology of Shame: Theory and Treatment of Shame based Symptoms*, New York: Springer Publishing Company.
Kaufman-Osborn, Timothy V. (2010), 'Political theory as profession and as subfield?', *Political Research Quarterly*, 63: 3, pp. 655–73.
Kent, Susan K. (1987), *Sex and Suffrage in Britain 1860–1914*, Princeton, NJ: Princeton University Press.
Koopman, Colin (2013), *Genealogy as Critique: Foucault and the Problem of Modernity*, Bloomington: Indiana University Press.
Lenker, Lagretta T. (2001), *Fathers and Daughters in Shakespeare and Shaw*, Westport, CT: Greenwood Press.

Lloyd, Moya (1999), 'Performativity, parody, politics', *Theory, Culture and Society,* 16: 2, pp. 195–213.
Lloyd, Moya (2008), 'Towards a cultural politics of vulnerability: precarious lives and ungrievable deaths', in Terence Carver and Samuel Chambers (eds), *Judith Butler's Precarious Politics: Critical Encounters*, London: Routledge, pp. 92–107.
Locke, Jill (2007), 'Shame and the future of feminism', *Hypatia*, 22: 4, pp. 146–62.
Locke, Jill (2016), *Democracy and the Death of Shame: Political Equality and Social Disturbance*, New York: Cambridge University Press.
Lorde, Audre (2009), *I Am Your Sister: Collected and Unpublished Works of Audre Lorde*, in Rudolph Byrd, Johnnetta B. Cole and Beverly Guy-Sheftall (eds), Oxford: Oxford University Press.
Love, Heather (2007), *Feelings Backwards: Loss and the Politics of Queer History*, Cambridge: Harvard University Press.
McWhorter, Ladelle (2013), 'Post-liberation feminism and practices of freedom', *Foucault Studies*, 16, pp. 54–73.
Mahmood, Saba (2005), *The Politics of Piety: The Islamic Revival and the Feminist Subject*, Princeton, NJ: Princeton University Press.
Manion, Jennifer (2002), 'The moral relevance of shame', *American Philosophical Quarterly*, 39: 1, pp. 73–90.
Marcus, Sharon (2007), *Between Women: Friendship, Desire and Marriage*, Princeton, NJ: Princeton University Press.
Marberry, M. M. (1967), *Vicky: A Biography of Victoria C. Woodhull*, New York: Funk and Wagnalls.
Margalit, Avishai (1996), *The Decent Society*, Cambridge, MA: Harvard University Press.
Marilley, Suzanne M. (1996), *Woman's Suffrage and the Origins of Liberal Feminism in the United States, 1820–1920*, Cambridge, MA: Harvard University Press.
Mason, Michael (1994a), *The Making of Victorian Sexuality*, Oxford: Oxford University Press.
Mason, Michael (1994b), *The Making of Victorian Sexual Attitudes*, Oxford: Oxford University Press.
Massad, Joseph (2007), *Desiring Arabs*, Chicago: University of Chicago Press.
May, Todd (1993), *Between Genealogy and Epistemology: Psychology, Politics and Knowledge in the Thought of Michel Foucault*, Philadelphia: Pennsylvania State University.
Mazlish, Bruce (1975), *James and John Stuart Mill: Father and Son in the Nineteenth Century*, New York: Basic Books.
Miller, D. A. (1988) *The Novel and the Police*, Berkeley, Los Angeles: University of California Press.
Mineka, Francis E. (1944), *The Dissidence of Dissent: The Monthly Repository, 1806–1838*, Chapel Hill, NC: University of North Carolina Press.

Mineka, Francis E. (1972), 'John Stuart Mill and neo-Malthusianism, 1873', in John M. Robson and Michael Laine (eds), *The Mill News Letter*, VIII: 1, pp. 3–10.

Muñoz, José Esteban (2009), *Cruising Utopia: The Then and There of Queer Futurity*, New York, London: New York Press.

Nussbaum, Martha (1999), 'The professor of parody', *New Republic* (02.22.1999), <http://www.akad.se/Nussbaum.pdf> (last accessed August 14, 2013).

Nussbaum, Martha (2001), *Upheavals of Thought: The Intelligence of Emotions*, Cambridge: Cambridge University Press.

Nussbaum, Martha (2004), *Hiding from Humanity: Disgust, Shame and Law*, Princeton, NJ: Princeton University Press.

Nussbaum, Martha (2010), 'Mill's feminism: Liberal, radical and queer', in G. Varaouxakis and P. Kelly (eds), *John Stuart Mill – Thought and Influence*, London: Routledge, pp. 130–45.

Okin, Susan (1979), *Women in Western Political Thought*, Princeton, NJ: Princeton University Press.

Packe, Michael St. John (1954), *The Life of John Stuart Mill*, New York: Macmillan.

Passet, Joanne (2003), *Sex Radicals and the Quest for Women's Equality*, Urbana: University of Illinois Press.

Phillips, Anne (2001), 'Feminism and liberalism revisited: has Martha Nussbaum got it right?', *Constellations*, 8: 2, pp. 249–66.

Popa, Bogdan (2015), 'How to interrupt happy nationalism: from Butler's performative contradiction to radical cosmopolitanism', in Tamara Cărăuș and Elena Paris (eds), *Post-foundational Cosmopolitanism*, Routledge Studies in Social and Political Thought, London: Routledge, pp. 240–54.

Puar, Jasibir K. (2007), *Terrorist Assemblages: Homonationalism in Queer Times*, Durham, NC: Duke University Press.

Reeves, Richard (2008), *John Stuart Mill: Victorian Firebrand*, London: Atlantic Books.

Rancière, Jacques (1999), *Disagreement: Politics and Philosophy*, trans. Julie Rose, Minneapolis: University of Minnesota Press.

Rancière, Jacques (2001), 'Ten theses on politics', *Theory and Event*, 5: 3.

Rancière, Jacques (2011), *Staging the People: The Proletarian and his Double*, New York, Verso.

Rancière, Jacques (2012), *Proletarian Nights: The Workers' Dream in Nineteenth Century France*, New York: Verso.

Rawls, John (2005), *Political Liberalism*, New York: Columbia University Press.

Republican, The (1825), *The Republican*, vol. XI (January 7 to July 1, 1825). London: printed by R. Carlile.

Ring, Jennifer (1985), 'Mill's "The Subjection of Women": the methodological limits of liberal feminism', *Review of Politics*, 47: 1, pp. 27–44.

Ross, Alison, 'Why is "speaking the truth" fearless? "Danger" and "truth" in Foucault's discussion of parrhesia', *Parrhesia*, 4: pp. 62–75, <www.parrhesiajournal.org> (last accessed December 11, 2016)

Said, Edward (1979), *Orientalism*, New York: Pantheon Books.

Sawicki, Jana (2013), 'Queer feminism: cultivating ethical practices of freedom', *Foucault Studies*, 16, pp. 74–87.

Saxonhouse, Arlene (2006), *Free Speech and Democracy in Ancient Athens*, New York: Cambridge University Press.

Schotten, C. Heike (2009), *Nietzsche's Revolution: Decadence, Politics, and Sexuality*, New York: Palgrave, MacMillan.

Scott, Joan W. (1999), 'Gender: a useful category of historical analysis', in *Gender and the Politics of History*, revised edn, New York: Columbia University Press.

Sedgwick, Eve K. (1990), *Epistemology of the Closet*, Berkeley: University of California Press.

Sedgwick, Eve K. (2003), *Touching Feeling: Affect, Pedagogy, Performativity*, Durham and London: Duke University Press.

Sedgwick, E. K. (2009), 'Shame, theatricality, and queer performativity: Henry James's *The Art of the Novel*', in David Halperin and Valerie Traub (eds), *Gay Shame*, Chicago: University of Chicago Press, pp. 49–62.

Simons, Jon (1995), *Foucault and the Political*, London: Routledge.

Smith, Francis B. (1973), *Radical Artisan, William James Linton, 1812–97*, Lanham, MD: Rowman and Littlefield.

Smith, Elisabeth S. (2001), 'John Stuart Mill's "The Subjection of Women": a re-examination', *Polity*, 34: 2, pp. 181–203.

Smith, Anne Marie (2008), 'Missing poststructuralism, missing Foucault: Butler and Fraser on capitalism and the regulation of sexuality', in Terence Carver and Samuel Chambers (eds), *Judith Butler's Precarious Politics: Critical Encounters*, London: Routledge, pp. 79–92.

Stafford, William (2004), 'Is Mill's 'liberal' feminism masculinist?', *Journal of Political Ideologies*, 9: 2, pp. 159–79.

Stein, Arlene (2006), *Shameless: Sexual Dissidence in American Culture*, New York: New York University Press.

Stephen, Leslie (1968), *Some Early Impressions*, New York: Burt Franklin.

Tarnopolski, Christina (2002), 'Plato and the Politics of Shame', unpublished dissertation, University of Chicago.

Tarnopolsky, Christina H. (2010), *Prudes, Perverts and Tyrants: Plato's Gorgias and the Politics of Shame*, Princeton, NJ: Princeton University Press.

Theweleit, Klaus (1987, 1989), *Male Fantasies*, 2 vols, trans. S. Conway, Minneapolis: University of Minnesota Press.

Thomas, Megan C. (2016) 'Secrecy's use: using Bakunin to theorize authority and free action', *Contemporary Political Theory*, 15: 3, pp. 264–84.

Traub, Valerie (2016), *Thinking Sex with The Early Moderns*, Philadelphia: University of Pennsylvania Press.

Tully, James (2009), *Public Philosophy in a New Key. Volume 1: Democracy and New Freedoms*, Cambridge: Cambridge University Press.
Turner, Jeffrey A. (2010), *Sitting in and Speaking out: Student Movements in the American South, 1960–1970*, Athens, GA: University of Georgia Press.
Urbinati, Nadia (1991), 'John Stuart Mill on androgyny and ideal marriage', *Political Theory*, 19: 4, pp. 626–48.
Valdez, Inés (2016). 'Non-domination or practices of freedom? French Muslim women, Foucault, and the full veil ban', *American Political Science Review*, 110: 1, pp. 18–30.
Walkowitz, Judith (1980), *Prostitution and Victorian Society. Women, Class, and the State*, Cambridge: Cambridge University Press.
Warner, Michael (1993), 'Introduction', *Fear of a Queer Planet: Queer Politics and Social Theory*, Cultural Politics, vol. 6, ed. Michael Warner, London, Minneapolis: University of Minnesota Press, vii–xxxi.
Watson, Janell (2011), 'Psychoanalysis, secularism, and sexuality, an interview with Joan Wallach Scott,' *Minnesota Review*, 77, pp. 101–10.
Wiegman, Robin (1999), 'Feminism, institutionalism, and the idiom of failure,' *differences*, 11, pp. 107–36.
Williams, Bernard (1993), *Shame and Necessity*, Berkeley: University of California Press.
Young-Bruehl, Elisabeth (1996), *The Anatomy of Prejudices*, Cambridge, MA: Harvard University Press.
Zerilli, Linda M. G. (1994), *Signifying Women: Culture and Chaos in Rousseau, Burke and Mill*, Ithaca, NY: Cornell University Press.
Zerilli, Linda M. G. (2005), *Feminism and the Abyss of Freedom*, Chicago: Chicago University Press.
Zerilli, Linda M. G. (2008), 'Feminists know not what they do: Judith Butler's gender trouble and the limits of epistemology', in Terence Carver and Samuel Chambers (eds), *Judith Butler's Precarious Politics: Critical Encounters*, London: Routledge, pp. 28–45.
Zivi, Karen (2008), 'Rights and the politics of performativity', in Terence Carver and Samuel Chambers (eds), *Judith Butler's Precarious Politics: Critical Encounters*, London: Routledge, pp. 157–71.

Further Reading

Allen, Amy (2013), 'Feminism, Foucault, and the critique of reason: re-reading the *History of Madness*', *Foucault Studies*, 16: 15–31.
Brown, Wendy (2001), *Politics Out of History*, Princeton, NJ: Princeton University Press.
Bush, M. L. (1998), *What is Love? Richard Carlile's Philosophy of Love*, London: Verso.
Callcut, Daniel (ed.) (2009), *Reading Bernard Williams*, New York and London: Routledge.

Corbett, Ken (2009), *Boyhoods. Rethinking Masculinities*, New Haven and London: Yale University Press.
Heyes, Cressida J. (2013). 'Foucault Studies Special Issue: Foucault and Feminism', *Foucault Studies*, September issue, 16, pp. 3–14.
Jacobs, Jane E. (ed.) (1998), *The Complete Works of Harriet Taylor Mill*, Bloomington, IN: Indiana University Press.
Kingston, Rebecca and Leonard Ferry (2008), 'Introduction: the emotions and the history of political thought', in Rebecca Kingston and Leonard Ferry (eds), *Bringing the Passions Back In: The Emotions in Political Philosophy*, Vancouver: UBC.
Layton, Lynne (1999), *Who's That Girl? Who is That Boy? Clinical Practice meets Postmodern Gender Theory*, New Jersey: Jason Aronson, Inc.
Lloyd, Moya (2007), *Judith Butler: From Norms to Politics*, Malden, MA: Polity Press.
MacKinnon, Catharine and Andrea Dworkin (1988), *Pornography and Civil Rights: A New Day for Women's Equality*, Minneapolis, MN: Organizing Against Pornography.
Nussbaum, Martha (2000), 'The future of feminist liberalism', *Proceedings and Addresses of the American Philosophical Association*, 74: 2, pp. 47–79.
Ryan, Alan (1998), 'Mill in a liberal landscape', in John Skorupsky (ed.), *The Cambridge Companion to Mill*, Cambridge: Cambridge University Press, pp. 497–541.
Simons, Jon (2013), 'Power, resistance and freedom', in Christopher Falzon, Timothy O'Leary and Jana Sawicki (eds), *A Companion to Foucault*, Blackwell Companions to Philosophy, London: Wiley-Blackwell, pp. 301–19.
Stern, Donnel B. (2010), *Partners in Thought: Working with Unformulated Experience, Dissociation and Enactment*, New York: Routledge.
Urbinati, Nadia and Alex Zakaras (eds) (2007), *John Stuart Mill's Political Thought*, Cambridge: Cambridge University Press.

Index

abjection, 6, 17, 43, 105
abolition, 88, 97, 179, 180
abolitionist, 128, 157, 167, 169, 180
academia, 28
  neoliberal, vii, 183
activism, 6, 14–15, 20, 39, 127, 183, 189
  black, 41
  feminist, vi, 3–4, 7, 9, 13, 118–19
  genealogy of, 22
  nineteenth-century, 4, 23, 25
  normalization of, 25
  policing, 132–4
  political, 5–7, 12, 13, 24, 69, 106, 139
  progressive, 26, 153
  queer and democratic, 35
  queer feminist, 32, 37
actor, 8, 12, 31, 166, 186, 192
  rational choice, 39
  Victorian, 184
Adams, W. B., 40, 84–9, 91–2, 95, 97, 99–104, 109–10, 126, 164, 194
adultery, 46–8, 52, 94–5, 99, 104, 111, 114, 153, 157, 166–8
affair, 49, 74, 91, 94, 99, 100, 103, 104, 113
  Beecher affair, 163–7
  Fox affair, 82, 97–106
  sexual, 153, 158, 167–8, 171

affect, vii–ix, 6, 11, 27, 30, 75, 148, 152, 169, 183–6, 195, 199, 202
  and dispositif, 12
  and Rancière, 152–3
  disciplinary, 18, 35, 82, 185
  performativity of, 28
  policing, 4–5
  political, 5, 8–9
affection, 46, 86–7, 106, 151
  mutual, 94
affective, 5, 45, 75, 112, 147, 163, 179, 186
  intimacy, 45
  orientation, 190
  practice, 26
  relationship, 107
  responses, 75
  "turn", 26
  virtualities, 73
  wrong, 163
agency, 5, 19, 32, 34, 62, 75, 109, 188
  a conception of queer feminist, 13–17, 20–4, 28, 34, 41–4, 86, 149, 152, 169, 187
  and sex workers, 149
  and woman, 119, 131–2, 135, 146
  democratic, 192
  feminist, 188
  in political theory, 33
  liberal, 16, 23, 33, 71
  political, 3, 21, 41–4, 118
  poststructuralist, 16, 71

206 Index

agitation, 60, 133–4, 137, 144
agonism, 19
  politics of, 146
Althusser, L., 36, 183
anarchic, 6, 118
animal, 54, 60–1, 86, 155
  strange, 63
animality, 61
antagonism, 179, 190
anticipation, xi, 178
anti-feminist, 127–8
Antigone, x, 32, 199
  and Judith Butler, 111, 161–2, 180, 196
  and Sophocle, 33
anti-homonormative, 6
antinormative, 14
  arrangement, 107
  life, 52
  relationships, 45
anti-relational (in queer theory), 189
anxiety, vii, 50–2, 58, 107, 157, 168, 183
arrangement, 13, 31, 32, 45, 74, 85, 91, 100–1, 107, 117, 159–61, 168, 177–8
  coercive, 165
  concubinage, 138
  sexual, 50–3
  socialistic, 169
asexual, 55
autonomy, 18, 139, 140, 187
  in speech, 64
  legal, 125
  personal, 15
  sexual, 122, 139, 173

backlash, 169
  conservative, 78, 173, 178
  institutional, ix
Beecher, H. W., 153, 158–9, 163, 165–76, 178, 180
Beecher Stowe, H., 157, 158, 174

behavior, 9, 12, 62–3, 65, 75–6, 84, 116, 134, 139, 140, 157, 162, 172
  sexual, 104–5, 154–5
Berlant, L., ix, 26, 186–8, 190, 195
Bersani, L., 6, 26, 29, 187, 189, 195
binary, 36, 108, 134, 176
birth-control activist, 143
bourgeois, 113, 135, 153
bourgeoisie, 89, 143
Brown, W., xi, 7, 18–19, 22, 25–6, 29, 33, 35–6, 40, 62, 82–3, 98, 104–6, 109, 113–14, 117, 124–5, 132, 148–9, 191, 193, 195–6, 203
Butler, Josephine, x, 16, 24, 34, 39, 40, 96, 108, 115–19, 121–41, 145–7, 153, 163, 165, 171, 186–7, 195–6, 198
Butler, Judith, 6, 13, 15–18, 20, 22–3, 25–6, 28, 31–9, 41–7, 51–2, 54 , 62, 64, 66, 71–2, 74–5, 78, 82–3, 86, 90, 92–4, 98–9, 102, 107, 109, 111, 118, 123, 149–50, 152, 154, 160–3, 168–9, 172, 176, 178–80, 187–8, 192, 196–9, 200–4

camp, 74
  moralistic, 167
  theoretical, 17
campaign, 34, 53, 55, 58, 115, 120–2, 128, 132, 134, 158, 166, 195
capitalism, ix, 29, 183, 198, 202
caricature, 55, 58, 155, 157, 194
Chambers, S., xii, 3, 7, 11–12, 17, 22, 27, 29, 30, 33, 43, 64, 72, 74, 197, 200, 202–3
chastity, 85, 87, 110, 155
civility, 65, 69, 189
civilization, 68, 110–11, 158
closet, 13
  epistemological, 82, 85, 105, 107, 202
  sexual, 114

coercive, 94, 163, 165, 172
coming out, 13, 64, 105, 107
Comstock, A., 174–6
Comstock Law, 154, 172, 174–6
conservative, 20, 36, 50, 55, 60,
    67–8, 69, 74–5, 77–8, 81–2, 90,
    94, 114, 142, 157–8, 166, 173,
    175–6, 178
  activists, 153
  critiques of sex radicalism, 25
  enemy, 54, 114
  establishment, 175
  moralism, 143
  opposition, 172
  press, 157
  social practices and laws, 31
Contagious Diseases Acts (CD Acts),
    vi, 21, 25, 96, 111, 115, 120,
    128
contempt, 8, 9, 19, 65, 66, 68, 76–7,
    116, 124, 130–1, 133–4, 144
corporal, 31
counter-discourse, 129
counter-figure, v, 3, 12–13, 25–6, 71,
    79, 82, 108, 116, 147, 177, 184
counter-hegemonic, 94, 99
  gesture, 106
counter-normative
  relationship, 20
  term, 14
cross-dresser, 53, 55, 60, 155
cruel, 94, 170, 180
  optimism, 190, 195
cruelty, 130, 169
cynic, 18, 20, 37

debate, 14, 21, 25, 33, 35, 61, 68,
    96, 104, 111, 120, 132, 135–6,
    154, 161
decent, 41, 153, 158, 200
defective, viii, 16, 61–3, 97
democracy, 32, 63, 117, 132, 148,
    150, 185, 195, 197–200, 202–3
  radical, 23
despised, 9, 37, 99, 167

dettering, 45, 73
deviant, 65
  character, 108
  meaning, 72
  sexually, 37
dichotomy, 82, 105, 107, 116, 144,
    187
disagreement, xi, 3, 5, 13–14, 64–5,
    70, 159, 163, 199, 201
discipline, vii, 142, 184–5, 198
  academic, 191
disclosure, 45, 116–17, 163, 166,
    168, 178
disgust, 8, 9, 19, 30, 35, 69, 76–8,
    108, 116, 124, 130–1, 134,
    143–4, 172–3, 187, 201
dispossession, 151, 162
  mode of, 26, 162–3, 177, 196
dispute, 5, 15, 147
disruptive, 6, 7, 25, 27, 41, 161, 189
  capacity, viii
  force, 82
  gesture, 17
  intervention, 41, 154, 177
  moment, 61, 192
  potential, 184
dissent, 83, 102, 124, 126, 194, 200
  radical, 154
  sex, 106, 153, 172
Dissenters, the, 91, 112
distribution, 40
  of power, 73
  of vulnerability, 162
  places and roles, 4, 98, 179
  social positions, 107–8
division, 38, 60, 108, 159, 189, 192
  of sexual labor, 84
divorce, 48, 51, 85, 88–9, 91, 94,
    96–7, 99, 100, 109, 111–12,
    120, 137, 143
domination, x, 66, 86, 90, 95
  effects of, 149
  fantasies of, 148
  logic of, 12
  male, 96

domination (*cont.*)
  order of, 9, 27
  sexist, 38
  sexual, 129
  state of, 5, 145
  subject of, 15
drag, xiv, 15, 33, 39, 44, 52–5, 58–9, 63–4, 72, 74
dream, 147, 153, 159, 160, 168, 201

enemy, 88, 127, 133–4, 158, 171, 174–5, 190
  of the police, 185
enfranchisement, 26, 66–7, 77, 96, 122, 150
equality, viii, 4, 5, 10, 14, 15, 18, 23, 26, 68, 77, 94, 96, 111–12, 116, 118, 146, 177, 187, 188, 190, 194, 197, 199–201, 204
  egal, 69, 77
  gender, 65–6, 110
  of the working class, 146
  order of, 29, 63, 70, 73
  position of, 132
  rhetoric of, 131
  social, 40, 77, 110
  substantive, 72
  vocabulary of, 117
event, 5, 8, 10, 19, 48, 51, 61, 77, 162, 170, 201
experiment, 13, 50, 58, 101, 107
  in living, 21, 46, 73, 81, 107, 114
  intimate and sexual, 102
experimentation, 20, 114, 178, 189

factory, 98
failure, vii, 9, 58, 61, 67, 81, 203
fear, 8, 30, 45, 50–1, 68, 82, 102, 129, 130, 132, 143, 162, 171, 185
fearless, 73
feeling, vii, ix, 8, 12, 27, 30, 35, 49, 50, 51, 61, 69, 78, 109, 129, 130, 133, 138, 145, 165, 170, 172, 179, 183–4, 191, 197, 200

  bad, viii, xi, 185–6, 190–1
  inferior, 9, 14
  irritated, 185
  of humiliation, 75
  of subordination, 36
  painful, 126
  powerless, 191
  structure of, xi
  wronged, 190
feminism, v, 3, 5, 13–16, 21, 24, 26–7, 33, 38, 40, 55, 122, 128, 134, 150, 155, 184–6, 188, 195–9, 200–4
  Anglo-American, 3, 184, 186
  cultural, 148
  first wave, 186
  liberal, v, 3, 15, 20, 22, 34, 38, 118
  nineteenth century, 188
  queer, 38, 184
  US, 148
  Victorian, 83, 119
  Western, 15
feminist, v–vi, 15, 16, 19, 22–3, 33, 34, 38, 39, 46, 54–5, 58, 61, 72, 76, 81, 83, 90, 95, 101, 104, 106, 110–11, 115, 119, 122, 126–7, 129, 134, 137, 144, 146–7, 154, 165, 184–7, 192, 194–200, 203–4
  action, 25, 36, 118
  activism, 4, 7, 9, 25, 32, 118, 132
  activist, 15, 31, 67, 116, 133, 192
  agency, 13, 14, 16, 20, 21, 24, 34, 44, 149, 188
  canon, 22
  counter-discourse, 129
  democratic, 7, 192
  discourse, 20, 34, 149
  dissent, 39
  first wave, x, 23, 26
  liberal, 3, 15, 16, 20–4, 29, 33, 38–9, 40, 119, 134, 186
  male, 44
  manifesto, 68, 84

movement, 28, 37, 58, 75, 109, 121, 133, 135
nineteenth century, 16, 22, 26, 43–4, 46, 117, 153, 184, 187
philosopher, 60
political theory, 184, 188
queer, xi, 3, 5, 11, 13, 16, 20–3, 26–7, 39, 44–5, 63, 153, 186, 189
radical, 26, 90, 102, 133–4, 145, 147, 150
resistance, 33, 54
rhetoric, 19, 20, 26, 69, 118, 122, 135
scholar, 20, 97
scholarship, 4, 7, 9
second-wave, x
strategy, 24, 36–7, 67
tactics, 122, 163
theorist, 7, 8, 19, 20, 30, 75
theory, 4, 20, 14–16, 27, 33–4, 43, 71, 184, 188
Victorian, 23, 108, 116, 126, 153
Foucault, M., 3, 5, 10, 12, 14, 20, 27–8, 32, 37–9, 44–5, 52, 73–4, 82, 105, 108, 113–14, 117, 145, 148, 184–5, 198–9, 200, 202–4
Fox, W. J., v, 40, 50, 82, 83, 87–95, 97–106, 110–13, 161, 163, 194
free love, vi, 27, 40, 151, 153–5, 158–61, 164, 167–71, 173, 175, 178–80, 195
free lover, 147, 151–3, 155, 162–3, 165–6, 172, 176, 179, 187
free speech, 24, 66, 151, 174–5, 178, 202
freedom, vii, 15, 20, 21, 23, 36, 38–9, 76, 94, 108–10, 139, 146, 164, 171–3, 178, 180, 187, 195, 203
practice of, 3, 5, 20, 28, 38, 98, 113, 124, 139, 145, 200, 202
sexual, 108, 155, 158, 160
social, 151

freethinker, 69
friendship, 9, 46, 51, 74, 106, 200
future, vi, xi, 11, 26–7, 47, 49, 52, 94, 96, 99, 100, 103, 117, 131, 152, 172, 183–8, 192, 193, 197, 200, 204

Garrison, W. L., 128, 169
gay, 6, 13, 19, 29, 31–2, 36–8, 42, 47, 65, 105, 149, 161, 178, 189, 199, 202
gender, x, 12, 20, 28, 36, 46–8, 52, 54, 58, 71–2, 81, 86, 89, 90, 92–3, 98, 107, 119, 139, 146, 148–9, 154–5, 157, 160, 170–2, 179
discrimination, 15, 21, 86, 164
equality, 65–6, 110
hierarchy, 146, 178
identity, 54, 58, 149
inequality, 39, 87–8, 98, 146
marginal, 5
normativity, 90
norms, 11, 14, 54, 58, 60, 63–4, 73–5, 85, 106, 155
practice, 9, 31
trangression, 161
groan, 25, 60–1, 63
guilt, 18, 28, 36, 46, 149, 152

harm, 20, 65–6, 75–6, 112, 127, 130, 148, 152, 176, 191, 198
harmful, 9, 37, 69, 121, 149
healing, 93, 127–8, 151, 187
heteronormative, 13, 65, 74, 105
order, 52, 98
standard, 9, 23, 33
heteronormativity, 31, 52, 177, 197
heterosexist, 105
heterosexual, 12, 20, 30, 36, 105, 155, 180
ideal, 161
marriage, 46, 177
matrix, 54
monogamy, 32, 161–2, 171

heterosexuality, 53
  monogamous, 153, 177, 188
homoerotic, 82
homonationalism, 201
homonormativity, 29
homophobic, 42
  anti- , 178–9
homosexual, 11, 73, 82, 105, 197
human, xiii, 18–19, 28, 36–7, 60, 66, 69, 73–4, 76, 77, 108, 110, 116, 137, 158, 161, 164, 171, 178, 187–8, 191
  agency, 43, 62
  rights, 36
  sexuality, 50, 154, 163, 166, 169
  speech, 54
  vulnerability, 102–3, 109
humanist, 22, 34
humanities, 26
humanity, x, 9, 60, 151, 161, 201
humiliation, vi, 8, 9, 13, 19–20, 25, 29–30, 31, 35–7, 43–4, 63–5, 69, 75–7, 101–2, 108, 115–19, 123–4, 131, 134–5, 144–9, 175, 187–8
  of the self, 6
  public, 159
hypocrisy, 23, 124, 152, 166, 168–9, 170, 172

identity,
  policed, 117–18, 134, 149
  politicized, 7, 29, 148
  politics of, 7, 28–9, 33, 35, 124
immoral, 13, 48, 51, 74, 95, 103, 105, 108, 116, 123–4, 126, 139, 141, 155, 157, 162, 165–6, 168, 177, 180
immorality, 83, 85, 88, 94, 103, 104, 114, 117, 136, 160–1, 167, 173
imperialism, x, 34, 196
indecent, 99, 127
inequality, 5, 18, 23, 68, 88, 90, 92, 95, 98, 110, 121, 165
  gender, 39, 87, 93, 146
  sexual, 144

injury, 17, 36, 61, 118–19, 131, 148, 170, 179
  constructive, 76
  rhetorical, 116
  state of, 34, 195–6
insult, 8, 9, 17, 29, 37, 47, 68, 76–7, 99, 126, 145, 152, 171, 186
  performative, 68
insurrectionary speech, 39, 72, 169
intelligible, 10, 12, 53–4, 160, 162, 177
interpellation, 20, 47, 104, 147, 152, 162, 171, 183
interruption, ix, 14, 45, 53, 71, 82, 97, 184
  of the liberal order, 3
intimacy, 45–6, 49, 51–2, 71, 74, 83, 87, 95, 98, 103–8, 113–14, 154, 160, 170, 172, 176–8, 188, 197
invisible, viii, 10, 12, 98, 177, 186
irritated, 26, 184–5
irruption, 14, 64, 70

justice, 15, 40, 60, 66–7, 77, 94, 128–9, 130, 163, 166, 168, 178

liberal, viii, ix, 3, 12, 15–16, 18–20, 22–4, 29, 32–5, 38–43, 48, 62, 65, 70–1, 87–90, 99, 113, 118, 134, 139, 148, 150, 153, 184, 186, 197, 200–2, 204
  conception, 14, 64
  democracy, 7, 18
  dispositif, 12
  order, 3, 12, 14, 71
  political theory, 12
  politics, ix, 9, 53–4, 63, 69, 125
  theory, 12, 14
Liberal, 52, 55, 77, 122, 124, 141
liberalism, 14, 15–16, 21, 29, 34, 38, 139, 148, 195
  modern, 21
line of escape, vi, 26, 147, 151, 153–4, 159–60, 177–9

line of fracture, 159
literariy, 25, 63–4, 69, 70, 108, 118, 131
lover, 46, 53, 87, 138, 155, 161; see also free lover

marginal, 5, 40, 166
  knowledge, 32
marginalization, 126
market, 86, 180, 191
  academic, vii
marriage, 32, 45–7, 50–1, 71, 74, 81, 83–92, 94–8, 100, 103, 106, 109–12, 124, 143, 152, 154–5, 158, 160, 163–9, 170–2, 177–8, 194, 200, 203
  same-sex, 23, 114
masturbation, 154
melancholia, 152, 162, 179
method, 3, 10–11, 32, 48, 82, 104
  genealogical, 38
  interpretative, 26, 39
middle class, 84, 98, 134–5, 139, 143, 149
  opinion, 84
  respectability, 84, 98
  woman, 135, 139
migrant, 84, 158, 189–90
  sexual, 189
militant, 39, 122
Mill, J. S., v–vi, ix–x, xiv, 4, 9, 12, 15–16, 20–6, 31, 33–4, 38–41, 44–63, 65–71, 73–8, 81–5, 88–90, 95–114, 115, 118–21, 124–7, 129, 132–51, 153, 155, 160–1, 163, 165, 178, 186–7, 189, 194–5, 198–204
Miller, D. A., vii, 185, 200
monogamy, 26, 32, 45, 83, 155, 161–2, 165, 171, 177, 180, 190; see also heterosexuality: monogamous
Monthly Repository, the, v, 24, 26, 40, 71, 81, 83–4, 86–90, 94, 96, 103, 161, 163–4, 194–5, 200

moral, viii, 15, 35, 84, 94–5, 105, 110, 112, 116, 124, 130–1, 141–2, 157, 161, 164, 167, 176, 200
  norms, 95
  panic, 121
  perfectionism, 167
  philosopher, 49
  progress, 69, 123
moralist, 103, 154, 158, 185
morality, 18, 48, 51, 89, 94, 104–5, 116, 121, 155, 157, 159, 161, 173–4, 180
mourning, 28, 162, 179–80, 196
Muñoz, J. E., 26, 160, 189–90, 198, 201

negative, 3, 7, 46, 82, 85, 126, 142, 153, 163, 173, 187–8
  emotion, 4, 72, 130, 179
  feeling, 30
  liberty, 38
  other, 85
  outcome, 61
neoliberal, 183
  present, ix
  time, ix
normalization, 10, 12, 117
  dispositif of, 10
  frames of, 191
  of activism, 25
Nussbaum, M., 7, 15–22, 24–5, 29, 30–1, 33–5, 38, 40, 48, 54, 63, 71, 74, 81–2, 90–1, 93, 102, 104–5, 107, 109, 114, 118, 147–9, 192, 201, 204

obscene, 48, 65, 75, 174
obscenity, 36, 48, 154, 157, 172, 174–6
officer, vii, vii, ix, xi, 36, 135, 183–5

pain, 29, 37, 50, 60, 93–4, 102, 118–19, 126–7, 129, 130–2, 140, 148, 187

paranoid, 185
Parks, R., 41–4, 63–4, 73
parody, 15, 33, 39, 54, 74, 200–1
parrhesia, 5, 145, 202
partition, 14, 60
  of powers, 7, 13
  of the sensible, 53
  of the sexually accepted, 153
  of the sexually visible, 84
  of the visible, 12, 53
performative, 4, 8, 28, 43–4, 53, 62, 72, 82, 93, 95–7, 99, 104, 109, 111, 119, 123–5, 152, 162, 165, 196–7, 201
  act, 14, 17, 43, 86, 185
  action, 42, 72, 82, 95, 163, 169
  capacity, 6, 13, 171
  de-officialization of the, 93
  event, 48
  force of the, 47
  gesture, 28, 37, 46, 99, 188
  insult, 68
  intervention, 4, 41–2, 49, 51–3, 65, 86, 95, 106, 123–4, 150, 162, 185
  practice, 116
  promise of the, 43
  rhetoric, 24, 124,
  silence, 71, 97, 105
  slur, vi, 3, 13, 25–6, 63, 70, 92, 108, 115–16, 119, 123, 135, 146, 186
polemic, 185
polemical, 15, 27, 33
polemicization, 186, 195
police, the, 36, 76, 104, 122, 136, 138, 183, 185
police, the, vi–viii, xi, 3–7, 9–12, 14, 17–18, 20–3, 25–7, 39, 52–4, 60, 63–4, 66, 70–1, 82, 84, 96, 109, 117, 149, 152–3, 172, 175–6, 183–91, 200
  order, 11, 70–1

political, viii–ix, 4, 5, 7–10, 12, 15, 17, 20–1, 22, 24, 26, 28–9, 31–3, 34–6, 39–40, 45, 53–5, 60–5, 70–2, 75, 76, 78, 86, 88, 92, 94, 96–7, 99, 102, 106, 108–9, 111–13, 116–17, 119–21, 124–5, 127–30, 133–5, 137, 139, 141, 143–7, 149–50, 152–5, 158, 162–73, 176–9, 184–7, 189–90, 194, 196–98, 200, 202–3
  action, viii, 4, 6, 8, 14, 19, 23, 29, 41, 43, 64, 66, 95, 105, 122, 154, 162, 176–7, 186–7
  agency, 3, 15, 21–2, 41–3, 118, 146, 188
  argument, 54, 65, 69, 93, 97, 118, 122, 146
  category, 15
  conflict, 4, 61, 64, 66, 70, 146–7, 153
  contestation, 24, 46, 93, 172
  culture, 29
  disagreement, 13
  discourse, 34, 53, 62, 117, 131
  domination, 66
  elite, 10, 119, 124, 130, 141, 163–5
  emancipation, 49, 84, 176
  enemy, 101, 133, 144
  establishment, 90, 146
  event, 8
  imagery, 55
  impotence, 29
  interruption, 3
  intervention, 4, 9, 11, 16, 21, 23, 39, 43, 65, 77, 119, 133–4, 141, 148–9, 163, 172, 178, 186, 188
  judgment, 35
  liberalism, 38, 201
  norm, 5, 93, 154, 171, 176
  power, 23, 28, 39, 41, 90, 121
  radicalism, 40
  rally, 122

refugee, 49
resistance, 17, 42, 47, 90, 118
revolution, 24
rhetoric, vi, 9, 16, 114, 118, 123, 130, 134, 135
science, 191
speech, 62,
strategy, 7, 25, 93, 103, 119, 144, 147, 149, 163, 165, 169
subject, 6, 10, 14, 25, 30, 41, 44, 53, 63, 70, 73, 108, 117–18, 131–2, 145–6, 166, 186
tactic, 127
theorist, viii, xi, 4, 7, 12–3, 18, 21, 33, 38–9, 63, 72, 118, 147, 184, 186–8, 191, 193
theory, v, x–xii, 3–4, 7, 12–13, 17, 20–1, 25, 30–1, 34, 38–9, 54, 71, 183–8, 191, 195–7, 199, 202
thought, 27, 184, 201, 204
trangression, 44
politicalization, 149
politics, viii–ix, 3–8, 11–19, 22–5, 27–30, 32–3, 37, 39–40, 42, 44–5, 53–4, 58, 60–5, 68, 70–3, 75, 82–85, 87, 89–90, 97, 102, 111, 118–19, 131–2, 134, 144–7, 149, 154–5, 157–9, 171, 175–8, 185–7, 189, 190–1, 194–204
American, 40, 176
anarchist, 33
anti-black, 27
anti-homophobic, 178
as-usual, viii, 187, 192
class, x
coalition, 147
emancipatory, 42
equality-oriented vision of, 26
gay and lesbian, 178
legislative, 39
liberal, ix, 3, 9, 53–4, 63, 69, 125
liberal theory of, 14
Marxist, 33
progressive, 39, 54, 60, 124, 192
racial, x

redemptive, 189
revolutionary, 158
subversive, 149
theatrical, 187
transformative, 7
poststructuralism, 21, 202
poststructuralist, 15–16, 28, 33, 71
power, 3–5, 13–17, 19–20, 22, 28, 30, 33–7, 39, 41–2, 44–5, 47, 55, 60, 64–6, 68, 70–4, 86, 88–90, 93, 95, 99, 101–2, 104–6, 111–12, 118–19, 123, 126–7, 129–30, 135–6, 142–3, 145–6, 149, 152, 162, 172–3, 176, 178, 184, 187–8, 192–3, 195–6, 204
disciplinary, 44, 54, 185
dynamic, 5, 19
independent, 99, 102, 104, 129
inequalities of, 19, 64
relations, 5, 16, 23, 145
powerless, 55, 58, 148, 183, 191
practice, iii, v, ix–x, 4–5, 8–16, 18–20, 21–2, 24–29, 31, 34–9, 42–4, 47, 52, 54–5, 62–5, 68–9, 71–2, 76, 85–8, 90–4, 97, 107, 109, 112–13, 123, 134, 137, 139, 142, 147, 150, 154, 160, 163, 165–6, 170, 177, 184, 186–9, 192, 204
Cynic, 18, 20
historical, 6, 32, 43
of disrupting *the police*, 70
of excess, 63–4, 191
sexual, 52, 123, 141, 147, 161, 166, 170; *see also* queer: practice; freedom: practice
priest, 164–5
privacy, 46, 139, 151, 171
private, 36, 51, 74, 83, 100, 105, 108, 125, 132, 136–7, 139–40, 161, 168, 171, 180
production, vii, 7, 15, 19, 149, 180, 185
of prostitution, 130

214 Index

production (cont.)
  of queers, 6
  of the subject, 6, 108
property, 71, 110–11, 120, 122–3, 150, 160
  land, 150
  private, 180
  rights of, 74
promiscuity, 123, 153, 173
prostitute, 23–4, 85–6, 96–7, 112, 115–17, 120–1, 126–32, 134–42, 144–6, 150, 158, 162–5, 175–7
prostitution, 26, 34, 84–6, 89, 96–7, 110, 112, 115–16, 119, 121–6, 130–2, 134–43, 157, 164–5, 175, 195, 199, 203
  laws, 164
punishment, 27, 31, 36, 66, 185
puritanical, 172

queer, viii, x–xi, 5–8, 10–13, 15, 17–18, 20–2, 27–9, 30–1, 33–7, 47, 52, 58, 65, 81–3, 98–9, 108–9, 149, 152, 155, 160, 172, 178–9, 184, 197–8, 200–1, 203
  agency, 14, 23, 42, 44
  apparatus, 6
  experience, 47
  feminism, 38, 184, 202
  feminist, xi, 3–5, 7, 11, 13–14, 16, 19–24, 27, 32, 39, 45, 63, 149, 153, 186, 189
  genealogy, v, xi, 8, 10–14, 25, 27, 41, 43, 72–3, 183, 186
  intervention, 25, 52–3, 107
  performativity, 82, 202
  political theory, v, viii, x, 1, 4, 6, 13, 21, 26, 183, 185–91, 193
  practice, v, ix, 3–4, 8, 12, 14, 20, 23, 25–6, 30, 43–4, 46, 63, 71, 84, 116–19, 134, 141, 145–6, 186
  radicalism, 74
  studies, 45, 52, 178–9, 184, 198
  temporality, 160

  theory, 3–7, 14–15, 18, 27–8, 62, 82, 149, 152, 184, 186, 189–91, 193, 197
  utopia, 189–91
queering, vi, 7, 21, 26, 38, 181
Queer Nation, 29
queerness, 7, 13, 16–17, 152, 189

Said, E., 109, 202
Sedgwick, E., ix, 6, 26, 28, 47, 61–2, 82, 105, 107, 185, 192, 202
scandal, 13, 17, 49, 83, 100, 113, 153, 159, 161, 165, 167, 169, 170, 176, 179
scandalous, 82, 94, 180
  impure, 94, 111
  intervention, 32
  technique, 37
seductive, xi, 157
sex x, 11, 29, 31–2, 52, 67, 99, 104–6, 122, 124, 131, 143, 168, 179–80, 189, 193–4, 196, 198–9, 202
  anal, 6
  and self-shattering, 6
  discrimination, 21
  dissent, 54, 106, 153
  genital, 9
  norms, 14
  radical, 74, 153, 155, 164, 166–7, 174–5, 179, 201
  radicalism, 176
  slurs, 13
  wars, 16, 34,
  work, 116–17, 139
  workers, 129, 131–2, 134, 138, 149–50
sexism, 35, 38
sexual, 13, 28, 31, 35, 37, 45, 47–8, 55, 73–4, 87, 94, 104, 108, 110–11, 114–15, 121–2, 124, 129, 130, 139, 141, 143, 152, 158, 162, 164, 167, 172–6, 178–9, 195
  cross-dresser, 55
  deviance, 48

Index   215

difference, 21
diseases, 119, 136, 140–2
dissent, 26, 75
education, 64, 154
experience, 163
experiment, 102
experimentation, 20, 114
freedom, 108, 110, 158
hierarchy, 127, 189
impurity, 95
inequality, 144, 146
infidelity, 167
injustice, 82
intercourse, 74, 87, 164, 173
labor, 84
liberation, 87, 166
marginality, 47
minority, 9, 31, 58, 65
moralism, 84, 142
norms, 13, 25, 45, 46, 58, 86, 122, 153, 155, 158, 164, 176–7
pleasure, 32, 36, 136
politics, 83, 85, 155, 158, 161, 196
property, 160
radicalism, 25, 40
relations, 45, 98, 155
relationship, 12–13, 26, 48, 74, 103, 107, 114, 154, 161, 178, 180, 188
respectability, 53, 83–4
revolution, 147, 198
shame, 6, 107, 130, 189
subversion, 177
transgression, vi, 48, 83, 101, 154, 161, 189
villain, 160
visibility, 109
sexuality, ix, 6, 9, 11–13, 20, 23–4, 26, 32, 34, 45–7, 50, 52, 55, 58, 71, 74–5, 82–3, 85–7, 96, 98–9, 103–7, 110, 116, 119–23, 125, 127, 129, 138, 140–4, 146, 149–50, 152–5, 157, 159–66, 168–9, 171–4, 176–9, 183, 189, 197, 202, 203
studies, 11

Victorian, 143, 200
shame, iii, v, vii–x, 1, 3–14, 17–20, 22–7, 29–32, 35, 37, 39, 43–9, 51–5, 58, 60–2, 65, 67–9, 71–3, 75, 78, 82–3, 85–7, 91–3, 95, 99, 101–5, 107–9, 111, 115–16, 119, 126–9, 130, 134–5, 138, 140, 147–8, 152, 155, 162, 165, 168–9, 171–3, 177, 179, 181, 183–90, 192, 198–203
a queer conception of, 118
a queer practice, 141
as a disciplinary affect, 18, 35, 185
as a line of escape, vi, 147, 151–3, 177–8
as dislocating positions, 186
as dispossession, vi, 162–4, 177–8
category of, ix, 18
constructive, 18, 91–3, 104
disturbing, 183, 192
flattering, 147
harsh, 145–6
performativity of, 5–6
primitive, 7, 18, 35, 105, 109
respectful, 7, 130
servants of, 123
shameless, 35, 69, 90, 126–7, 166, 202
silence, v, 4, 7, 8, 12, 13, 19, 20, 23, 25, 30, 36, 43–4, 53–4, 60–3, 75, 81–5, 96–9, 102–3, 105–7, 109, 113, 116, 126, 153, 161, 165, 186–7, 189
disrupting, 64
disturbing, v, 3, 13, 25, 63–4, 82–4, 97–8, 103, 106
performative, 71, 97, 105–6
slavery, 34, 68–9, 77, 85, 87–8, 90, 95–7, 111–12, 128, 153, 166–70, 180, 195–6
social reformer, 69, 89, 93
subjectivation, 25, 44, 70, 149
subjectivity, 27, 36–8, 42, 93, 152, 179, 188, 198
queer, 47

subversive, 69, 78, 117, 149, 167
suffrage, 24, 39, 88–9, 95, 111,
    132–4, 144–5, 149, 195,
    199–200

racial, x, 41, 43
    assumption, 41
    discrimination, 41
    distribution of power, 73
    inequality, 88
    slur, 42, 92
Rancière, J., viii, 3–7, 11, 17, 25–7,
    39, 43–4, 53, 60, 63, 69–71,
    75, 82, 84, 97–8, 108, 113,
    117–18, 131–2, 146, 148–50,
    152–3, 158–60, 163, 166, 176,
    179–80, 183, 186, 189, 192,
    197, 199, 201
recognition, x, 19, 44, 61, 70, 147,
    160, 162
redemptive, 6, 187, 189
rejection, 15, 36, 50–1, 104, 117,
    130, 145
relational, 30, 52, 73–4
    rights, 74
religion, 34, 73, 125, 179, 194,
    197
religious zealots, 124
representation, 22, 40, 67, 75, 106,
    120, 126, 132, 143, 154
    a theory of, 72
repression, vii–viii
reputation, x, 23, 37, 48, 69, 74, 85,
    104, 107, 117, 159, 166, 169,
    175–6
resignification, 13, 19, 23, 28–9, 32,
    34, 37–8, 42–3, 46, 64–5, 69,
    72, 78, 90, 95, 109–10, 116,
    128–9, 140, 149, 152, 167,
    176, 188
resistance, vii, 12, 17, 20, 23, 27,
    36–7, 41–2, 47, 72, 90, 98,
    118, 204
    cultural, 74
    feminist, 33, 54

rhetoric, v–vi, 9, 16, 19, 20–1, 23,
    25–6, 34, 61–6, 69–71, 85,
    96–7, 108, 111–19, 122–5,
    127–8, 130–2, 134–6, 138,
    146, 153, 163–4, 168
    Islamophobic, 36
    of shame, 23
ridicule, 48, 51, 60, 69, 101, 159,
    162, 192
risk, xiii, 5, 14, 17, 36, 38, 44, 52,
    61, 63, 105, 117, 124, 131–2,
    135, 139, 145, 149, 160, 172–3,
    177–8, 190–1
Royal Comission, 119, 124, 126,
    135, 139–41, 143
rumor, 103, 167

safe space, 62
sans-part, 117–18, 131, 166, 186,
    190
scholarship, ix, 4, 7, 9, 22, 26,
    54, 58, 108, 134, 153, 184,
    191
secrecy, 105, 109, 137, 166,
    202
self, 5–6, 19, 21, 27, 30, 75, 148,
    152, 163, 189
    practices of, 28
slave, 68, 77, 90, 92–3, 96, 112,
    122, 167
    auction, 167
    market, 180
slavery, 34, 68–9, 77, 85, 87–8, 90,
    92, 95, 97, 111, 128, 166–70,
    180, 195–6
slur, 8, 13, 19–20, 23, 37, 63,
    66, 71–2, 108, 116, 146,
    152, 178; *see also*
    performative: slur
    as a practice of excess, 63, 70
    humiliating, 7
    queer as a slur, 17, 42
    racial and gendered, 92
soul, 124, 126, 128–9, 150–1,
    183–5, 192

state, 13, 23, 27, 36, 45–6, 60, 63, 65–6, 68–9, 121, 125, 135–6, 139, 142, 158, 196, 198
  and queer feminists, 19, 36, 40, 66, 125
  attorney, 174
  power, 23, 72, 178
subject, 4–6, 9–11, 19, 27, 36, 41–2, 46, 64–5, 94–5, 114, 125, 131, 135–6, 149–50, 159, 166, 168–9, 179, 184–5, 188, 189–90, 198, 200
  bourgeois, 135
  of domination, 15
  of liberal politics, 12, 16, 102
  political, 6, 10, 14, 25, 30, 41, 44, 53, 63, 65, 70, 73, 108, 117–18, 131–2, 145–6, 158–9, 166, 186, 188–9
  queer, 17, 28, 31–2, 44, 46–7, 52, 93, 118
  sovereign, 62
subjectivation, 25, 44, 79, 149
subjectivity, 27, 38, 42, 152, 179, 188, 198
  and women, 93
  formation of, 36–7
  queer, 47
surprise, viii, 26, 44, 52, 176, 184–5, 188, 192

tactic, 7, 10, 13, 16–17, 23, 32, 37, 63, 106, 108, 116, 126–7, 130, 132–4, 137–8, 144–7, 152–3, 159, 165–6, 169, 171–2, 180, 189
  civil rights, 40
  feminist, 122, 163
  of sexual exposures, 175–8
  resignification, 140, 167, 188
  shame-based, 44
  shaming, 102
Tarnopolsky, C., xii, 7, 19, 25, 29, 35, 63, 116, 118, 130, 147–9, 202

Taylor, H., 9, 15, 25, 31, 38, 44, 46–7, 49–53, 55, 66–7, 70–1, 76, 83–4, 87, 96, 98, 100–1, 104, 106–8, 114, 160–1, 189, 195, 204
theater, 74, 117, 132, 198
theatrical, 167, 177
  act, 166
  disorder of the senses, 26
  performance, 176, 187
  politics, 187
  production of subjects, 6
transformative, 27, 117, 148, 187, 192
  politics, 7
  strategy, 99
trauma, 126, 187–8, 197
trope, 11, 25, 68, 82, 85, 90, 92, 97, 108, 125, 136–7, 141
truth, 5, 52, 68, 73–4, 102, 109, 113, 117, 128, 130, 151, 198, 202

Unitarian, v, 25, 39–40, 71, 83–4, 87, 89, 91, 99–101, 113, 125, 161, 194, 198
universal, 27, 38, 89, 150, 154
unpredictable, 7, 50, 169
upper class, 23, 70, 91, 116, 118, 123–4, 132, 135, 146, 172
utilitarian, 61, 136

visceral, 4, 14, 27, 186
vocabulary, 20–1, 117, 152, 154, 161, 186, 188
  exclusionary, 155
vote, 22, 24, 32, 39, 54, 67, 77, 89, 96–7, 113, 115, 120–1, 132–3, 135, 137, 144, 146, 150, 154
vulgar, 50, 110, 122, 133–4, 138, 144–5, 155, 158, 186

war, 16, 34, 48, 86, 97, 102, 109, 123, 171

Westminster, 53, 55, 60–2, 68, 71, 121, 141, 187, 197
women, x, 12, 14–15, 19, 23–4, 26, 33–4, 37, 40, 47, 49, 53, 55, 58, 65–70, 75–8, 81, 84–97, 100, 108–13, 115–16, 118–26, 128, 130–41, 143, 145, 148–50, 152, 154, 157–9, 163, 165–6, 170, 172–4, 176, 178–80, 187, 194–204
- agency, 119, 132, 135, 146
- black, 154
- emancipation of, 49
- married, 24, 95–6, 112, 120, 164, 172
- movement, 21, 26, 39–40, 58, 120, 126, 132–5, 137, 145–6, 154, 167
- rights 24, 39–40, 55, 68, 77, 89, 96, 113, 115, 120–1, 129, 135–6, 144, 154, 167
- suffrage, 24, 67, 134
- working class 91, 125–6, 138–9
worker, 48, 54, 65, 70–1, 84, 88, 91, 98, 116–17, 125–6, 131–2, 134, 138–9, 143, 146, 149, 150, 153, 158–9, 179–80, 201
wound, 127–8, 185, 195
wrong, 3–6, 9, 14, 29, 44, 60, 65, 76, 118, 124, 126–7, 130, 147, 159, 163, 165, 184, 186–7, 190, 192

Zerilli, L., 20–1, 33, 38, 110, 134–5, 137, 143–4, 203

EU representative:
Easy Access System Europe
Mustamäe tee 50, 10621 Tallinn, Estonia
Gpsr.requests@easproject.com

www.ingramcontent.com/pod-product-compliance
Lightning Source LLC
Chambersburg PA
CBHW051116230426
43667CB00014B/2600